Virgin Nation

Virgin Nation

*Sexual Purity
and American Adolescence*

SARA MOSLENER

OXFORD
UNIVERSITY PRESS

OXFORD
UNIVERSITY PRESS

Oxford University Press is a department of the University of Oxford.
It furthers the University's objective of excellence in research, scholarship,
and education by publishing worldwide. Oxford is a registered trade mark
of Oxford University Press in the UK and in certain other countries

Published in the United States of America by Oxford University Press
198 Madison Avenue, New York, NY 10016, United States of America

Library of Congress Cataloging-in-Publication Data
Moslener, Sara.
Virgin nation : sexual purity and American adolescence / Sara Moslener.
p.   cm.
ISBN 978–0–19–998776–4 (hardback)
1. Sex—Religious aspects—Christianity—History. 2. Social movements—United States—
History. 3. Values—United States—History. I. Title.
BT708.M67 2015
241'.6640973—dc23
2014036841

1 3 5 7 9 8 6 4 2

Printed in the United States of America on acid-free paper

For my parents
For always letting me go, and come back again.
And for my sister, Martha,
Who loves without fear.

Contents

Acknowledgments

WHEN I STARTED this project seven years ago as my doctoral dissertation at Claremont Graduate University, I had no doubt that many people would find it compelling and intriguing. However, I had no idea how many people would express an ongoing interest in my work by providing critical feedback, emotional support, and unbridled enthusiasm, especially at times when my confidence faltered. My first debt of gratitude is to my earliest readers, my dissertations group at CGU, comprising two of the most intelligent and steadfast women I know, Katrina Van Heest and Jacqueline Hidalgo. I am especially thankful for a vibrant cohort of Americanists during my time at CGU, including Fay Botham, Sara Patterson, Jocelyn Newsome, Amy Hoyt, Julia Parnell, Laura Ammon, Amy Black Vorhees, and Ann Taves, who guided all of us through our doctoral studies. I am indebted to numerous other friends whose own work and various interests provided for hours of good conversation and much-needed frivolity, including Gianluigi Guggliermetto, Tara Prescott, Devin Kuhn, Jeremy Hustwit, Wendy Nafziger, Emily Bennett, Garth Reese, and Stephanie Sleeper, my former writing consultant who continued to read and respond to my work even when she no longer got paid for it.

Two seminars were especially helpful in providing me with colleagues who gave my work serious attention and offered time and space for developing my ideas. I am especially grateful to Steven Warner and the Calvin Seminars in Christian Scholarship, and to Mark D. Jordan and the Seminar in Religion and Sexuality at Emory University. These opportunities were instrumental in my own development as a writer and scholar and introduced me to some of the greatest people currently working in our field, many of whom I now consider friends.

The only disappointing part about being a historian in the digital age is that projects like these require fewer trips to archives than they used to. For that reason, I am especially grateful to Bob Shuster and the staff at the

Billy Graham Center Archives for giving this young historian a bona fide archival experience. I am eternally grateful for the librarians at each and every institution I've been a part of, who have patiently filled my seemingly unending interlibrary loan requests and maintained a cheerful disposition whenever I appeared before them to pay my fines. I am especially grateful to the librarians at the Honnold Library at the Claremont Colleges for forgiving a couple hundred dollars in fines I incurred when, during a research trip, I found myself unable to return to campus due to a family crisis. I am also grateful for Carla Tracy and Stacy Nowicki, the fearless leaders of the libraries at Augustana and Kalamazoo Colleges, respectively. They not only know how to manage great libraries, but expressed a great deal of enthusiasm when a new, young professor inquired about using library space for a class project. For these and many other reasons, I have many times harbored fantasies of becoming a librarian.

At least once a week, I am filled with gratitude that Amy DeRogatis extended her stint as an outside reader on my dissertation committee into a long-term mentorship and friendship. Academics often toil in isolation, so the gift of having a colleague who would accompany me to yet another sexual purity event is invaluable.

Various readers and responders to my work have tended to the mechanics and content of the final mansucrit with great care. Among these are Katie VanHeest, Amy DeRogatis, and Anne Dickey. Finally, I would like to thank my colleagues, past and present, at Augustana College, Kalamazoo College, Western Michigan University, and Central Michigan University. I am especially thankful for Robert Haak, Laura Hartman, Eric Stewart, Kristy Nabhan-Warren, Lendol Calder, Carol Anderson, Taylor Petrey, Charlene Boyer Lewis, Janelle Werner, Susan Freeman, Stephen Covell, Brian Wilson, Kelly Murphy, and Laurel Zwissler. They have all shared with me endless advice, support, and, in one case, a zombie walk in downtown Denver.

Virgin Nation

Introduction

SEXUAL PURITY AND NATIONAL SECURITY

SINCE THE NINETEENTH century, sexual purity has been a rallying cry for feminists, Cold War ideologues, social Darwinists, Protestant revivalists, physicians, and Christian psychologists. Though this history spans more than a century and numerous fields of inquiry and social critique, sexual-purity rhetoric has maintained consistent themes. The recurrent themes of American nationalism and civilizational decline, with frequent references to apocalypticism, complicate assumptions about the cultural work that sexual purity performs. Often portrayed by advocates and scholars alike as a commitment and experience limited to the personal desires and fulfillments of individual adolescents, sexual-purity work and rhetoric has a deeper hold on the American political landscape.

Contemporary Christian sexual-purity campaigns have given teenage virgins in the United States a platform for declaring their commitment to God, family, and their future spouses. Though sanctified through the authority of personal choice, sexual purity is not ultimately about what is best for individuals seeking safe passage through adolescence. Modern-day purity campaigns, like their nineteenth-century predecessors, are opportunities for Christian evangelicals to assume a primary role in securing a strong and superior nation-state. Public policies for sexual education, teen pregnancy, and adolescent health give statistical benchmarks that shape outcomes for public health. These, in turn, are alternately supported and refuted by religious activists, whose use of therapeutic and medical language allows evangelical purity activists to insert religious instructions regarding premarital sex into the public sphere. So, while public discourse focuses on goals and outcomes for public health, Protestant evangelical organizations use sexual purity to maintain their ties to Republican supporters by asserting ostensibly biblical ideals of marriage, family, and sexuality as integral to national well-being. Protestant evangelicals have employed this strategy since the nineteenth century by appealing to a longstanding logic that asserts a causal link between sexual deviance and national decline, a trope that has proven rather useful in an array of historical contexts in which evangelicals have sought to assert their own visions for the nation's moral trajectory.

The organization Silver Ring Thing, which has traveled the country presenting its message of purity and repentance since the early 1990s, succinctly incorporates this political ideology into its extravagant media presentation. At a Silver Ring Thing live event, an original video presents a jaunty song with an accompanying narrative that portrays condom use as a threat to national security. In just one stanza, the organization summarizes over a century of purity rhetoric:

> *The world says use a condom*
> *If we told you you'd be fine / we'd be lying to your face*
> *It's like playing with a nuclear bomb*
> *You could wipe out the whole human race*

These lyrics assume a foregone association between personal sexual practice and national—even global—security, a resonance that is neither explained nor defended by its producers. This short lyric and a subsequent interview with the organization's director in which he offered insights into his own beliefs regarding civilizational decline and imminent apocalypse, prompted me to search for an explanation as to how and why this connection is presented as axiomatic. Scholars of LGBT history have examined the supposed causal relationship between sexual immorality and national security within the context of antigay policies beginning in the Cold War.[1] However, this conservative political discourse emerged at an earlier time, from nineteenth-century social or sexual-purity campaigns. Though it became and remains a staple of antigay platforms, this discourse is ultimately grounded in the rhetoric of sexual-purity rhetoric, which since its earliest days, has upheld the white, middle-class, heterosexual, nuclear, Christian family as the foundation of American national strength.

For much of their history, sexual purity movements have been calls for collective action and social change, calls that have drawn upon theories of race and gender, formulations of national identity, and evangelical theologies in order to articulate the ways in which the nation's future is imperiled by sexual immorality. Rooted in fears of national instability and civilizational decline, the idea of sexual purity has been most compelling at points in history when evangelical theologies of the end-times provided viable explanations for widespread cultural crises. Likewise, the accompanying value system offered the most promising solutions in these dangerous times. For nineteenth-century purity advocates, it offered a way to address the fear of declining Anglo-Saxon privilege; for twentieth-century fundamentalists, the threats were nuclear destruction and communist invasion; and, for later evangelicals, the paramount concerns involved the excesses of the sexual revolution coupled with lingering Cold War concerns. In each case, sexual-purity rhetoric proved an asset to evangelicals seeking to maintain political and cultural supremacy. By asserting a causal relationship among sexual immorality, national decline, and impending apocalypse, evangelical leaders shaped a purity rhetoric that positioned Protestant evangelicalism as the salvation of American civilization.

It is no surprise, then, that initial efforts to launch purity campaigns in the late twentieth century were transparently political. In 1993, several dozen young evangelicals representing the Southern Baptist denomination's newest Sunday-school initiative, True Love Waits, pounded over 100,000 pledge cards into the lawn of the National Mall. The action was reported as religious, political, countercultural—even radical—by observers, some of whom heralded a new chapter in the sexual revolution. What for many signaled a return to the traditional value of premarital chastity also marked a new form of public expression among evangelical youth. What was new was not the private belief that one must abstain from sex until marriage, long a mandate of most conservative religious cultures. No: here, for the first time, were evangelical teenagers making this personal choice into a public and political declaration as a form of religious testimony.[2]

Both movement leaders and scholars mark the emergence of the evangelical purity movement as a response to the perceived excesses of the 1960s counterculture; however, the shift from premarital chastity as private choice to sexual purity as a public and political declaration was the culmination of several shifts in evangelical life in the twentieth century. Scholars who see the movement's genesis as a response to the 1960s situate it within a form of postboomer evangelicalism that prioritizes the individual choice and self-fulfillment, what I call the individualistic turn in American evangelicalism.

Because contemporary purity advocates portray their efforts as a response to the counterculture that hastened the degeneration of sexual morality and American family life, most studies of the movement follow suit.[3] For this reason, conclusions about evangelical purity culture are circumscribed by a particular narrative of evangelical history. The individualistic turn in American spirituality that accompanied the cultural revolution infiltrated all corners of the US religious landscape, none more so than evangelicalism. Evangelical purity culture is both an outgrowth of and reaction to the sexual revolution, but it maintains a primary concern for the countercultural values of personal growth and individual transformation. Media reports, scholarly analysis, and purity advocates portray the movement as firmly situated in the quest for spiritual enlightenment and sexual fulfillment.

In *Virgin Nation*, I propose that sexual purity needs a far broader historical trajectory for us to adequately understand its cultural and political impacts. When I began this project I, too, assumed that the narrative of the contemporary purity movement began with the sexual revolution and the individualistic turn in American evangelicalism. The purity organizations whose literature I examined and whose events I attended oozed with the optimism and good feelings of a religious tradition infused with the therapeutic tonality of modern life. Only after several months of my study did another mood emerge, one of fear that signified the possibility of large-scale destruction. I recognized the language of apocalypticism and began to investigate how it might be connected to the rhetoric of sexual purity. My investigation pushed me beyond my own starting point, because studies and documentation of late-twentieth-century evangelicalism could not fully explain the persistence of apocalyptic rhetoric in post–Cold War, mainstream evangelicalism. I found that a rhetoric of sexual purity, or more precisely a rhetoric of sexual fear, connecting sexual immorality with national insecurity and impending apocalypse, had been prominent among Cold War fundamentalists. Even further back, nineteenth-century purity movements had asserted the very same formulation, this time addressing widespread fears of Anglo-Saxon decline.

These initial findings led me to conclude that contemporary evangelicals who embrace sexual purity are more than beneficiaries of the religious right's ability to coopt countercultural rhetoric. This book demonstrates that, throughout the history of American evangelicalism, sexual purity has secured a place for itself within numerous platforms for social and political change.

Regardless of historical context, the ideological connections drawn between sexual immorality and national security include several cooperating impulses: evangelical political activism, deep anxiety over gender roles and changing sexual mores, fear of moral decay, apocalyptic anticipation, and American nationalism. These phenomena converge at points in US history when evangelical Christians have sought to restore or maintain their political influence. In each case, purity advocates have asserted sexual immorality as a cause and consequence of national decay, responding with moral regulations derived from religious values and nationalist ideologies. Sex and national survival are the poles around which evangelicals have constructed an American identity, asserting their own value system to be the cornerstone of a thriving nation-state. At this intersection of nation and religion, purity reformers have employed theories of rise and decline in order to position sexual purity and its purveyor, Protestant evangelicalism, as the salvation of civilization.

Sexual Purity and American Adolescence

Few scholars and observers of the contemporary purity movement, not to mention purity advocates themselves, acknowledge the significant precedence of the nineteenth-century campaigns. Historically situated between the Victorian and Reform eras, social-purity campaigns marked an important shift in the locus of authority and, more importantly, how people negotiated that shift. As David Pivar, who has written the most extensive studies on these movements, has shown, by the end of the 1800s, Protestant evangelicalism was losing its place as the religious establishment in the United States, in part because purity reformers transformed the value systems of Protestantism—gender complementarianism, domestic piety, and social improvement—into mainstream American values.[4] At the same time, advocates of civilizational advancement recognized that scientific language of evolution did not hold the same moral authority or emotional appeal as did traditional revivalism.

In this same era, G. Stanley Hall's work on child psychology was equally characterized by shifts in the locus of cultural authority. His extensive work on adolescence, published in 1910, exhibits one scholar's attempt to negotiate shifting modes of cultural authority. Adolescence, as Hall introduced it, became a cultural category that represented a new stage of human development and created a space for the anxieties of a culture transitioning from innocence to maturity. In crafting the notion of the adolescent, Hall established significant linkages between religious conversion, sexual awakening, and civilizational advancement that help unpack subsequent arguments for sexual purity.[5] Hall was careful in his writing to use words that evoked the transformative experiences of revivalist tent meetings, known for their passionate displays of religious faith, by describing adolescence as a new birth. Hall himself advocated for "a new religion" rooted in the quest for human advancement, and he felt the need to impart the authority of evangelicalism into these new scientific endeavors. In doing so, he asserted that adolescence was marked as a unique stage of human development because of the concomitant development of sexual and spiritual awareness.

Hall's theories of adolescence did not remain relevant to the field of psychology for very long, especially because of his use of religious metaphor, but his ideas do remain relevant to the study of religion and adolescence. Before Hall, sexual purity was the act of a dutiful family member who sought to protect his or her own family from disgrace. But, by the early twentieth century, when adolescents functioned more independently from their family structures, sexual purity became the unique task of adolescents, whose youth and vitality were seen to provide the greatest hope for American civilization.

The therapeutic claims of the evangelical purity movement owe a significant debt to Hall's initial work in the field of adolescent psychology. Those claims are especially instrumental in allowing evangelicals to assert the precariousness of adolescent development and to articulate the innate connections between adolescent psychological, spiritual, and moral development. The movement's ability to maintain its cultural influence—especially in a culture whose mainstream already imbues self-care and therapeutic processes with an almost sacred status—depends on psychological and therapeutic processes. Purity advocates employ a rhetoric that fuses the psychological language of self-care, self-development, and self-improvement with the spiritual message that authentic personal transformation is only possible with the assistance of Jesus Christ.[6] In this framework, sexual purity takes on preemptive healing capabilities that protect the practitioner from the physical and emotional traumas that purity advocates presume accompany premarital sexual activity.

When G. Stanley Hall first conceived of adolescence as a battleground between sexual desire and religious conversion, he used the language of revivalist Christianity. His goal was to promote what he termed the "new religion" among traditionalists, but he only succeeded in creating an ideology that was quickly outdated within the emerging progressive movement. Like Hall, the contemporary purity movement asserts a dilemma for adolescents, one that positions sexual desire and religious belief within conflicting moral spheres. The purity movement promises assistance with that dilemma by providing young evangelicals with a concrete belief system and a set of behavioral practices that ideally outweigh the curiosities and demands of sexual desire. As with Hall, the primary goal of adolescent psychological development for purity advocates is the suppression of sexuality for a greater good.

The purity movement's attention to psychological and mental health discourses reveals a tactic similar to Hall's: an attempt to translate religious belief into the discourses of mental health and psychological development. By doing so, the movement is able to move beyond its evangelical foundations and into the secularized mainstream. In this way, religious ideologies impacting adolescent sexuality enter into the public sphere under the guise of mental health or therapeutic discourses, giving them credibility beyond their initial religious context.

Sexual Trajectories

Hall, in his work on adolescence, maintained a disdainful distance from the social-purity movement of the nineteenth century, yet there is ample evidence to suggest that the same ideological configuration linking moral character, civilizational advancement, and Protestant family life underscored both projects. *Virgin Nation* begins in chapter one with the first national campaign for sexual purity by a coalition of women's-rights activists, educators, clergy, and medical professionals. As a feminist initiative, purity work was an auxiliary service of the Woman's Christian Temperance Union and the Young Men's Christian Association, which sought to increase women's political and social position by asserting their moral authority over men. Victorian gender ideologies presumed that male and female sexuality were not only distinct but also antagonistic. Women's natural inclination for sexual virtue indicated to many Victorian feminists that women—at least white women—were especially suited to temper the sexual excesses of American men, whose liberties of appetite threatened domestic tranquility. As moral reformers, purity advocates sought to improve the habits and manners of men—to create a single standard of sexual behavior whereby men adopted the feminine attribute of purity, a tactic that raised deep concerns among social Darwinists and would precipitate a masculine makeover of American Protestantism.

The idealized white, middle-class family, free of relational strife, venereal disease, illness, drunkenness, feeblemindedness, infidelity, and other
consequences of moral degeneracy, represented the hopes for a nation
that likewise sought to vanquish the moral and social threats to its own
stability and flourishing.[7] The nationalist discourse of these reformers
capitalized on racialized and sexualized fears of national decline and asserted a causal relationship between sexual immorality, Anglo-Saxon decline, and national decay.[8]

The new psychology of adolescence was a cultural project seeking to
ensure sexual purity, including proper heterosexual development and
racial virility. It reflected fears of women's increased role in public life (especially teachers), which precipitated Hall's own masculinist anxieties.
Concerns about new sexual attitudes and gender roles, the replacing of
religious belief with scientific inquiry, and fears of declining and rising
birthrates among white Protestants and immigrants, respectively, were
all expressed in the civilizing work of sexual purity and in the psychology
of adolescence. The great white hope was not a white boxer hoping to
defeat Jack Johnson, but adolescents, whose evolutionary stage was primed
for the development of superior traits that could be passed on to later
generations.

Despite the humiliation of the Scopes trial in which fundamentalists
were excoriated for their refusal to accept the scientific claims of evolutionary thought, they continued to seek new avenues for public and political influence. Among the most successful was evangelical outreach
toward adolescents, whose lives were now shaped more than ever by peer
influence and leisure time. The emergence of a postwar evangelical youth
culture was valuable in its ability to mark American patriotism with
youthful, religious enthusiasm. Youth-focused evangelical movements,
such as Youth for Christ, orchestrated a confluence of American national
identity and Christian revivalism.

Fundamentalist leaders Torrey Johnson, Billy Graham, and Carl F. H.
Henry were especially instrumental in shaping adolescent identity by
adopting a rhetoric of sexual purity that alerted teenagers to their crucial
role in facing the emerging threats of the Cold War era. Nineteenth-
century purity crusaders agonized over the decline of Anglo-Saxon superiority and deployed the virtues of purity to reauthorize racial supremacy.
Likewise, fundamentalist leaders feared the internal demise of American morality and the consequent invasion of the Soviet Union. They refined their premillennialist theology to encompass revitalized theories

of rise and decline and positioned sexual immorality as a symptom of national decline. By linking sexual deviance, national vulnerability, and the expectation of imminent apocalypse, fundamentalists were able to reinterpret nineteenth-century sexual-purity rhetoric for a nuclear age.[9]

Graham was an ardent anticommunist, and his early preaching career was characterized by denunciations of sexual immorality for increasing the likelihood of communist invasion and nuclear war. He affirmed congressional anticommunist initiatives that sought to expel homosexuals from government posts. Like Joseph McCarthy, Graham was convinced that homosexuals, as sexual deviants susceptible to blackmail, were a threat to national security. This link between sexual deviance and national security would remain a salient trope through the mid–twentieth century and soon find even greater prominence with the rise of the Christian right.[10]

Historian Jason Bivins has introduced the idea of a religion of fear: as a descriptor of Cold War religiosity, it is even more apt than when applied to late-twentieth-century evangelicalism, the target of Bivins's analysis. Bivins is not incorrect, but, like scholarship of the purity movement, his historical timeline does not extend back far enough. The religion of fear that remains germane to today's evangelicals is primarily found in evangelical popular culture such as the *Left Behind* book series and Hell House, a haunted house franchise that provides a creative venue for religious proselytizing.[11] As popular cultural expression of conservative political ideologies and fundamentalist theology, the contemporary iteration of the religion of fear works primarily in representations of older theological tropes of human fallibility and cultural decline. By returning to these older themes that addressed the confusion and dread that Americans felt in this face of possible nuclear war and communist invasion, contemporary evangelicals work to reclaim their political and cultural significance. As historian Angela Lahr has shown, the cultural and political influence of evangelicals is directly related to their ability to effectively address widespread fears that were most effective at the height of American Cold War anxieties.[12] To see remnants of the religion of fear in a post–Cold War world indicates that evangelicals persist in their desire for continued relevance to contemporary concerns.

As their influence declined along with threat of the Cold War, fundamentalist and neoevangelical Christians shifted their attention from international conflict to domestic affairs.[13] Most histories of twentieth-century evangelicalism contend that this shift was due to the alarm with which the architects of the Moral Majority responded to the countercultural movement of the 1960s and 1970s. They claimed that American families and the American nation-state were facing an internal threat greater than any posed by the Soviet Union: sexual immorality.[14] The notion of "family values" as the solution to sexual immorality gained relevance when already-established tropes of national insecurity and sexual immorality were drawn upon. At the same time, "family values" owed its new status in the cultural zeitgeist to the increased prominence of therapeutic processes brought about by the counterculture.

As forces were galvanizing the Christian right with their talk of moral decay and national decline, believers were contending with another new turn in conservative evangelicalism—what sociologist Donald Miller calls the new church. In Miller's formulation, the countercultural values of individualism, antiestablishmentarianism, and personal transformation found their way into mainstream evangelicalism, prompting a new ecclesiastical structure (or antistructure) and an emphasis on personal spirituality. By the 1970s, evangelicalism and American therapeutic culture had developed a kind of syncretism that garnered for evangelicals an even greater degree of authority and popularity. Late-twentieth-century evangelicalism, typified by megachurch structures that resemble corporate headquarters and shopping malls, attests to the movement's ability to commodify new paradigm spirituality.[15]

When I refer to the individualist turn in evangelical spirituality, I am marking Miller's new paradigm and evangelicalism's embracing of the counterculture as a turning point in evangelical self-understanding. I use the term *spirituality* instead of *religion,* because the new paradigm was facilitated by shifts in American religious life away from traditional, collective structures and theological traditions, and toward personal quests for self-revelation and personal fulfillment. Though sociologists chart this move across numerous forms of religiosity, I am particularly interested in how evangelicals adopted a spiritual orientation—the celebration of human potential that came to contend with and coexist alongside more established notions of moral decay and national decline.

The concept of family values emerged as a way to bridge the harsh rhetoric of the Cold War era and the therapeutically infused theology of the 1970s. The connection between domestic stability and national security emerged as a mainstay of evangelical rhetoric in that decade. More than ever before, the American family was at the center of American political life, as calls for its restoration made allies of Republican politicians and evangelical leaders. Domestic ideology as political strategy among conservative evangelicals has been well documented by numerous historians of the Christian right.[16] It combined the new therapeutic values of evangelicals who were helping young churches grow at exponential rates with the lingering Cold War anxieties that cast a shadow over significant political events. Political strategists were instrumental in and deliberate about constructing the ideology of family values. But the more significant and long-lasting contribution was the development of a therapeutic evangelical culture led by experts in the areas of parenting, family life, and adolescent psychology. More than anything, this development created a new mode of evangelical faith practice and a new kind of evangelical leader, the Christian psychologist whose expertise provided families with Bible-based advice for securing a faithful home life and a godly nation.

Since the mid-1980s, mainstream evangelicals have designed and marketed sexual purity by carefully calculating appropriate amounts of cultural resistance and accommodation. When I refer to some evangelical groups and individuals as mainstream, I am speaking of those evangelicals who, like their nineteenth-century counterparts, exhibit a desire to move closer to secular values and representational systems in order to assert a nationalist ideology that privileges the values of evangelical Christianity. Sociologist Christian Smith has asserted that evangelicals seek to create tension between themselves and the secular world, a tension that is evident when evangelicals position sexual purity alongside the sexual beliefs and practices of most Americans. New paradigm spirituality aids Smith's thesis by explaining how the countercultural values of individualism, self-transformation, and antiestablishmentarianism became emblematic of a contemporary suburban evangelicalism that caters to the tastes, comforts, and concerns of middle-class conservatives. Using Smith's argument, I would conclude that the vitality of the purity movement is located in its ability to maintain its distinction while in close proximity to the mainstream. Twenty-five years ago, the purity movement was an exemplar of evangelicals' attempts to move conservative religiosity closer to the mainstream.

However, more recent scholarship on evangelicalism and sexuality complicates Smith's argument. Lynn Gerber's study of Christian weight-loss and ex-gay movements demonstrates that socially conservative evangelicals seek not only to maintain an oppositional stance to mainstream American life, but also to establish and maintain evangelical identity at the center of American cultural life.[17] *Virgin Nation* furthers Gerber's thesis by demonstrating how evangelicals have successfully deployed both cultural and nationalistic strategies to situate sexual purity as a religious and therapeutic practice not as oppositional, but as foundational to American national identity.

I begin my examination of contemporary evangelical purity culture as an outgrowth of new paradigm spirituality by analyzing the purity organizations True Love Waits and Silver Ring Thing. Though the politicized history of these groups is evident at the outset, their commitment to the new paradigm emerges in their primary efforts in evangelical cultural activism. As self-proclaimed grassroots activist organizations that profited from a favorable political climate, Silver Ring Thing and True Love Waits need to be examined as outgrowths of the counterculture that reshaped itself according to a subset of conservative ideology.

Not every advocate for sexual purity aims for political acknowledgement. But this narrative indicates that the movement sought a place within the US political landscape. Purity advocates sought some kind of recognition that this commitment was more than a personal choice—it was inherently part of one's religious identity and therefore demanded not only special protections but an open door into public and political discourse. But their attempts to create political ties were short lived. Though the movement was assisted by some key federal decisions and funding opportunities, its leaders have never established themselves as key political players. Their predecessors of the 1970s fought for moral restoration by controlling supposedly disordered bodies with political and moral persuasion, but contemporary purity advocates seek transformation through the body, believing that the transformed bodies of sexually pure adolescents hold the promise of a similarly transformed society. Purity leaders found themselves entering a new era in which it was more productive to work as cultural activists reinforcing a particular value set independent of political affiliation, though by no means challenging the established norms of the Christian right.

By permitting youth to take their place as the mediators of American national identity and morality, organizations like Silver Ring Thing and True Love Waits have actualized what, for the Moral Majority, was only rhetorical. As members of a self-proclaimed minority, sexually pure adolescents draw upon ideologies of individualism, personal well-being, and sexual freedom and assert a subaltern sexual identity that demands respect and political voice. When they initially elected to work in the public and political spheres, sexual-purity advocates chose to use the countercultural rhetoric of the sexual revolution. This is not to say that they are endorsing the cultural impacts of that revolution—just the opposite. However, it's important to note that their rhetorical strategies are heavily indebted to both the feminist and gay-rights movements. By adapting the rhetoric of personal rights, the purity movement has framed itself as the latest chapter of the sexual revolution.

The focus of sexual-purity work on the young may at first seem self-evident, but the reasons for this focus cannot be clearly articulated without understanding the nature of adolescence itself. For the contemporary movement, adolescence is a precarious stage of development in which unformed psyches and moral codes are vulnerable against the adult urges brought on by puberty. For evangelicals, the transition from child to adult is especially precarious if an adolescent is not supported with proper spiritual guidance. Advocates of sexual purity insist that maintaining one's sexual integrity is a nearly impossible task given the temptations of internal sexual urges and an external culture that teases young people with the titillations of sexual experimentation. The only foolproof guard against these pitfalls is not a piece of jewelry or even the public proclamation of commitment often solicited by groups, but a connection to the core of evangelical Christianity: a personal relationship with Jesus Christ.

The project of adolescent spiritual formation pervaded by the therapeutic mode of new paradigm spirituality is the imperative of sexual-purity groups. Evangelicals time and again seek the assurance of salvation for themselves and their loved ones, a task made easier when the goals of self-help are attached as signifiers of spiritual development. The sexual-purity movement is one effort in which an outward bodily commitment evidences the state of one's soul. By framing sexual purity as a therapeutic process, purity advocates entered a new arena of discourse and public scrutiny. Debates over the effectiveness of abstinence-only education versus comprehensive sex education bent eagerly toward social scientific data that, depending on a reader's bias, prove or disprove the claims of both sides. Sociologists and public-health experts of course seek to qualify and quantify the impact of sexual purity in order to provide the public and legislators with an accurate assessment of effective sex education. Though purity advocates heralded those findings that upheld the legitimacy of their work, they quickly backed away from scientific study as a validation of their work.

The therapeutic work of sexual purity operates in service to the goals of adolescent spiritual formation as conceived of by purity leaders. When the therapeutic establishment failed to recognize the contribution of sexual purity to adolescent health and well-being, purity advocates were able to fall back on their spiritual principles. Sexual purity isn't, after all, about what ultimately is good for the physical and psychological well-being of the individual. Sexual purity, with its promises of marital bliss and sexual ecstasy, is a most compelling metaphor for the Christian faith and the promise of eternal salvation. By situating spirituality, and not merely adolescent sexuality, within the zeitgeist of therapeutic culture, the evangelical purity culture gained the technique of gleaning conclusions from research findings without usurping its primary concern for adolescent spiritual development.

Perhaps the only other manifestation of evangelicalism that exhibits the tradition's penchant for cultural accommodation is its use of popular media and technology. An abstinence road show that travels nationwide and has made several trips to South Africa and the United Kingdom, Silver Ring Thing is a quintessential example of today's evangelical youth culture. A Silver Ring Thing event is scaled and crafted according to the mandates of the media consumed by most American adolescents. Although it is only one organization within the evangelical purity culture, I end my study by focusing on Silver Ring Thing because the group exemplifies all the components of the evangelical purity culture. Among smaller organizations, these components exist only in part. Even True Love Waits, because of its primary role in providing resources for parents, schools, and church- and community-based organizations to use at their own events, does not provide a comprehensive look at the evangelical purity culture in the way that Silver Ring Thing does.

The study of religion and popular culture has allowed scholars of religion to investigate how media representations enact social obligation and cultural criticism. An analysis of the organization's use of popular media, including its own original presentations, allows us to decipher how purity culture facilitates adolescent transformation. Because of its heavy dependence on popular media and technology, evangelical purity culture is exemplary of contemporary mainstream evangelicalism. Likewise, its emphasis on personal well-being, cultural relevance, and therapeutic spirituality situates the movement squarely within a historical trajectory originating with the counterculture of the 1960s and 1970s.

And, yet another narrative has emerged, one that evidences the continued influence of a rhetoric of sexual fear that has aided evangelicals in their attempts to maintain political relevance. The moral economy of sexual purity is equally shaped by the fear-based theologies of Cold War America and the accommodationism of new paradigm spirituality.[18] By using the religion of fear, purity culture demonstrates how sexual immorality poses a legitimate threat to the individual and to the collective well-being of the American citizenry. In doing so, evangelical purity culture marks adolescent sexual purity as a venue rife with opportunities for personal transformation, national revitalization, and, quite possibly, the salvation of American civilization.

Evangelical purity culture is firmly situated at the intersection of political activism, nationalism, and millennialist theology. This convergence occurs at points in US history when evangelical Christians have sought to restore or maintain their political influence and when they have been able to map theological frameworks onto widespread cultural crises. In response to the threat of moral and national decline, the movement provides ethical regulations derived from religious values and nationalist ideologies. At this intersection of nation and religion, purity reformers, now and in the nineteenth century, employ theories of rise and decline in order to position sexual purity, and the adolescents who embody it, as the greatest hope for restoring America's lost innocence.

Chapter One

Sexual Purity and Civilization Work in the 19th Century

THE HISTORY OF sexual purity in the United States begins with a reversal of traditional teachings about men and women. For centuries, the story of Adam and Eve has portrayed a woman, and therefore all women, as morally and spiritually inferior, a theological anthropology that reinforced gender hierarchies in both church and society. The reversal of this formulation was useful to burgeoning capitalist society, where separate spheres worked to offset the quasi-nefarious dealings of men in public life with the nurturing nature and piety of women who maintained the domestic sanctuary. The virtue of purity as a uniquely feminine asset was part of the larger project to alleviate Protestant anxieties about personal wealth and engagement with the market economy. Women's ability to maintain the virtues of religious piety and sexual purity allowed white, middle-class men to pursue economic success and thus reassure white middle-class Protestants of their cultural dominance.

That the first wave of feminism coincided with the earliest purity movement is curious to contemporary observers, who recognize the conservative political affiliation of most modern-day purity movements. Among the first purity reformers were women who used their own assumed superior status to control the sexual behavior of men. Rather than acquiesce to the domestic realm and political irrelevance, these women used the claim of female purity to assert a moral authority beyond the confines of their homes.

On an even more fundamental level, the introduction of sexual purity as a Christian ideal allowed Protestants to assert women's presumed lack of sexual desire as a foundation for Protestant continued cultural dominance. Subsequent religious groups have reaffirmed the essentially pure state of female sexuality in order to secure their religious and cultural superiority. In the same way that American Protestants established their own superiority through bodily regimens of diet and exercise, so, too, has female purity denoted the boundaries of evangelical orthodoxy.[1]

As the mythology of innate female purity has receded, though not disappeared, from the American imagination and been entirely rejected by later feminist initiatives, the monitoring and control of female sexuality has become more pronounced. As with the 19th-century purity and other social reformers who sought to maintain cultural and economic dominance, the control of sexuality through religious teaching has remained a significant strategy for evangelicals facing the gain or loss of their own cultural capital.

Representing the privileged classes of numerous Protestant denominations, social-purity advocates emerged from an already established network of reformers and grafted the concerns of social purity onto their existing agendas. By 1886, both the Woman's Christian Temperance Union (WCTU) and the Young Men's Christian Association (YMCA) had established chapters addressing the need for social purity. Influenced by the successful campaign within the Church of England, American reformers adopted the programmatic structure of the White Cross Army. In doing so, American purity reformers developed campaigns that sought the political elevation of women by controlling the moral actions of men.[2]

Ideal manhood and womanhood were the currencies of sexual purity, offering social and political equality through the restoration of virtue. The women and men of the early purity movement were unique within the history of purity movements in that they were gender egalitarians who believed that a civilized society required a single standard of sexual behavior. An advanced civilization valued the feminine virtue of sexual purity and sought to expand women's moral authority by extending those virtues to the male sex. The progress of America as a nation-state, then, was dependent upon the proper negotiation of gendered roles and morality.[3]

As part of the narrative of American secularization, the earliest purity movement demonstrated a shift in the locus of morality away from the Protestant churches. Religious institutions were losing their exclusive rights to morality, and movement leaders recognized the need to reorganize their rhetorical strategies around more universal claims.[4] Within Protestant circles, the religious rhetoric of sexual purity and social Darwinism allowed reformers to connect their own race and class privilege with the well-being of the United States. Sexual purity, they contended, was most prominently exhibited in the cultural, physical, and moral superiority of their own Anglo-Saxon race. As a result, purity rhetoric of this era equated social uplift with assimilation into white Protestant culture. However, this status was tenuous, because reformers viewed themselves as the direct beneficiaries of classical civilizations felled by sexual licentiousness; reformers therefore interpreted the fall of these civilizations as a potent warning for their time.[5]

Changing ideals of womanhood were central to this project, because reformers sought to relocate women's domestic piety to the public sphere. The movement tried to increase the public influence of women and promoted purity as a "social salvation" that promised to elevate all worthy parties to the status of white, middle-class Protestantism. Revivalist piety, the related benevolence movement, and the promises of social and human evolution all shaped discourses of sexual purity in the nineteenth century. Missionary ideologies that were infused with imperialistic assumptions about the racial and economic privilege of white, middle-class Protestants compelled reformers to view their work as a religious duty. At the same time, scientific theories explaining the cultural categories of civilization and savagery created a moral dimension to the science of evolution that folded the concept of civilizational advancement into the premillennialist theology of nineteenth-century evangelicals.[6]

Domestic education in morals and manners for the young, extended educational opportunities for young men and women, the sentimentalization of childhood, and raising the age of consent created a new cultural space inhabited by young people, no longer children, yet not fully mature. This age between youth and adulthood took on primary significance for reformers, educators, and clergy who sought interventions that would offer safe passage between the two phases of life and inculcate the proper values and virtues for promoting a healthy citizenry.[7] Not until the emergence of the field of psychology was this stage of life given a name: adolescence.

An opponent of the purity movement (though not of the concept itself) and its accompanying initiative for gender equality, G. Stanley Hall developed the concept of adolescence in much the same way purity reformers had asserted purity—by marrying religious piety with the goals of advancing the human race, culturally and genetically. The civilization work of the purity reformers and of Hall generated a cultural trope linking adolescence, sexual purity, and civilizational or national advancement.[8] Understanding these linkages is of primary importance for understanding their later manifestations in the twentieth and twenty-first centuries.

Ideal Womanhood and Manhood

Ideals of manhood and womanhood were integral to middle-class Victorian Americans seeking respectability. Primarily, gender complementarianism was the foundation for the social order of a burgeoning capitalist society. Even purity reformers committed to reshaping gender roles and relations used these ideals as rhetorical support for their work. Marriage and a harmonious domestic life were unqualified social goods that supported economic vitality and civilizational advancement. As a white, middle-class ideal, domesticity linked the well-being of the white race with the well-being of the nation-state and allowed immigrants, newly freed men and women, and other nonwhites the opportunity to achieve middle-class status by adopting a set of practices established by the dominant class.

The protection of women, marriage, and the home was the special purview of the WCTU and Frances Willard, who commented often on the degenerative effects of drinking and promiscuity. Prostitution and other kinds of female exploitation, alcohol, and sexual impurity were threats to domestic harmony and its ability to act as a civilizing agent. Men who were unable to curb their "inflamed natures" and threatened the security of their homes, wives, and families exemplified the kind of social chaos that, according to Willard, characterized the Roman Empire just prior to its collapse.[9] These habits and circumstances kept women from claiming their "right to womanhood" by fulfilling their domestic duties as mothers and wives and claiming their own moral authority.[10]

Because of their biological imperative to procreate and nurture future generation, women were especially suited to lead the work for social betterment. In the pages of the *Philanthropist*, the flagship publication of the purity movement, physician Elizabeth Blackwell made the argument that women and men had equally strong sexual urges. However, woman's desire for sex was rooted not in lust but in her need to participate in what Blackwell called "her special racework."[11] As the bearers of the next generation, women were compelled to focus their creative energies toward the future of the race.

Sexual-purity work began with the presumption that white, middle-class women personified ideal womanhood and that the behavioral ideals for men were fraught with sexual license and moral laxity. This formulation was problematic for reformers, who believed that men and women were created as complementary parts. To allow men to rely on women's spiritual and moral authority, while relaxing men's standards, created a social disharmony that threatened the work of social reform. Frances Willard, president of the WCTU and leading purity reformer, drew upon the creation story from Genesis to lament the lack of unity between men and women in the fight for purity. Women's work, she told the audience at the International Council of Women, was incomplete without the efforts of men. Because men and women were created together by God to complete one another, any task undertaken for the purpose of achieving the new millennium, or age of peace, required cooperation between the sexes.[12]

The idealization of womanhood was fulfilled in the duties of motherhood, described in the flowery language of Victorian sentimentality and in the dutiful rhetoric of work. As the first educators of their children, mothers were expected to create environments and objectives that would transmit the values necessary for character development, including religious instruction and personal purity. The early efforts combined physical and religious development, inoculating the young against diseases of mind and body.[13]

The protection of body and mind were equally important for young women, as attested by numerous advice letters and pamphlets distributed by social-purity organizations. Ideal young women demonstrated modesty in dress and behavior, were concerned with maintaining physical health, and enjoyed spending time with children. The association between ideal womanhood and motherhood required that young women were trained according to the physical and moral demands of bearing and raising children. Because women's moral authority was predicated upon their ability to mother, the establishment of mothering as a location and practice of moral development played a central role in the advancement of women's rights. Women for the most part lacked political authority, but those who held social, class, and race status enjoyed a degree of moral authority in Victorian culture. Women's rights activists harnessed this authority for the purposes of expanding their influence and power beyond the mothering role. Led by these women, social purity coalesced as a movement around the virtues of women's moral authority and sought to create a universalized standard of moral practices and sexual behaviors. The movement codified this arrangement through the rhetoric of sexual purity, a term that encompassed all favorable habits and dispositions that Victorian culture associated with ideal womanhood.[14]

If women, reformers believed, were using their moral authority to claim political and public authority, then the inverse was also the case:

men needed to use their political and public authority to claim their own moral authority. However, public action was not sufficient for achieving the gender cooperation that purity reformers desired. Numerous evangelists, religious leaders, authors, and reformers sought to reframe masculine ideals. The purity movement was heralded by purity publications as a "new era of accountability for men" that was "destined to revolutionize old customs, and old statutes, which have so long perpetuated the stand of moral inequality for the two sexes."[15]

Other Victorians shared purity reformers' desire for social progress but were concerned about the effects of a feminized and overcivilized society. Psychologist and educational theorist G. Stanley Hall epitomized the resistance to women's increased access to education and public life. The goals of social Darwinism made him and purity reformers strange bedfellows in the work of social progress, even as he proclaimed the reformers' work a hindrance to the cause. Not unlike purity reformers, Hall's views on women were dominated by a biological essentialism that imposed the primacy of motherhood on all women. As an evolutionary psychologist, Hall recognized that women's health and well-being were paramount to the genetic improvement of the human race. But Hall's understanding of and appreciation for women was not simply utilitarian. In numerous writings, he depicts female physiology with the sentimentality of a Victorian poet. In describing a young girl's menstrual cycle, he wrote,

> Then, actually though unconsciously, if entirely healthful, she is more attractive to man; and as the wave of this great cosmic pulse which makes her live on a slope passes, her voice, her eye, complexion, circulation, and her very dreams are more brilliant. She feels her womanhood and glories in it like a goddess.[16]

As Hall gloried in the mysteries of womanhood, he also attempted to circumscribe women's roles to protect their greatest asset, reproductive capabilities.

As a result, his pedagogical goals for women's education were focused primarily on sexual hygiene.[17] Education, through which young people were given opportunities to achieve optimal health and proper social and moral development, was the key to social progress. For women's part, lessons in personal hygiene, physical well-being, and moral teachings reinforced middle-class values of ideal femininity and physical preparedness for marriage and motherhood. Threats to a young woman's virginity were not immoral because they threatened her social respectability, but because they threatened her ability to contribute to the improved condition of the human race.

In an era when women organized for and achieved increased social, religious, and political influence, many men felt threatened by the loss of their own positions of leadership and sought to restore their dominance. One of many responses to the perceived feminization of American culture, Hall's work in developmental psychology established a biological, pedagogical, and evolutionary foundation that necessitated female submission to the goals of social Darwinism. Hall was hardly alone in his concerns, as many evangelicals perceived women's political contributions and the purity movement as threats to male privilege. Within the conservative branch of evangelicalism, critics of liberal theology expressed fear of feminized theology and a female-dominated laity. The "feminization of religion" was problematic for men who resisted the gender complementarianism of the social reformers. Their solution was to promote the idea of muscular Christianity popularized by the Victorian British novelists Charles Kingsley and Thomas Hughes, whose works fused athleticism, patriotism, and religion and emphasized the importance of training the body for the purposes of protecting the weak and furthering righteous causes. Muscular Christianity, according to Hughes, comprised four ideals: manliness, morality, health, and patriotism. Hughes was especially concerned with Christological formulations that positioned Jesus as the highest form of manliness.[18]

Muscular Christians were propelled by fear and disdain for what they saw as the effeminate Christology, clergy, and hymnody characterizing mainline Protestantism. As a reaction against women's religious leadership and a response to the influx of immigrants, Protestant men saw themselves as men of action and aggression who, unlike the feminized Victorian gentleman, could stand up to the challenges of modernity in the same way that Christ stood up to the challenges of the Roman Empire.[19] Working-class Victorian manliness valued physical prowess, pugnacity, and sexuality. While working-class men chided middle-class men as weak and effeminate, middle-class Victorians dismissed the rough masculinity of the working class as coarse and backward.

Muscular Christians, like many Americans of the day, feared the decline of the Anglo-Saxon race. Newly arrived immigrants posed a threat to Protestant hegemony and exhibited a physical vitality that was not part of Victorian masculinity. Hence, muscular Christianity appropriated a fearless and primal quality tempered by subservience to God's will that could confront both the feminization of the church and the growing dominance of immigrant Roman Catholicism.[20]

There is some debate whether muscular Christianity was adopted by evangelicals in an attempt to challenge the growing authority of women or to refine men's behavior in favor of women's authority.[21] The revival work of Dwight Moody provides some insight into this query, not only because his revivals sought to draw men back to Christianity, but because of his affiliation with Frances Willard just prior to the beginning of her tenure as president of the WCTU.

The founder of the Chicago bible institute named after him and a prominent evangelical leader in the late nineteenth century, Moody became a proponent of muscular Christianity while doing mission work in Chicago during and after the Civil War. As a key leader in the YMCA, Moody embraced muscular Christianity as a tool of evangelicalism; the combination of the two propelled him to national attention. In 1865, Moody was elected president of the Chicago branch of the YMCA; two years later, he traveled to England and met John Nelson Darby. The impact of Darby's dispensationalism on Moody played a central role in the development of muscular Christianity, though this meeting held greatest significance for the eventual emergence of Protestant fundamentalism.[22] As a muscular Christian, Moody initially embraced the postmillennialist view of Christian theology also held by social-purity reformers. However, as an inherently premillennialist ideology, dispensationalism espoused the idea that social decline was a harbinger of the return of Christ. After the Civil War, Protestantism was split into pre- and postmillennial camps. Upon this shift in his theological orientation, Moody maintained his affiliation with muscular Christianity and in doing so precipitated the split in the muscular Christian movement.[23]

As a revivalist, Moody's masculine attributes appealed to male audiences and demonstrated the importance of physical virility to religious piety. During the Chicago World's Fair, Moody's revivals were especially focused on the working class—groups of men whose behavior threatened the social stability and moral order of the city.[24] Like purity reformers, Moody hoped to restore masculinity of all classes to a Christian ideal characterized by self-control, morality, and religious piety.

Moody's deployment of muscular Christianity was not an attempt to challenge women's authority. He explained urban decay as a result of men relinquishing their responsibilities to home and family. Men and women, according to Moody, held distinct, yet complementary traits: without the influence of female piety on their lives, men would be overcome by the vices of uncontrolled masculinity. Muscular Christianity, for Moody, was not so much a reordering of gender traits as the reification of gender roles that reinforced the naturalness of female piety and male integrity.[25]

In 1877, Frances Willard resigned as president of the Chicago WCTU and worked for Moody's evangelistic team. He encouraged her to preach both temperance reform and suffrage, but when she invited a Universalist to address her meeting, Moody recognized that he and Willard's theological differences were insurmountable and terminated her position. Moody supported the evangelical work and education of women, but he didn't support the idea of groups like the WCTU that established themselves independent of men's authority. Willard insisted on gender equality and deployed the moral authority of womanhood to justify her evangelistic work, which was characterized by the theological flexibility that would eventually lead to her departure from Moody's ministry. Though their conflict was initially theological, Moody later expressed his disgust for the WCTU because it did not conform to his expectations for male authority and female submission. Reform organizations like Willard's threatened Moody's understanding of divinely ordained gender roles: as in the domestic sphere, female evangelists and reformers were to submit to the authority of their male counterparts. Moody's contestation was not primarily about biblical adherence but about threats to worldly male authority that organizations like the WCTU represented.[26]

Although conservative evangelicals like Moody adopted muscular Christianity in order to reinstate male authority, this form of Christianity was a mainstay of liberal Protestants and their social reform agendas. Rather than superseding women's authority by adopting feminine virtues as conservatives did, liberal muscular Christianity reinforced men's moral accountability. The purity movement utilized muscular Christianity to reconstruct ideal manhood. Alongside the cultural realities of women's vulnerability and dependence on men, muscular Christianity served the purposes of purity reform by demanding men's moral accountability. As manhood was reconstructed according to the virtues Victorians traditionally assigned to women, the locus of authority shifted, creating new cultural spaces open to women's participation.

Purity reformers believed that social improvement required gender complementarianism that endorsed equality between men and women.

Even though Willard presided over an extensive organization run solely by women, she maintained that any significant social change required the cooperation of the sexes.[27] When speaking about the goals of the White Cross Army, both at home and abroad, she spoke of a desire to elevate fatherhood to the same spiritualized status as motherhood. Imbuing manhood with the same moral and spiritual standards held up for women made the man an "equal sharer in the cares that have so ennobled women as to make some of them akin to angels."[28] While conservative Protestants adopted muscular Christianity to address the presumed feminization of Christian theology and institutions, purity reformers utilized it to persuade men that sexual purity and moral living were not anathema to, but requirements of, real manhood.

As a step toward achieving women's independence from men, purity reformers wrote extensively about women's economic and political dependence upon men. In addressing this failure of gendered realities, purity reformers situated women as the more vulnerable sex whose well-being was contingent upon men's morality. As gender complementarians, purity reformers made use of gender stereotypes that appealed to women's need for security and men's desire to protect. Ellice Hopkins promoted the White Cross as an army of men whose valor and strength were best demonstrated through self-restraint and moral fortitude. The White Cross Army wanted to appeal to the working class, in the presumption that lower-class men were coarser in manners and morals. Purity, for Hopkins, was about educating men toward a more noble kind of masculinity, and she deployed tropes of knighthood to imbue the concept with a special status. Like muscular Christianity, Hopkins's purity rhetoric illustrated the battle between flesh and spirit that men faced in their attempts to assert mastery over their baser selves.[29]

Though the White Cross in the United States dropped the word "Army" from its name, the trope of knighthood frequently appeared in the speeches and writing of reformers. Willard told one audience that the White Cross used the language of chivalry to appeal to men's nobility:

White Cross work contemplates a direct appeal to the chivalry of men: that they shall join this holy crusade by a personal pledge of purity and helpfulness: that boys shall early learn the sacred meaning of the White Cross and that the generous knights of this newest and most noble chivalry shall lead Humanity's sweet and solemn song.[30]

Membership in the knighthood Willard spoke of was a special status for men who committed themselves to purity. Purity reformers did not adjust their assumptions that sexual restraint was challenging for men, nor did they presume that women's purity was no longer innate and fragile. Men were chastened by the idea that taking a woman's innocence was worse than committing murder, as both her body and soul would be destroyed. One writer implored, "Incest differs from impurity only as fratricide differs from ordinary murder."[31] Reformers challenged their culture's permissive approach to male sexuality—the cultural assumption that created the theater in which the drama of masculinity often unfolded. By reframing male sexual permissiveness as immoral and weak, the movement problematized the means by which manhood was achieved, though not the ideal itself. Men's self-indulgence led to the misery of physical weakness, emotional corruption, nervous tendencies, and lack of will—all characteristics that rendered them unable to love and accept love. Self-control, on the other hand, promised health, happiness, and a wholesome (i.e., married) life.[32] Tropes of chivalry and knighthood established a rhetorical link between male sexual restraint and masculine attributes of strength and aggression without negating the moral mandates of purity.

Allusions to medieval nobility romanticized gender roles, and purity publications often characterized ideal manhood as a chivalrous duty toward the weaker sex. As part of their knighthood, men who took the White Cross pledge were expected to protect the pure, a job not to be undertaken except by those who were themselves pure. Out of necessity, men in the movement were required to take responsibility for the formal legislative aspects of sexual purity. Yet, regardless of the legal status of prostitution or age-of-consent laws, men were expected to accept the mandates of purity as "a law unto themselves," that is, as a law that transcended both natural inclination and legal sanction. Ideal men considered every woman a sister, and they were committed to defending her purity regardless of her social and economic status.[33] Amid efforts to raise the age of consent, one author argued that chivalrous men were more effective than the law at protecting women and girls against corruption.[34]

As an outgrowth of muscular Christianity, the idea of knighthood encoded Christology with the ideals of manhood. Muscular Christians displayed anxiety over portrayals of Jesus that feminized his features and behavior, as was common in the Victorian era. Evangelists, authors, and businessmen imbued Jesus with masculine traits like leadership, business acumen, and physical strength.[35] Though purity reformers did not express similar fears, they did assert Jesus as an exemplar of ideal manhood because his virility was exhibited through his physical and spiritual purity.[36] Authors employed other biblical figures as standards of male purity: Joseph, the son of Jacob, was sold by his brothers and ended up working in the household of an Egyptian officer. When the officer's wife attempted to seduce Joseph, he rebuffed her, and the wife had him arrested on a false accusation of sexual misconduct. One author in the *Philanthropist* offered Joseph as an exemplar of the "strongest manhood" because of his ability to "draw the curb on the jaw of fierce desire till the fiery Bucephalus of passion steps as tame as a lamb."[37] Borrowing from the rhetorical strategies of muscular Christianity, purity rhetoric equated virility with the virtue of self-control and challenged the idea that men were bound by their carnal impulses.

A commitment to sexual purity was a commitment to cooperation between the sexes. Ideal manhood and womanhood increased the social stability of marriage and family life. The quality of domestic life, according to purity reformers who witnessed firsthand living and working conditions plagued by sexual impurity, hinged on the development of proper habits of male self-restraint.[38]

> Blessed are the pure in heart, for they only can see and know the sacred happiness of that perfect union for heart and life which is so pure and holy that it could be made the sublime love of the divine Christ for his people.[39]

This sentiment echoed the Victorian belief that marriage was a divinely sanctioned institution reflecting the relationship between God and the believer. Domestic ideologies, then, were not simply about right relations within the home but also about locating the site of spiritual and moral transformation. Domesticity was a way to distinguish the civilized from the savage and gave women a special role in marking that delineation. Women like Catharine Beecher and Sarah Josepha Hale, the editor of *Godey's Lady's Book*, promoted a form of domestic piety that sanctioned the work of Manifest Destiny, a project of white, middle-class expansion across the North American continent. By locating safety and morality within the home, Victorian proponents of domesticity coded the nondomestic, or foreign, as unsafe and immoral. Beecher and Hale described home life in imperialistic terms—the home was an empire of the mother that thrived under her regal authority.[40]

The postmillennialist theology of revivalist Protestantism shaped reformers' expectations for change. The optimistic tenor of liberal Protestantism promoted the idealization of family life and gendered norms. To
facilitate this, the purity movement crafted useful characterizations of the
sexes and domestic piety that were rooted in Victorian sentimentality and
refinement. Egalitarian forms of marriage and domestic life held eschatological significance, seen as signs that American society was moving
toward an era of peace and prosperity, which, according to premillennialist theologies, would precipitate the return of Christ. The reform of gender
roles and the institution of a public domestic piety imagined increased
political authority for women and increased moral authority for men.
More importantly, gender egalitarianism and domestic ideology signified
an advanced civilization and a secure nation-state.

The home and family were for Willard the locus of this transformation, with fatherhood and motherhood providing evidence of God's goodness and promising hope for social progress. Ideas about gender and
family life had evolved, Willard contended, to a higher state—one that
more closely resembled the perfect union first shared by Eve and Adam.
Willard recognized that this ideal was not yet complete, which allowed her
to situate gender equality and divine marital union as marks of a new
stage of human existence. New ideals of womanhood and manhood called
for a companionate relationship in which the partners shared traits of
purity and moral responsibility. Willard's eschatological vision of domestic, married life was influenced by social Darwinist theories, which allowed her to mark gender inequality as a sign of a less-evolved civilization.
Her argument for women's equality was based upon the belief that wom-
en's civilizing work was needed throughout society. The greater the opportunity for women to impact cultural and political life, the greater a
society's ability to achieve a level of fitness required for survival and cultural supremacy.[41]

Gendered Vice and Virtue

Though ideal womanhood and manhood played significant roles in shaping eschatological visions of family and society, purity reformers also developed strategies for using gender inequalities to shape the movement.
The contrast between the vices and virtues associated with masculinity
and femininity provided the rhetorical infrastructure for the movement.
Masculine ideals were related to professional success, not religious piety,

while purity workers entered political life with moral fortitude as their primary persuasive tool. They were seeking to change not just men but traditional male spheres of engagement. If men could be reshaped according to the mandates of female virtue, then women could have access to all arenas of public life. Sexual-purity rhetoric used gendered virtues and vices strategically to both influence men's behavior and make a case for women's political rights.

Ellice Hopkins, the founder and most prominent activist in the Church of England's White Cross Army, worked toward increased political status for women through the refinement of male sexuality. The name of her organization helped to dispel any confusion that one could not be sexually continent and reach maturity as a man. Hopkins's intent was not to disrupt the gender ideologies that supported middle-class Victorian culture, but to rearrange the social locations of gendered vices and virtues. Morgan sought to extend feminine virtues into the public sector and, in so doing, modify men's private and public conduct in accordance with the virtues of sexual purity and religious piety. Women reformers had no intention of relinquishing their own claim to these virtues, but instead used their supposedly natural inclinations to assert their moral authority over men. According to Hopkins, the best men could integrate the best qualities of womanhood into their own character, and this would assure women the ability to preserve their own moral integrity.[42]

The restoration of morality required the full cooperation of men in resisting the "almost universal belief that license is venial, even necessary to men."[43] At the second National Purity Congress, Emily Blackwell impressed upon the audience that the systems that regulated and maintained the legitimacy of prostitution presumed the inequality of men and women. Advocates of legalization drew upon the argument of historian William Lecky, who described prostitutes as a necessary evil. The prostitute was a "priestess of humanity charged with the mournful office of bearing the sins of the people."[44] These kinds of sociohistorical assessments assumed men's lack of self-restraint, while burdening women with the task of attending to the moral refuse of society. In order for women to achieve equal access to political and public authority, this sexual double standard had to be be eradicated.[45]

Women's reputation as the weaker and more vulnerable sex supported their claims to sexual purity and religious piety, the foundational elements of women's moral authority. Men were characterized as the source of sexual depravity and the natural antagonists of women's virtue. Susan B. Anthony articulated this position as early as 1875 in a talk she delivered as part of the Sunday afternoon Dime lecture series in Chicago. She defined women as less capable of, but more vulnerable to, the ills associated with drunkenness and sexual impurity. Though less prone to these forms of wickedness, their economic dependence on men rendered them highly vulnerable to their effects. In the workforce, women had access to their own income but continued to be exposed to similar dangers from male coworkers and supervisors. Whether or not a woman worked, her purity was always easily threatened. Domestic intemperance, poverty, and harsh working conditions created untenable living and working situations. Chances to work with the promise of comfort and luxury were strong temptations for impoverished and working-class women. Anthony thus portrayed prostitutes and other women who worked in the public sector as victims of male debauchery and economic inequality. Likewise, she said, women were often lured into marriage with similar promises and as few rights. The solution was equal access to the political process. Only women could effectively represent their own needs. A male family member could not do so on their behalf. A woman's moral failings were always traceable to a man's doing, a harsh economic situation, or both. Anthony sought to create a more transparent ethical system in which women had equal rights and responsibilities for their actions.[46]

Popular among purity reformers was the cautionary tale that warned young women of the ways they could be lured into prostitution or other illicit activities. These were often represented in the *Philanthropist* by works like Grace H. Dodge's "A Portion of a Confidential Letter to Girls." After praising the ideal behavior of young women, she describes how easily even the most pure women could be deceived into inappropriate sexual relationships. She warns her readers against enjoying the attentions of strangers, receiving expensive gifts, and "carrying on" with male companions who are not well known to them. She tells the story of a young woman who was courted by a young man: after numerous dates and increasing physical intimacy, he gave her some lemonade, "which strangely excited her" and resulted in shame, remorse, and an unwanted pregnancy. Without the needed social sanctions, promises of marriage, even an engagement, could coerce a young woman into sexual activity. Since marriage, family, and home life were the foundation of a woman's moral authority, premarital indiscretions threatened the "little kingdom of which the wife is to be the queen and half-creator."[47]

An anonymous author in the *Philanthropist*, simply called "a friend," wrote with more urgency. "Girls, beware, oh beware!" the article began. It went on to describe scenarios in which a young woman's desire for material possessions results in her exploitation and defilement. Advertisements for jobs, according to the author, were often a cover for prostitution rings, offering abundant pay without specifying the kind of work available. Any promise of material goods, through either work or benefactors, was suspect. Though middle-class respectability was often associated with the possession of material goods, unbridled desire for those goods could lead to a woman's ruin.[48]

While young women were offered advice to help them resist the temptations of male attention and material wealth, purity reformers worked to adapt men's behavior through public condemnations of their activities. The *Chicago Tribune* printed a reformer's remarks peppered with outrage and moral indignation:

> While evil men are at large to plot and plan their deeds of ruin, while by the tens of thousands they were free to deceive, drug, force, tempt these "cuckoos in the nest" for their own foul ends. Society had branded the women. Very well, if you will pin the scarlet letter upon her poor breast with your ruthless hands. I demand in the name of the God of Justice that you pin it also on the coat of the man! Nay! Brand it upon his very brow, that he may forever bear the mark of Cain.[49]

A frequent topic was the myth of young men's need to "sow their wild oats."[50] An article reprinted from the *Pioneer*, the publication of London Purity Society Alliance, spoke plainly to young men, calling "wild oats" sins deserving of God's wrath and not to be dismissed as small transgressions. Purity reformers needed to debunk the popular belief that men required a sexual outlet in order to achieve physical maturity. This author argued the elective nature of sexual activity by pointing to the social restrictions placed on women. If women could be expected to abstain and even thrive from sexual purity, then so, too, should men. The expectation that women remain pure while men did not was indefensible.[51]

Frances Willard used this rhetoric in her condemnations of men's drunkenness and sexual promiscuity, calling them makers of women martyrs. She frequently described womanhood as defenseless, weak, and in need of protection as a way to emphasize the evil effects of alcohol and the sexual double standard. Home, family, women, and children needed special protection because they played a central role in the cultivation of personal and collective morality.[52]

Purity reformers adopted three strategies to prevent the corruption of innocents: purity pledges, written advice, and education; rescue work with fallen women; and legal action toward the eradication of prostitution and raising the age of sexual consent. The White Cross exemplified the purity pledge strategy. As crafted by Ellice Hopkins and promoted by the American branches of the organization, purity pledges called upon men to reform their conduct, protect women, and embrace purity.

> 1) To treat all women with respect, and endeavor to protect them from wrong and degradation. 2) To endeavor to put down all indecent language and coarse jests. 3) To maintain the law of purity as equally binding upon men and women. 4) To endeavor to spread the principles among my companions, and try to help my younger brothers. 5) To use every possible means to fulfill the command, "Keep THYSELF pure."[53]

Each of these stipulations was an attempt to instill in men the feminine qualities of purity, compassion, and restraint. Different pledges for women, boys, and girls included variations on the White Cross pledge, though the strongest efforts were aimed at men. As men adapted their behaviors according to the expectations of sexual-purity reforms, women's moral status achieved greater social and political significance. This movement focused on getting young men to commit to lives of sexual purity, but it did so under the aegis of women's moral superiority.

Male reformers also used the rhetoric of female vulnerability and male debauchery. Gendered vice and virtue meant that separate spheres were needed to protect the vulnerable. Any breach of that separation created new anxieties. The entrance of young women into the industrial workplace was especially worrisome for Victorians, who were still leery of situations that regularly put men and women in close proximity to one another. This breach of separate spheres heightened women's vulnerability and also threatened the locus of their moral authority, the home.

The *Philanthropist* frequently ran columns about the vulnerability of working women. Aaron Macy Powell, president of the American Purity Alliance and coeditor of its journal, the *Philanthropist*, encouraged the development of a society to focus especially on working women and ensure their protection from the advances of lecherous male coworkers. In the journal, Powell and his coeditor and wife, Anna, wrote about the threats facing working girls, who were easily enticed by the new entertainments and leisure activities available to them. "They do not themselves see or anticipate danger; are impatient of restraint, and are not readily amenable to advice from the older and more experienced," the Powells wrote. To the purity movement, these women were not newly emancipated to a life of personal income and elective leisure, but naïve and uneducated about a world of lurking evils. Powell warned that young women were easily lured by the affections of supervisors or coworkers into "a life of sin." In one case, three different women named the same factory foreman as the father of their newborns.[54]

The new social order that gave women opportunities for work and leisure complicated the arrangement of gendered vice and virtue. The male seducer was no longer solely responsible for the moral corruption of girls. Reformers and social workers determined that working-class living and working conditions were more determinative of a young woman's sexual propriety than male influence was.[55] Reformers were also aware that young women influenced one another's choices. The Reverend J. W. Richardson preached about a young woman who warned another that if she refused the attentions of licentious men, she would never receive any attention at all. By this anecdote, Richardson sought to demonstrate the ways that young women can lead one another astray without proper oversight.[56] Even as reformers recognized the complexity of young men's and women's sexual awareness and behavior, they retained the tropes of female vulnerability and male aggression. Even as they published cautionary articles for both men and women that acknowledged this complexity, these tropes performed a strategic political function by supporting women's moral authority.

Women who worked as prostitutes also complicated the rhetoric of gendered vice and virtue. The Reverend Anna Garlin Spencer wrote that prostitutes were both sinners and sick patients, a characterization that ranked the prostitute alongside the drunkard. Both the prostitute and the alcoholic were powerless against their physiological and pathological cravings. As men could be addicted to alcohol, degraded women could become addicted to sex. But drunkenness was neither illegal nor always detrimental to a man's social status, whereas a prostitute's sexual appetite always put her at odds with the law and destroyed her position. Garlin believed these vices should be offered the same treatment, providing victims with a cure rather than incarceration.[57]

Purity reformers called alcohol and prostitution "the Siamese twins" of social iniquity, but, as gendered vices, they had very different repercussions.[58] Purity reformers sought to extend female virtues to men in order to awaken their sense of responsibility. At the same time, they needed to protect women from male vice, which reformers understood as inherently male attributes in excess. The problem of prostitution was not only that it victimized and degraded women, but that it imbued women with the masculine vice of uncontrolled lust.

The trope of women's vulnerability and men's sexual aggression was consistent with Victorian gender ideologies that supported women's social inferiority and men's spiritual inferiority. Female reformers used gendered vice and virtue to urge the reformation of men's behavior. At the same time, women used sexual-purity reform to challenge male privilege within their own organizations and American culture at large. Julia Ward Howe noted the problematic nature of male-dominated, antiprostitution organizations.[59] Women reformers believed that men could not adequately legislate controls over other men, especially in matters of sexuality.[60] But Howe's critique was addressing not primarily legislative challenges but, rather, women's access to positions of political power.

Gender, Domesticity, and the Market Economy

Though religious rhetoric reinforced the biblical mandates of female domesticity and male leadership, this arrangement was idealized primarily because of its benefit to the economic and moral status of middle-class family life. With a burgeoning capitalist economy, middle-class households struggled to reconcile their growing personal wealth with the traditional austerity of Protestant evangelicalism. Catholic immigrants boasted an array of images and objects that displayed their piety. Protestants now set aside their reticence and began to purchase items that would demonstrate their own religious dedication.[61]

Most of these religious goods were displayed in the home as part of the tableau of female domesticity. As her own piety was centered on her domestic responsibilities, an evangelical woman engaged the market in order to demonstrate the moral status of her family.[62] For men, the responsibility to offer care and provisions for his family required absence from the hallowed space of his home, while his wife's commitment to the maintenance of domestic piety provided the necessary counterbalance to his public and commercial ventures. The separate-spheres arrangement supported the economic success of middle-class families by uniting a woman's domestic piety with a man's public and commercial ambitions.[63]

Given the centrality of the home in these formulations of piety and morality, middle-class Protestants were especially troubled by families whose economic situation did not allow home ownership and required the earned income of women and children. It was these urban, often immigrant, families whom purity reformers targeted with their work for social uplift. The benevolence work of middle-class evangelical women rested on the assumption that individuals and families without the amenities of a middle-class family life were more vulnerable to the social ailments that plagued urban environments.

Through an ideology of moral motherhood, Protestant women sought to restrain the excesses of a male-dominated capitalist system that relied on the existence of an underclass. Using their elevated status as white, middle-class women, social reformers worked with less-fortunate women to enable their ascent to middle-class respectability. Unbridled capitalism also endorsed a system of commodification in which all leisure goods could be purchased, including a woman's body. Purity reforms sought to provide a system of checks and balances to curb the excesses of capitalism that exploited the weak, especially poor women.

Benjamin DeCosta, rector of the Church of St. John the Evangelist in New York City and president of the White Cross Society in the United States, was direct in his criticism of capitalism as it related to the welfare of the economically vulnerable. He preached about the evils of a social order that exploited the labor and bodies of disadvantaged women.

> Capital is to-day forcing its victims to work on starvation wages in factories and shops that are sinks of iniquity, and in which purity is impossible and no girl's virtue is safe. Capital has a distinct employment of the hellish kind, providing the houses and means, and appointing the pimps and panders, coining great profits out of the misery and shame, plunging their employees lower and lower, day by day, until the miserable victims, inebriated fiends, become a danger and menace to society, and in self-defense the White Cross Society is obliged to proceed against them.[64]

As part of the Protestant liberal effort to shape church teachings around concern for the poor, DeCosta's ministry revealed a deep affinity between purity work and the social gospel movement. Earlier, Kate Bushnell, a medical doctor and evangelist for the WCTU's department of social purity, addressed the organization's fifteenth annual convention with a sermon decrying middle-class ignorance of poverty. Bushnell called WCTU women to awaken to the moral and economic degradation faced by poor women and their families. With the fierce eloquence of an open-air revivalist, she implored them to act according to the mandates of divine justice, which required Christians to open their eyes to the plight of the downtrodden. Middle-class Christians who prospered from capitalism could easily isolate themselves from the degrading circumstances of those who did not. Purity reformers and social gospelers confronted middle-class apathy with prophetic calls to social reform and Christian compassion: "(I) charge it against this day and civilization, that we are constantly condemning to eternal death a class of people whose story we will not allow ourselves to hear."[65] Bushnell moved seamlessly from the curse of economic degradation to the sexual double standard and called upon mothers in particular to "bring the world to a higher level of purity."[66]

In the last quarter of the nineteenth century, American Protestants found themselves increasingly divided over understandings of Christian piety. The optimism that animated the social reform of postrevival Protestantism continued as a staple of the social gospel movement. Christian piety for revivalists and reformers prioritized good works over orthodox belief, an orientation that other evangelicals found disconcerting. Like new scientific discoveries and other modernist approaches to truth, liberal Protestantism faced increasing hostility from conservatives, who believed that religious orthodoxy was threatened by an overemphasis on social concerns. By the time social-purity work was part of the constellation of social issues for Protestants, the tradition was divided into distinct conservative and liberal camps. Sexual purity was allied with progressive Christianity, not because conservatives didn't value sexual restraint and deplore sexual promiscuity, but because the purity movement had its theological foundation in liberal Protestantism.

Domestic Piety and Anglo-Saxon Superiority

In cities like New York, Chicago, Denver, and San Francisco, reformers visited red-light districts to report on the degraded state of these enclaves and offer women religious or medical services; sometimes, they left with prostitutes in tow, hoping to find them a better life.[67] These groups established rescue homes for "fallen women," as former prostitutes were called, where they would be indoctrinated into the opportunities of white, middle-class womanhood. They would learn domestic skills, establish Christian faith practices, and, ideally, meet genteel Christian men who would establish them as the respectable, married women reformers idealized.

The reality was usually not so rosy. Women brought to these homes were often expected to leave their communities of racial or ethnic origin and return only when they could do so with a proper Christian husband. They ended up occupying a liminal social space in which they were not fully accepted into the white, Protestant middle class but could not return to their communities of origin without falling back into the economic circumstances that led to their initial degradation. Moreover, the cultural boundaries of their values and definitions of womanhood were not recognized by white, middle-class women. Cultures that treated their women differently from Victorian standards were characterized as "heathen."[68] Likewise, home mission women who centered all of women's value on the role of mothering could not comprehend cultures in which women achieved status through other roles.[69] Sharp distinctions were made between moral and immoral women, and many women—including Mormon women who defended polygamy, Chinese women who bound their daughters' feet, Navajo women who practiced traditional rituals, and working-class women who had premarital sex without compunction—were deemed immoral according to Victorian ideology steeped in Anglo-Saxon superiority.[70]

Missionary efforts also reached out to newly freed blacks in the South, where white, Northern missionaries worked to ameliorate the aftereffects of slavery by encouraging the adoption of middle-class values. The work of women missionaries consisted of domestic and religious education, often with little distinction between the two. Though most purity reform occurred in Northern cities, missionaries gave purity a prominent place in their agenda. Northern missionaries in the South were motivated by Victorian belief in the necessary cooperation of domestic integrity, religious piety, and social uplift. Women like Catharine Beecher and Mary Lyon had developed the ideal of domesticity into an educational and moral system for middle-class women. Numerous domestic practices and behavioral norms demonstrated how white Protestants had imbued middle-class norms with sacred significance. Female missionaries sought the salvation of freedmen and freedwomen at the convergence of domestic and religious education. Salvation was not limited to the salvation of individual souls, nor was domestic instruction merely a tool for achieving a tidy and ordered home. Rather, the work of domestic salvation was a program in racial uplift rooted in the belief that the ill effects of slavery could be overcome by the adoption of those virtues associated with white, middle-class women.

Mary L. Sawyer, a missionary teacher at the Talladega School in Alabama, addressed the American Missionary Association (AMA) on the topic of "women's work for women" in 1882.[71] In her talk, Sawyer urged the importance of domestic instruction at her school. Her primary concern was that her students learned the value of cleanliness and order. Concerning her mission, she wrote, "Personal neatness is to be inculcated; dress, deportment, speech, expression, manner, must be watched and toned by careful teachers."[72] Sawyer challenged Northern assumptions about the degraded state of black life in the South, and, at the following year's meeting, began her comments with a direct challenge to the portrayal of Southern black women as backward, unrefined, and immoral. She argued that her branch of missionary work in the AMA was succeeding in its efforts to transform coarse, uneducated girls into noblewomen for Christ.

Another AMA missionary, Laura Parmelee, a math teacher at the LeMoyne School in Memphis, also contributed reports on "women's work." Like Sawyer, she placed a heavy emphasis on order and cleanliness. However, she also expressed a special concern for sexual purity as a domestic and personal virtue. She strongly advocated sending girls away to boarding schools to develop habits of domestic piety and social purity, in light of the ease with which her work was undone by the influence of students' home lives. Prioritizing etiquette, comportment, and fashion, Parmelee saw her work as the transformation of her students from "animals to thoughtful young women."[73] Parmelee's primary objective, however, was to impart to her students the value of bodily respect and chastity.

Purity reformers received reports from missionaries describing a post-slavery culture in which moral laxity among whites and blacks was normative. In slavery, few blacks had marriage rights, but many witnessed the sexual exploits of their masters and adopted these practices for themselves. Reports published in the *Philanthropist* claimed that black men had been trained to be lustful, and that women had acquiesced to their degraded status. Married, white men pursued black women and seduced

them with gifts and attention. Black girls and women, according to reformers, bore the burden of men's sexual vices.[74] Parmelee addressed this
concern by instituting lessons on sexual hygiene and human reproduc-
tion and advocating chastity as a "responsibility toward God." In her address to the Women's Meeting of the AMA, Parmelee called for a full-time
physician who could continue the health education of her students and
their mothers, someone who would travel the area giving lectures on
health, personal hygiene, nutrition, and the importance of sexual purity.[75]
Though there is no evidence to suggest that such an individual was secured for this work, the LeMoyne School went on to institute a program
in nursing. One physician who assessed the program admired the students' preparation and remarked that many of the women were prepared
to be not only nurses but physicians. In response, Mary Sawyer remarked
that the goal of the program was not to train young black women for professional life, but to compensate for their mothers' inability to teach their
daughters the value of personal health and sexual purity.[76]

The *Philanthropist* endorsed this view by reprinting the comments of a
Southern preacher published in the Atlanta African American newspaper
the *Weekly Defiance*. Like Southern white missionaries, Reverend C. N.
Grandison lamented the impact of slavery on black mothers and their
daughters:

> Mothers know how hard it is to train their daughters to virtuous
> lives, simply because the treatment of the whites towards their race,
> in and since the days of slavery, has been such as to imbue them
> with the idea that they are not expected to be as good as white ladies.[77]

According to white purity reformers and missionaries, slavery rendered
Southern blacks not culpable for their immoral behaviors. Marriage practices among Southern blacks dismayed white Protestants, but blacks
themselves were not held accountable. Rather, the degrading circumstances of slavery, and especially the examples set by slave masters, explained the prevalence of unmarried partners.

A problematic correlation between prostitution or "white slavery" and
the institution of African chattel slavery in the South resulted in a variety
of responses to the purity movement among African Americans.[78] Reverend Grandison's approach was just one example of how blacks challenged the racialized assumptions of purity reform while also endorsing
the law of purity for blacks. He used the phrase "white ladies," indicating

his awareness that the ideals of purity and domestic piety were reserved for white, middle-class women. Yet, he also applauded black women who embraced this moral standard and acknowledged them for providing "the future blessings of the race."[79]

At the 1893 Parliament of the World's Religions, Fannie Barrier Williams, one of the few blacks to participate in the Chicago World's Fair, criticized its white Protestant organizers for its exclusion of black participants. She was especially critical of white, middle-class domesticity, the very thing on display at the American Purity Alliance's meeting held concurrently with the fair. She challenged the movement by calling into question white women's special claim to moral authority—a position, she argued, that was obtained at the expense of black women. White women's moral authority implied the moral inferiority of black women. Domesticity, not ideals of white, middle-class womanhood, was the key for social and moral uplift for Southern blacks.

> We do not yet sufficiently appreciate the fact that at the heart of every social evil and disorder among colored people, especially of the rural South, is the lack of these inherent moral potencies of home and family that are the well-springs of all the good in human society.[80]

Historian Louise Michele Newman has demonstrated that social movements such as temperance, social purity, and suffrage were part of a larger project of "civilization-work," which presumed the moral and social superiority of white, middle-class women.[81] Although purity reformers rejected any argument for their subservience to men, they assessed other racial and class groups based on their adaptation of traditional gender roles. Middle-class women of color like Williams and Grandison's daughters had to embody Victorian ideals of womanhood to signify their race's capacity for civilizational advancement and to pursue their own social reforms. By claiming the female virtues of domesticity, purity, and piety for themselves, black women reformers challenged white women's exclusive claim to moral authority.[82]

Purity, Civilization, and the Invention of Adolescence

As David Pivar has shown, the cultural shifts in late-nineteenth-century America meant a rearrangement of the locus of moral authority. The influx of Roman Catholic immigrants and especially the advancement of the biological sciences meant that America no longer depended upon Protestant evangelicalism's exclusive claim to truth and moral authority. Yet, for a significant amount of time, discourses of morality were encoded with both traditional revivalist themes and social Darwinist theories. The millennialist hopes of liberal Protestants, first awakened during the extended revivals of the midcentury, were a mainstay of purity reformers' assertion of ideal manhood, womanhood, marriage, and domestic life. Postmillennialist theologies envisioned a perfect society characterized by gender equality, economic parity, and universal moral standards—the very ideals evoked by Frances Willard and other reformers. Unlike their conservative counterparts, liberal Protestants did not resist the new science of evolutionary biology. It provided a self-evident rationale for their goals of moral reform. At the end of the nineteenth century, sexual-purity rhetoric was complemented by the concept of sexual hygiene, which recognized the scientific and medical contributions to the problem of social decline.[83] At the time, the languages of social Darwinism and purity reform were often indistinguishable and were frequently used strategically to transfer the moral authority of Protestant piety to science, medicine, and health without undermining Anglo-Saxon superiority. Purity reform amalgamated the concepts of social Darwinism and Christian civilization to create a particular claim on the American people: America's civilizational advancement as a nation-state was dependent upon the thriving of the Anglo-Saxon race, made possible through the practice of sexual purity.[84]

The racialized rhetoric of social Darwinism was used to assert Anglo-Saxon superiority. In historical events, international travel, and evolutionary biology, white, middle-class Protestants found evidence for their own moral and genetic superiority. Unlike colonialist ideologies that asserted a fixed distinction between more and less advanced civilizations, social Darwinists believed that civilizational advancement was open to any group that successfully adapted to the superior culture. Likewise, a civilization could fall from its advanced position in the social hierarchy, making the work of civilizational maintenance equally important. Discourses of civilizational decline and advancement attached easily to nationalist ideologies that promoted the United States as the height of Christian civilization.[85]

The desire for human progress grew organically out of Protestants' millennialist inclinations for social advancement. Science was beginning to displace religious claims to truth and knowledge at the end of the nineteenth century. However, liberal Protestants found that social Darwinism could be used to support the idea of Christianity as a civilizing agent. Prominent child psychologist G. Stanley Hall's work on adolescence is especially relevant to the history of sexual purity. As a social Darwinist, he developed his theory of adolescence in tandem with particular goals of civilizational advancement. At the same time, he recognized that traditional religiosity held a great deal of rhetorical power. Therefore, he often deployed religious, even revivalist, language in his work, introducing evolutionary theory as, in effect, a new religion. Though highly skeptical of revivalist religion, Hall recognized humanity's need for salvation. The salvation he advocated, however, was achieved through evolutionary rather than spiritual means. Moreover, he believed in religion as an effective prophylactic, a hindrance to unsanctioned sexual activity; for that reason alone, religion held merit. Religion was created by and for humanity, contrary to the more orthodox belief that humanity was created by and for God.

During the Progressive Era, Hall was part of an educational reform movement that sought to break the code of silence that prevented public conversations about sex. Alongside the purity movement, the sex-hygiene reformers worked to stem the tide of venereal disease that threatened family and national stability. Hall's recommendations for teaching sexual hygiene, about which he spoke and wrote at length, show how the concept of adolescence entered the twentieth century at the intersection of religious conversion, social Darwinism, and Victorian gender roles. He and other educational leaders brought purity rhetoric into the modern age by inserting the moral idealism of Protestant evangelicalism into the evolutionary goals of sexual hygiene.[86]

Hall recognized that the success of his plans for sexual hygiene was contingent upon his ability to couch them in evangelical language. His address to the Meeting of the American Society of Sanitary and Moral Prophylaxis shows how he carefully employed evangelical theology to frame his own social Darwinism as a religious system. Beginning with the Old Testament, Hall reminded his audience of the covenant between Abram and Yahweh, which centered on God's promise to bless Abram with generations of descendants. This relationship was the beginning of what Hall referred to as "the romance of humanity and God," in which God acted as the reproductive force moving humanity toward posterity. God, Hall asserted, was posterity personified, and human beings show their reverence by participating in their own propagation.[87]

Hall recognized the importance of continence for the production of healthy progeny. Despite his criticism of the purity movement, Hall found its language of corruption, pollution, and sin easily adaptable to his own evolutionary ideology and affirmed that religion was the most effective sexual deterrent for young people. Despite his wariness of evangelical religion and purity reform, Hall recognized that "those who have been most truly righteous have most sought purity and alliance with the power that works righteousness."[88] Even if religion proved to be a creation of humanity, its ability to protect humanity from its own corruption was invaluable.

This didn't keep Hall from asserting his own progressive view that a "new dispensation of sexual theory and practice" was required. That new dispensation was a new religion centered on the relationship between the individual and the future of the human race. Again, Hall positioned this shift within the evangelical tradition of revivalism by claiming that this momentous transition would require "a national, industrial, social, political as well as religious revival, such as the world has seen but once or possibly twice since the Renaissance."[89]

Hall's use of religious language to support his campaign for sexual hygiene was sincere but also strategic. Sexual hygiene played a very prominent role in his Darwinist conceptions of religion as civilizational advancement. It was also a way to shift moral idealism, a value indispensable to the hygiene movement, away from the salvific claims of Protestant evangelicalism. The goal of Hall's work in sexual hygiene was shared by religion and social Darwinism: the salvation of the species.

For purity reformers and social hygienists, social evolution was another way to equate Anglo-Saxon privilege and Christianity with civilizational advancement. The marker of an advanced civilization was the treatment and protection of women that allowed for their physical, intellectual, and moral development. The laws governing Christian nations provided the greatest opportunities for women; thus, Christianity and gender parity were the primary agents of evolutionary advancement.[90]

Social Darwinists within the purity movement worked to demonstrate the relationship between sexual impurity and civilizational decline. The Reverend William T. Sabine, a movement leader, spoke most often on the topic of social vice and national decay. A proponent of social evolution theory, Sabine believed that individual change and social change were integrally connected. Shifts in personal behavior that led to the moral decline of the individual would also lead to collective downfall. Social purity, as Sabine described it, was a citizen's obligation, because the individual's health could have direct consequences for the health of the nation. Morally and physically unhealthy men were incapable of leading proper domestic lives with thriving families and could not properly function as citizens.

> It follows, and there is no getting away from the conclusion, that where large sections of a population become physically and morally deteriorated through vicious and immoral practices, the strength and capacity of the State must be weakened in exact proportion. If the evil, unarrested, continues to spread in ever-widening circles; with every passing decade, involving hitherto untainted thousands in its curse; it is plain that the Nation must enter upon a period of decline, which allowed to proceed to its ultimate results can only issue in national ruin and extinction.[91]

Over several years, he crafted an argument that explained that nations and civilizations failed to thrive and faced inevitable decline because of sexual immorality. Numerous examples, including the greatest of civilizations—Greece, Rome, Babylon—demonstrated how moral depravity, sexual licentiousness, and venereal disease led to population decline, loss of moral stature, and loss of national cohesion.[92] Drawing upon these supposed historical precedents, Sabine was able to identify the kind of widespread behavior that rendered a nation at risk. Regardless of a nation's potential for or current state of civilizational achievement, abandoning the virtue of purity hastened its inevitable decline.

He drew further support for his argument from Joseph Cook's Boston Monday Lecture on the problem of prostitution. Deploring the ills of immigration and urban decay, Cook affirmed the cultural superiority of the Anglo-Saxon race, which he described as "the race that rules the world today."[93] With the high sentimentality of Victorian Protestantism, Cook depicted early Anglo-Saxons as a pure and natural race of people untainted by sexual impurity. Because this race's originators punished sexual immorality with great severity, he claimed, they emerged from the German forests a physically and morally superior race. Sexual purity was the "chief secret" of civilizational greatness because it promoted racial purity, genetic endurance, and a collection of superior moral and physical traits. Despite Cook's description of Anglo-Saxons as "pure as the dew the forests shook upon their heads," which naturalized their purity as an original state, he cautioned his audience on the mutability of human civilizations.

> If the Anglo-Saxon race has shown exceptional vigor, the chief
> secret of its power is to be found in its reverence for a pure family
> life. It will continue to have that power and rule the world it if con-
> tinues that pure life. Otherwise not.[94]

Connections between sexual purity, civilizational advancement, and the Anglo-Saxon race were also evident in the speeches and writings of Fran-ces Willard, whose travels confirmed her presumption of the sexual im-morality and inferiority of other races. She expressed concern at the rising number of such people coming to the United States. As immigrants and freed slaves gained more social leverage, Willard impressed upon her au-diences the importance of maintaining boundaries between whites and nonwhites. She even went so far as saying that an interracial couple could never live a "white life" together.[95] But, more often, she praised the achievements of her own race as the progenitors of a new and improved civilization made possible by the cooperation and parity of women and men.[96]

Purity reform crafted an evolutionary rhetoric that married Protestant idealism and scientific advancement, creating a nationalist ideology rest-ing on the generation of a better and stronger white race.[97] The work of child psychologists became increasingly relevant to the goals of sexual purity. As noted above, G. Stanley Hall was a severe critic of the sexual purity movement and the push for women's equality. His use of revivalist language to make evolutionary theories more palatable to traditional reli-gionists indicated the compatibility of Protestant millennialist theologies and social Darwinism. His most significant contribution to this project was his work in adolescence, a new category that helped parents and other adults explain the sometimes strange and erratic behavior of postpubes-cent youth. In crafting the notion of the adolescent, Hall established sig-nificant linkages between religious conversion, sexual awakening, and civilizational advancement that help us unpack the subsequent argu-ments for sexual purity.

Hall's conceptualization of adolescence was the centerpiece of his at-tempt to shift Victorian piety away from traditional evangelicalism and toward modernist views of civilizational advancement and racial enhance-ment. His descriptions of adolescents are soaked in evangelical language, which provides in conversion a potent metaphor for the developmental transformations that occur during these years. Religious conversion was not just metaphor for the experiences of adolescence; this stage of life was the most ripe and therefore the most suitable time for an individual's religious awakening.[98]

Hall's work on adolescence provides a unique case for studying the tensions between nineteenth-century evangelicalism and modern science. Hall himself leaned toward the latter, but he deployed evangelical language in order to ascribe spiritual and moral consequence to social Darwinism. Where traditional evangelicals saw salvation in conversion, obedience, and piety, Hall saw it in genetic improvement and human progress. Hall's use of religious metaphor to describe adolescence quickly went out of fashion. Though he introduced the concept, his work on adolescence lost favor because of his reliance on religious metaphor. However, precisely because Hall's definition of adolescence was rooted in evangelical language, his definition is a critical framework for understanding the ideas that shape the work and rhetoric of sexual purity for adolescents.

For Hall, the unique challenge of male adolescence was to weather the transition between childhood and adulthood with the appropriate balance between savage instincts and civilizational progress. Hall noted that the onset of male adolescence was an awareness of sexual desire, accompanied by awareness of sinful nature.[99] With the awareness of sin, especially sexual desire as sin, male adolescents required proper sexual and religious education. Borrowing from the work of George Coe, who observed that most religious conversions occurred between the ages of eleven and twenty-three, Hall argued that the onset of sexual awareness and religious awakening occurred simultaneously and therefore should be addressed in relation to one another.[100]

The religious character of adolescence emerges rather quickly in Hall's introduction to his treatise on the subject. Hall immediately frames adolescence as a "marvelous new birth," drawing upon the language of Protestant revivalism that marks an individual's transition from sinner to saved. Puritan clergyman Jonathan Edwards had popularized the concept of a new birth, or being born again, during the New England awakenings of the mid–eighteenth century. Though Puritan spirituality was characterized by quiet piety and inner contemplation, Edwards became worried about the spiritual state of his congregation and sought new ways of confirming their authenticity through religious experience. A new birth was precisely the kind of experience Edwards advocated, a way to name and mark the inward transformation from sinner to saved.[101]

This experience began with the individuals' conviction of their own sin and the desire to escape the control of sin. Hall advocated that young boys be allowed to indulge their natural inclinations or savagery. The introduction of sex created a new landscape in which personal development and human progress required greater controls. Sex was an entirely creative and destructive force that "works its havoc in the form of secret vice, debauch, disease, and enfeebled heredity."[102] These new sexual urges destabilized the young person, whose childhood constancy was replaced with violent changes in physical and emotional states. The child now found adult activities and ambition enticing, had few resources for achieving them, and searched for a recognizable identity. Hall called this disruption the "storm and stress" of adolescence.[103] Emotional volatility signified the individual's awareness of limitation and helplessness, the trial from which a new birth emerged.

This new creature now exhibited the traits necessary to achieve full sexual, moral, and psychological development. Though sexuality held the potential for great destruction, Hall was careful not to reinscribe the sexual shame he endured as a youth. By using the concept of the new birth, Hall framed sexual awakening as an initiation into the human race and its march toward progress. Here again, Hall was adapting traditional evangelical language to his social Darwinism. The new birth was not a spiritual transformation from sinner to saved, but a physiological transition in which the child was reborn as a full contributor to the progression of the human race.[104]

Chapter Two

From Adolescence to Lost Innocence: Religious Revival and Sexual Deviance in the Cold War Era

Are you prepared to meet the consequences, multiplied by the lives of thousands of other Christians, find America steeped in an age of wonton debauchery such as she has never known? And are you prepared to meet the consequences that will come to your own Christian experience?

—TORREY JOHNSON, "Torrey Talks to Teen-Agers"

ACCORDING TO THE traditional historiography, fundamentalists, shamed and hardened by popular reactions to the Scopes "monkey" trial, receded from public and political life in the early twentieth century. Depictions of fundamentalists as unintelligent, even ignorant, militant cultural separatists populated the imaginations of journalists like H. L. Mencken, who transmitted this image via paper and radio to households across the nation. Noting the loss of fundamentalism's cultural caché, believers, it was said, left the rest of the world to its own devices. However, later historians tracing back the arc of fundamentalism from its resurgence in the 1970s discovered a vibrant subculture developing its own networks of schools, seminaries, denominational structures, publications, radio shows, and, eventually, television programming.[1]

The most vibrant of these developments were those focused on the evangelization of young adults, or adolescents,[2] an age group that had already been marked as ripe for religious conversion. Coupled with the victory of World War II and the return of young GIs, young adulthood became a monument to national strength and moral integrity. It was no surprise, then, that fundamentalists sought cultural rebirth through revival efforts targeting this age group. The result was the creation of an

evangelical youth culture that used its adolescent vitality to promote national pride and religious commitment, resulting in an increased number
of religious conversions and US foreign missionaries, as well as a revitalized confluence of Christian piety and US national identity.

Near the war's end, young adults found themselves with social opportunities unavailable to previous generations. Younger people, now
called teenagers, had developed their own, distinctly nonadult culture
characterized by social rather than familial relationships, immediate
self-gratification, and sexual opportunity.[3] The war economy provided
jobs for men and women alike, many of whom moved frequently in
order to fulfill employment opportunities. At the same time, youth of
a certain class expected to lead a full social life, autonomous from
family obligations and relations. That behavior included dancing, attending films, dating, consuming alcohol, and engaging in certain
forms of sexual activity. Though birth control was still rare and only
thinkable for married couples and prostitutes, young people expected
that sexual experimentation was part of the dating experience and did
not assume that its trajectory ended in marriage.[4] For many adults,
these were not welcome transitions; many suspected that libertine attitudes led to an increase in juvenile delinquency and a general decline
in morality among the young.

In the particular moment spanning the war's end and the postwar era,
fundamentalist leaders knew that continued separation from mainstream
culture would not grant them access to the young people who desperately
needed evangelizing. And so fundamentalist leaders in New York City
adapted older forms of revivalism that accommodated cultural innovations, such as radio, in an attempt to "wean bobby soxers from the temptations of Times Square."[5]

Among the most successful were events produced by Youth for Christ
(YFC), a revival movement that began in New York City but grew to maturity in Chicago under the guidance of Torrey Johnson, a pastor from Mid-
west Bible Church and graduate of Wheaton College (Illinois) and
Northern Baptist Theological Seminary. Fully aware of the social opportunities and temptations many young people faced, he feared the loss of
the young generation to worldly pursuits. But, rather than launch jeremiads against the evils of secular culture, Johnson sought to create an alternative to Saturday-night social options. During YFC's first series of events,
twenty-one Saturday-night rallies held in Chicago's largest performance
venue, the organization proved itself a viable contender for adolescent

audiences. Every weekly event included music especially selected to appeal to the bobby-soxer set, personal testimonies from military leaders and athletes, a sermon, and an altar call. Rallies also gained attention, and criticism, for their inclusion of popular and outlandish acts, including a horse that could answer Bible trivia (limited to those questions with numerical answers that could be transmitted via the stomping of a hoof).

And so, every Saturday night in the summer of 1944, Chicago's Orchestra Hall drew thousands of teenagers to an event that rivaled the excitement around juke joints and Frank Sinatra. In fact, many noted Johnson's own resemblance to Sinatra—his curly hair, bow tie, and vocal qualities that journalists simply described as "a Voice." More important, he spoke in the tone and language that resonated with the bobby-soxers.[6] Advertisements and short films boasted the resounding success of YFC by pointing to the number of individuals saved at each event, the number in attendance, the sales of Johnson's book, and the expansion of YFC into other states.[7] Even journalists hailed the organization's ability to inculcate Christian values in the younger generation: "Youth for Christ is drawing the bobby-soxers and their boy friends away from the juke boxes and dark-boothed hideaways to a streamlined revival of that indestructible thing— the human soul."[8] Even the nonreligious William Randolph Hearst instructed his newspapers to maintain continual coverage of YFC events, because he believed the organization held the greatest promise for overcoming the problems of juvenile delinquency.[9]

The Saturday event mimicked trends in popular entertainment while stressing the value of patriotism, revivalism, and missionary work. Promotional materials alerted potential audiences to this unique combination by claiming itself to be "Geared to the Times, Anchored to the Rock." Other materials referred to the event as a "date" and used sensationalist language to spark interest: "You'll thrill to the breathless tempo of Chicago's finest Saturday night program. . . . Imagine the thrill of meeting from all over the Chicago area. If you want the cream of the crop, here's where to find it."[10] As an alternative to other Saturday "date night" options, YFC marketed itself not only as a place to meet other Christian teenagers but also as providing the best options available for those seeking a Christian boyfriend or girlfriend.[11]

Much of this was out of step with the goals of earlier fundamentalists, who sought separation from mainstream culture. And this distance from previous fundamentalists was intentional. The success of YFC was rooted in its ability to present a new face of fundamentalism that could utilize the hooks of popular culture and still reinforce the message of Christian morality. The return to revivalist strategies allowed fundamentalists to step away from the heated political scene that had ensconced the Scopes trial. But, more important, it allowed them to revitalize the nineteenth-century evangelical strategy of endorsing mainstream culture to the extent that it could be utilized to bring people to Christ.[12]

However, to describe YFC rallies as only a favorable substitute for other social opportunities elides the greater stakes marked out by Johnson and his colleagues. Along with Hearst, Johnson was concerned with the increase in juvenile delinquency. In the early 1900s, adolescence was a newfound period of development in which young people, no longer children but not yet burdened with adult responsibilities, had a great deal of personal autonomy with regard to social and economic behaviors. Coupled with the introduction of automobiles, popular film and other forms of entertainment, and relaxed sexual mores, adolescent behavior was awash in new opportunities for personal fulfillment and immediate gratification. Like G. Stanley Hall, Johnson viewed adolescence as a period of great potential and equally great risk. As youth became more aware of their personal freedoms, they could also be made aware of their ability to choose correctly. All that was needed was the right hook to lead the young generation away from worldly pursuits and a way to convince youth to use their autonomy to choose the path toward righteousness. Thus, Johnson joined Hall in believing that religious conversion was the solution to juvenile delinquency—it just needed to be presented in a fashion that appealed to the target demographic.

YFC evangelists spoke condemningly of youthful indiscretions such as drinking and sex, often described in lurid detail. These narratives were cast to evoke penance from youth who had themselves wandered away from the moral teachings of Christianity, a temptation made even more alluring by the lack of supervision in wartime. Young people free to experiment with adult activities such as drinking and sex were the particular target of YFC. Too young to properly serve their country, these adolescents needed to be given their own marching orders. YFC's solution was to invoke the valor of person heroism, innocence, and loyalty—themes that amalgamated American nationalism and Christian morality. Borrowing popular patriotic themes, YFC rallies called upon young evangelicals to make responsible choices that positioned them to serve not only as effective global evangelists but as faithful Americans working to make the world safe for Christianity and democracy.[13]

Johnson did not perceive the dilemma of juvenile delinquency as only a threat to individual well-being and personal salvation. As he explained to those gathered for the first YFC convention in July 1945, "if we have another lost generation . . . American is sunk . . . we are headed either for a definite turning to God or the greatest calamity ever to strike the human race."[14] For Johnson, the well-being of the nation was dependent upon curbing the latest tide of adolescent irresponsibility. But even as he recognized the failings of the younger generation, he acknowledged the great contributions of youth during the war effort. As young heroes emerged from the theater of war, Johnson saw a new adolescent emerge, one who was valued as a citizen and contributor to national welfare. He cultivated the ideal of the Christian hero-citizen by inviting veterans to share their testimonies and by including patriotic anthems such as "God Bless Our Boys" and "The Battle Hymn of the Republic." Johnson even developed a segment in the program in which he invited the youngest serviceman in the audience to make a phone call to his family, live, in front the entire audience. One story that appeared on the rally's souvenir booklet recounted the testimony of sailor Kenneth Kirby. In a YFC radio braodcast, the sailor testified that, upon his conversion, he dedicated himself to leading his fellow sailors to Christ. According to the YFC report, Kirby wholeheartedly pursued this task as faithfully as he served his country, until the day he and his shipmates died in combat.[15] Stories such as these not only reinforced the importance of religious proselytizing, but also used the exigency of war to reinforce the urgency of salvation.

The unabashed patriotism of YFC events was not merely circumstantial; it was an effort to impart to young audiences the value of their Christian citizenship. The twenty-one Saturday-night events at Orchestra Hall culminated in the Victory Rally held on October 21, 1944. Though the referent for the victory theme remained vague, especially since the Allies had not yet won the war, the nationalist fanfare of the rally's advertising, YFC's organizational success, and the tallies of numerous saved souls stood soundly under the same banner of victory.

Regardless of whether or not a young person had served the war effort, YFC marked religious conversion with the pageantry of patriotic hymns, color guards, and returned war heroes. Reports of the Memorial Day rally at Soldier Field marking YFC's first anniversary described a nationalistic spectacle with a revivalist fervor on par with that of Billy Sunday and Dwight Moody. According to the *Chicago Tribune*, the event combined traditional church architecture (a large pulpit stood at the center of the venue), Hollywood and radio entertainment, military servicemen and their vehicles, and the large musical ensembles YFC had become known for.[16] Beginning the service, a youth-led color guard posted both American and Christian flags at numerous locations in the stadium. The first of many grand spectacles, 400 nurses dressed in white marched in the shape of a cross over the field, while song leaders conducted the crowd in singing "The Battle Hymn of the Republic." Later, two large stars were placed behind the pulpit: a blue star in recognition of soldiers on active duty and a gold star in memory of those killed in the line of duty. The pinnacle of the event, according to journalists, was the missionary pageant in which evangelist representatives from China, India, Africa, Russia, and the United States formed a large star in the center of the field. According to a YFC press release prepared by Carl F. H. Henry, the pageant singled out "groups representing the bleeding nations of the world, and disclosing their spiritual need."[17] Torrey Johnson valued his organization's international connections and the missionary zeal they inspired among young audiences. The military success of the United States translated, for Johnson, into a missionary mandate. YFC sent "invasion teams" of young missionaries to preach in Europe, Asia, Latin America, and the Pacific. By 1946, Johnson declared to *Time* magazine that YFC goals were no longer domestic, but sought the "complete evangelization of the world."[18]

However, the pinnacle moment, as planned by the organizers, was the altar call. As with all YFC events, the final moments offered audience members the opportunity to make an initial commitment to Christ or to renew that commitment. The Memorial Day rally, working at the convergence of piety and spectacle, offered its own unique approach to the conversion moment. As the lights of the stadium dimmed, a lighthouse placed in center field shone its spotlight into the crowd as if searching for lost ships at sea. The song leaders prodded the audience to accompany this display with the hymn, "I Wonder If the Lighthouse Will Shine on Me."

What is most remarkable about Youth for Christ is, not its spectacle or its numerical success, but that it was a *youth-based* movement that allowed fundamentalists to reemerge from their cultural separatism. The success of the movement stemmed from fundamentalist leaders' ability both to understand and to respond to the unique needs and interests of adolescents. The use of older revivalist strategies that permitted the use of mainstream cultural resources for the purpose of attracting people to Christian conversion was especially valuable in this enterprise. As a demographic, adolescents were increasingly autonomous, socially and financially. They were a vibrant new market, purveyors of entertainment, alcohol, and media; religion had to compete for the teens' allegiance, a struggle that further reinforced the belief that adolescence was an age of great moral danger and great spiritual opportunity.

This fundamentalist renewal was not just about moral and religious restoration for a generation flirting with danger; the restoration of national character and moral fortification were also understood to be at issue. The United States had defeated its enemies under the presumption that good triumphs over evil, only to turn its attention to domestic life and be overrun by the rampant immorality that had been normalized in wartime. Even before the Cold War had taken shape, political and religious leaders knew that the country's national security was contingent on its moral fortitude.

Fundamentalists did not seek to revisit the political and cultural battles of the Scopes trial. But neither were they satisfied with a separatist stance that kept them from engaging nonbelievers with the Good News. A return to nineteenth-century revivalism granted fundamentalists access to new audiences that promised the vitality of youthful optimism. Patriotic themes granted them access to postwar political discourse. Here, they began to mend the rent seam of Christian belief and national identity without reigniting the cultural battles of twenty years prior.

This mix of adolescent revivalism and patriotic religiosity proved to be a potent formula for fundamentalist renaissance. Within a year, YFC was filling stadiums, converting thousands, and sending hundreds into the mission field. At the Memorial Day rally on May 31, 1946, those missionaries transformed Chicago's massive Soldier Field stadium into an icon of Christian piety and national pride. Out of the group emerged one young missionary representing the United States who called for ongoing revival that would bring even greater glory to God and to the nation.[19] His name was Billy Graham.

Billy Graham and Youth for Christ

For Torrey Johnson, Billy Graham embodied the thrill, youthful charm, and charisma needed to maintain the vitality of Youth for Christ. Only twenty-four years of age and already a full-time employee of the organization, Graham's appearance during the Memorial Day rally was his first before a crowd of thousands. Graham was well received by teenage audiences because of his classically handsome appearance and his ability to imitate popular radio personalities. His dress, preaching style, and voice all resounded with the vibrancy of YFC, and his messages amplified the organization's desire to create a new generation of Christian citizens fortified with godly values and national pride. Graham's early sermons with YFC exhibited the commitments of the organization: youth revivalism, nationalism, and Christian piety. However, his concern for the spiritual and moral development of youth was a particular hallmark of his sermons and writings. Graham addressed youth and their concerns with great care; according to Johnson, no one had a greater ability to answer the quandaries of young people better than he.[20]

YFC events were known for their imitation of popular entertainment, and, in some ways, Graham did not differ from this programming structure. Not only were his sermons delivered in the fierce staccato of a radio personality: he often addressed themes of militarism, nationalism, heroism, and masculinity, as was common in the postwar era. However, other aspects of his sermons, especially those concerning sexual morality and Christ's return, allowed Graham to create a prophetic distance from mainstream adolescent culture, calling those within it to repentance.

Awash in patriotic fervor, YFC events sought to impart the value of Christian citizenship upon their audiences. Graham's use of military imagery, themes, and metaphors grew out of the organization's nationalistic commitments, but also from Graham's own valorization of military heroism as the most apt metaphor for the Christian life. In one sermon, entitled "Youth's Hero," Graham hailed the sacrifice of a young Marine who jumped on a grenade, saving the lives of fourteen others. The allusion to Christ's sacrifice was immediate, but Graham used the connection between military heroism and personal salvation to acknowledge the desires of his young audiences: "You know, there is something about American young people that makes us love heroes of every type, whether they be on the cinder track, the baseball diamond, the gridiron or in a tank."[21] Graham was careful to place himself within this demographic. At the age of twenty-four, he related well with young adults, because he was one. He drew upon his own personal concerns, questions, and aspirations to reach his audiences.

The Christian life, for Graham and many others in the postwar era, was a military battle, and he wasn't just looking for heroes, but seeking to make himself and other young people *into* heroes. Especially in the glow of victory, martial metaphors were most effective for using national military victory to reinforce the thrill of spiritual victory over evil.

Many of you can remember the shout of triumph that your soul gave when you first met Jesus Christ. How sure you were of victory then! How easy it seems to be more than a conqueror through him who loved you! Under the leadership of such a great general you can never be foiled in battle. . . . [22]

His descriptions of the Christian life harnessed the energy of military victory by emphasizing the threat of evil, the thrill of battle, and the glory of triumph.

While the creation of this Christian hero-citizen was not of Graham's own design, he was the most effective purveyor of it because he himself had experienced Christian conversion in this way. When Graham shared his own conversion story, he used military and athletic metaphors as a way to affirm his gender identity:

I had always thought of religion as being more or less "sissy" and a fellow who was going to be an athlete would have not time for such "sissy" stuff. It was alright for old people and girls, but not for a real "he man" with red blood in his veins.[23]

After being convicted of his sins at a revival meeting, Graham spent a night wrestling and fighting with the draw toward Christianity. It was this battle that convinced him that giving one's heart to Christ was not a sissy game, but an invitation to live a life of "zest, push, adventure, excitement, gaiety, and thrills." For Graham, this was the life he had always sought as a young man and feared Christianity would not provide. Upon discovering what historians now call muscular Christianity, Graham found a way to reconcile his masculinity and his Christian faith.

Graham's anxiety over "sissy" Christianity was hardly a new one. The fear that Christianity required men to adopt feminine attributes had been apparent in the 1800s. Numerous historians have described the "feminization" of nineteenth-century Protestantism as a consequence of an increasingly industrial market economy in which masculine virtues of competition, courage, and risk were considered the most valuable. "Lesser" cultural tasks—child-rearing, house-holding, and religious instruction—became the purview of women, whose feminine attributes were more suited to these tasks. As described in the previous chapter, these "separate spheres" constituted the gender ideology of the Victorian white middle class, a time period and demographic that permitted men some release from exacting piety in order to fulfill their professional and public duties. Women, on the other hand, protected from the harsh world of commerce and politics, could uphold standards of piety within the church and home.[24]

However, the ideology and practice of gender rarely matched, especially as women utilized their moral authority to assert greater political and religious leadership roles. Muscular Christianity, the most pointed response to the perception of the feminization of religion, emerged in the last quarter of the nineteenth century. Liberal and fundamentalist Protestants alike reacted fearfully against the increasing religious authority of women, but for different reasons. Concerned that "women have had charge of the church long enough," liberal Protestant men sought to reclaim Christian piety within the context of their professional work, mainly market capitalism. Victorian Protestants sought to engage the market economy as consumers and purveyors of material goods that helped them to established their religious and class status. Trained in the values of thrift, Protestants shifted their views of Christian piety to incorporate outward displays of piety, a shift that allowed for the consumption of commercial goods. For mainline Protestants, the contribution of muscular Christianity was to make capitalism compatible with Christian piety.[25]

For those Protestants who would later be known as fundamentalists, the assertion of male piety and religious leadership was not economically advantageous but biblically mandated. Alarmed at forms of progressivism that granted women more religious and moral authority than men, conservative evangelicals asserted Christian faith practice as a virile and heroic enterprise, a pointed counter to the perceived feminization and moral laxity of mainline churches and the culture at large.

The impact of muscular Christianity on the emergence of Protestant fundamentalism rests in a historical understanding of how conservative evangelicals created a subculture intent on repudiating the corruptions and compromises of the Protestant mainstream in particular and US culture in general. US religious historians have argued that fundamentalists sought to maintain Victorian gender ideologies that valorized women's domestic work and natural piety. As Victorian values began to fade, however, fundamentalists clung tightly to the ideology of separate spheres, insisting that this ordering of family life was a biblical mandate.[26] However, Margaret Lamberts Bendroth demonstrated that fundamentalism emerged as a reaction against this very notion of feminized piety. Conservative Protestants were deeply suspicious of a theology that elevated the

morality of women over that of men, especially when most of Christian
history was characterized by belief in women's spiritual inferiority. The
moral authority that women garnered from Victorian conceptions of
virtue and piety allowed them to issue correctives to men's moral and religious leadership. For fundamentalists, this was a dangerous inversion
that threatened the natural order of creation, which asserted male headship over women.[27]

By the 1920s, fundamentalists had successfully utilized the ideology of
muscular Christianity to usurp the Victorian model of feminine virtue to
assert women as psychologically and spiritually vulnerable and reaffirmed
men's rightful position as religious leaders.[28] However, many fundamentalists were uncomfortable with the worldly emphasis on athletics that characterized muscular Christianity. Popular evangelist Billy Sunday, a former
professional baseball player, seemed a natural advocate for the movement.
However, Sunday's decision to reject a baseball contract in favor of a career
as an evangelist with the YMCA was due in part to his belief that the values
of Christianity were incompatible with those of professional sports.

As fundamentalists, Billy Graham and YFC smoothed the harsh edges
of the tradition in order to increase their popular appeal. They sought both
engagement with and prophetic distance from the mainstream, a tension
that resonated with Graham's attempts to reassure men that Christianity
did not require the compromise of their God-given, masculine traits. That
Graham had to address these concerns indicated the continued influence
of nineteenth-century gender ideology that placed the mantle of Christian
piety upon women alone. Unlike many fundamentalists who embraced
muscular Christianity, Graham did not reject the value of women's piety.
Yet when he preached, the protagonists of his sermons—the Christian
hero-citizens whom he idealized—were always male. Likewise, his sermons remained in step with mainstream attempts to establish a postwar
nuclear family model that reified masculine virility and feminine domesticity. However, his endorsement of professional athletes and other forms
of popular entertainment proved an early sign that his affiliation with a
rigid fundamentalism would not last.

Billy Graham and Sexual Purity

Graham's separation from fundamentalism was still a decade away in
1947, and, despite his reification of the heroism of youth, he also recognized that young people required straight talk when it came to sexual

morality. Many in the postwar period, including Graham, were convinced that the rise in juvenile delinquency posed a great threat to America's future, a fear that grew out of changing sexual norms. Working with youth of various ages, Graham's advice and warnings about sexuality and sexual misbehavior were frequent.

Like other YFC preachers, Graham's moral jeremiads covered a range of temptations and possible failures for young people who were not on their guard against the power of "youthful lusts."[29] Often the most impassioned part of his sermons, Graham sought to convict the bobby-soxer generation of its moral failings as a reminder that only Christ could provide victory over sin. He spoke to his audiences knowingly, lifting up their collective misdeeds and calling those present to choose another way:

> In this day when young people are living, "wild, strange, foreign-flavored, globe-girdling, radio-riding," lawbreaking, frivolous, superficial lives, it is glorious to see a young man or women living a clean, honest, uncompromising spiritual life for Jesus Christ, a life which will result in constant daily victory over sin and inward rest of soul.[30]

Despite his use of the moral jeremiad, Graham critiqued that notion of modern legality that required complete separation from worldly amusements, including dating.[31] He wanted young Christians to live full, adventurous lives and to embrace physical attractiveness for the purposes of attracting others to the Christian life. Later in his career, he reassured advice seekers that dating was a natural process in which youth should be free to engage in order to develop relationships with numerous Christians of the opposite sex. He chided parents who disapproved of dating and asserted that parental interference could disrupt the maturation process of adolescence.[32] Graham endorsed the social practice of dating, but not the accompanying sexual practices to which many adolescents felt entitled. Neither did he endorse long-term relationships for young people. Intimacy of any kind between young people of different sexes required a strict code of purity. For Graham, purity flowed from the holiness of God and involved moral cleanliness, a discipline that required both physical and mental restraint.[33]

In other advice he gave to teenagers, Graham's guidance is even more explicit. He openly objects to the practice of petting, which he considered sexually immoral, injurious to the conscience and nervous system of both

parties, and a gateway to further degradation. To regulate the sex drive—
the strongest of human urges next to self-preservation, according to
Graham—the Bible offers guidelines for sexual regulation, violation of
which results in "weakness, mental dullness, insanity, and vile diseases."[34]
While Graham advised young adolescents to forgo intimate relationships,
he did not draw firm boundaries between sanctioned sexual practices in
engagement and marriage:

> If intimate love-making was deferred until late engagement or
> marriage, there would not be so many unhappy marriages. Don't
> play fast and loose with your emotions and passions. Let them be
> under the control of Christ, and your life will be fuller and richer.[35]

An initial review of Graham's advice to teenagers and young adults indicates his primary concern for the spiritual and emotional well-being of
his advisees. However, communication to that audience only accounts for
part of Graham's thinking on sexual immorality. In numerous sermons
and writings, Graham does not divorce the issue of sexual immorality
from larger nationalistic concerns. In doing so, he further developed the
rhetoric of sexual purity that first emerged from nineteenth-century
purity movements.

Moral Decay and National Decline in the Cold War Era

To some degree, the valorization of youth in the postwar era was part of
an adjustment period in which Americans recognized the loss of national
innocence. The United States as a nation had left the naiveté and security
of childhood and entered into a period of great adolescent potential and
equally great risk. Religious leaders like Graham crafted the ideal of the
Christian hero-citizen within the context of the adolescent experience on
individual and national levels. In his YFC sermon "America's Hope,"
Graham charted a course for America, one that he would reiterate to numerous audiences as the Cold War developed. The theme of civilization's
rise and decline, also prominent in nineteenth-century purity speeches,
emerged as a guiding question for Graham: does the United States have
what it takes to be a world leader? Believed to be at the height of its power,
the nation stood in view of the entire world, and Graham in his prophetic
role attempted to predict the US trajectory from this point onward.
"America's Hope" comprised numerous scenarios that traced the rise and

decline of great civilizations throughout history. In each case, Graham followed the same formula: (1) listing and extolling the civilization's initial virtues, (2) describing the forms of immorality that corrupted those virtues, (3) asserting a connection between moral decay and national decline, and (4) including frequent references to Sodom and Gomorrah, highlighting the sexual nature of US moral decay.[36] The purpose of this genealogy was not to disparage previous civilizations but to mark out similar signs of decline in American culture.

In "America's Hope," Graham situated his preaching style firmly within what Paul Boyer has denoted as the twentieth-century prophecy tradition. These writings and sermons carefully listed the sins Graham perceived as unique to the era, including sexual immorality, moral collapse, changing status of women, homosexuality, and, eventually, abortion and New Age movements. The themes of prophecy teachings shifted according to current events, so that preachers and writers could explain those events through biblical predictions. For Graham, this meant using the biblical text of Ezekiel to explain the rise of the Soviet Union and cast it as the aggressor in a spiritual battle between Satanic forces and godly truth: "Ezekiel 38 and 39 may be well describing Russia and the mighty power of Communism—the greatest, most well-organized and outspoken foe of Christianity that the church has confronted since the days of pagan Rome."[37]

But America's greatest enemy was not the Soviet Union, Graham said, but the decadence and degeneracy of American morality. Religious revival, lost since the days of Moody, had ceased to inform American political and social life, commencing an era of decline that left the country morally bankrupt. In this, Graham was not alone: political leaders like J. Edgar Hoover, Harry Truman, and Douglas MacArthur addressed the dangers of rampant religious apathy in the midst of the emerging geopolitical crisis. Loss of religious faith and the rise of atheism due to belief in the theory of evolution were the main culprits, according to Graham, and they resulted in moral decline and the breakdown of the home: "In her dress, manners, and morals, America has become sex-conscious." As in human adolescence, the emergence of sexual awareness required the tempering effect of religious revival.[38]

Graham learned how to be an evangelist to audiences of bobby-soxers and young GIs, crafting an effective formula for religious conversion in which he situated the call to repentance at the crossroads of individual and national adolescence. The revelations of youthful indiscretions evoked conviction, and the thrill of Christian adventure piqued curiosity. Placing his audiences in a state of apprehension and expectation, Graham offered an apocalyptic vision that addressed deep national and individual anxieties. He called individuals, and America as a whole, to repentance with warnings of Christ's judgment and reassurance that worldly threats would be rendered ineffectual. Concluding "America's Hope," Graham regarded his audience not as a collection of adolescent individuals but as America, itself, on guard, humbled, and expectant:

> America, I present you with a spiritual call to arms. "Come let us return unto the Lord: for he hath . . . smitten, and he will bind us up." America cannot organize her way out, nor buy her way out. She must pray her way out.[39]

The theme of civilizational decline and moral decay would remain a staple of Graham's early evangelistic career, though America, not ancient Rome, was more frequently portrayed as the civilization in decline:

> America is truly the last bulwark of Christian civilization . . . if America falls, Western culture will disintegrate . . . if you would be a true patriot, then become a Christian. If you would be a loyal American, then become a loyal Christian . . . America cannot survive, she cannot fulfill her divine purpose, she cannot carry out her God-appointed mission without the spiritual emphasis which was hers from the outset.[40]

After leaving Youth for Christ and establishing the Billy Graham Evangelistic Association (BGEA), Graham's sermons reached an even higher crescendo in order to address fully the coming global crisis. Just prior to the BGEA's Los Angeles Crusade in 1949, President Truman announced that the Soviet Union had successfully tested a nuclear bomb. Graham's revivalist formula, shaped during his time at YFC, was already primed to address this heightened stress level. His sermons during the crusade echoed similar themes: the degeneracy of the young, the moral crisis, and national insecurity—all with an increasingly anticommunist bent.

Graham called the timing of his LA campaign providential, believing that the impending threat of nuclear destruction served as a resounding reminder that human beings were more capable of destroying than saving themselves. He spared his audiences no moment of relief from the sense of danger and offered a secondhand prediction in which Western civilization ended in five to ten years: "Communism is a religion that is inspired, directed and motivated by the Devil himself who had declared war against Almighty God."[41] The world was thus divided between communists and Christians; a spiritual battle was being played out in global politics. But for local Angelenos, the threat was even more imminent: Graham informed them that the city was third on the USSR's list of US nuclear targets, not because it was an important industrial or military target, but because of its reputation as a "city of wickedness . . . known around the world because of its sin, crime, and immorality."[42] Graham ran through a litany of sexual sins in order to illustrate the convergence of moral, political, and spiritual problems. Sexual immorality threatened the young, who were "going to the dogs morally" because popular media made sexual images more accessible to them. The result, juvenile delinquency, carried a young generation away from religious and national obligations, but also provided an apt metaphor for the nation's own moral delinquency.

A related problem, increasing rates of divorce, indicated by the nation's growing disregard for biblical teachings, also presented a threat to the nation: "The home, the basic unit of our society is breaking and crumbling, and the American way of life is being destroyed at the very heart and core of society."[43] In a later sermon, "The Home God Honors," Graham elaborated his belief that threats to family and home were threats to the nation. He asserted, as he would many times, that the greatest menace facing America was not communism alone but an unsatisfactory family structure. Again drawing upon themes of human development, Graham noted that greatness begins not in battle but in the nurturing an individual receives in the early years of life. Communism and moral degeneracy both could undermine the nurturing influence of the home and stunt the developmental process by which young men transformed into the Christian hero-citizens whom Graham valorized:[44] "One of the goals of communism is to destroy the American home. If the Communists can destroy the American home and cause the moral deterioration of this country, that group will have done to us what they did to France when the German armies invaded the Maginot line."[45]

Obedience to biblical prescriptions for marital order was essential to a strong family life, Graham continued. Domestic stability that contributed to national stability required obedience to God's word. "Dictatorial wives," he warned, subverted biblical mandates for wifely submission and male headship. Graham's own prescriptions required that wives should run to greet their husbands, be modest and delicate, be attractive, keep current with world and national events, keep the house clean, not spend all of their husband's money, not nap, and not complain. Husbands, Graham asserted, must claim spiritual headship of the household, including the use of a family home–altar and the regular practice of family prayer.

Graham's understanding of gendered responsibilities provides further insight into how he perceived his audiences. His use of muscular Christian rhetoric and his identification with heroism and militarism initially presented a universalized, though masculine, believer. But his assertion of family gender roles demonstrated a deeper theological commitment to male headship in which women's spiritual progress required a male agent: "I don't think God will ever hold a woman responsible, it's the husband before God, as God's representative, as head of the home, who should establish the family altar."[46] Graham's dismissal of women's religious piety reflected fundamentalist trends to overturn Victorian gender ideologies that grew out of a strict separation between domestic and public life. Domestic, feminine virtues of submission and nurturance were insufficient for providing a secure home life. Men's piety, characterized by virility, heroism, and moral fortitude, was more suited to this role in an era when national security was dependent upon the shared stability of domestic and public life.

Though Graham was not initially well received by the Oval Office, his close relationship with President Eisenhower made him especially effective at sculpting a national self-understanding of being a key player in a divine drama.[47] Graham had set out to revive Christian influence on public and political life by restoring the public image of fundamentalist Christianity. Historian Angela Lahr argues that Graham and other fundamentalists adapted biblical prophecies as a way to renegotiate their relationship to the US mainstream and to create for their own benefit a national identity that integrated patriotism and Christian piety. The image of the nuclear bomb had imprinted itself on the American imagination, and millennialist theologies helped Americans interpret and respond to this new fear. Even young people could articulate the precarious nature of the era when asked to do so. In an essay competition for a revival magazine, one young writer acknowledged how close the human race was to nuclear destruction and asserted that seeking personal salvation was the only solution. Another drew upon prophetic themes of immorality that emerged as a sign of Christ's return. Cold War documents later declassified revealed that even the State Department used religious language when drafting policy documents. Situating the Cold War as a spiritual battle between a Christian America and godless communism was not the work of revivalists alone, though this formulation, as Graham noted in 1947, opened up unparalleled evangelistic opportunity.[48]

Graham was not the only Cold War fundamentalist to interpret world events in light of prophetic traditions, and even prominent liberal Protestants recognized their failure to adequately address eschatological issues.[49] Nor was Graham the architect of what historian Jonathan P. Herzog has called the spiritual-industrial complex. Herzog shows that early Cold War revivalism was unlike earlier populist revivals in that it was constructed not by religious leaders but by the government, business interests, educators, and the media for the sole purpose of providing a solution to a current political crisis. And while Graham and other revivalists used the spiritual-industrial complex to grow their audiences and establish cultural respectability, these ambitions allowed the spiritual-industrial complex to utilize religion to secure a national identity that required the cooperation of conservative politics and fundamentalist religious values.[50]

Restoring Intellectual Veracity

National politics was not the only avenue through which Graham and others sought respectability. The triumph of science over biblical inerrancy, and the consequent early fundamentalist separation, garnered the tradition a reputation for ardent anti-intellectualism. Fundamentalists like Carl F. H. Henry and Billy Graham helped draw fundamentalists out of their isolation; Henry by calling fundamentalists to transform the world, rather than abandon it, and Graham by drawing fundamentalists into political discourse. Both Henry and Graham began their respective careers—Henry as a journalist and academic, Graham as a preacher—as dyed-in-the-wool fundamentalists. However, by the 1950s, both were shedding the label in favor of the less militaristic moniker *evangelical*. Both made prolific use of prominent intellectuals, whose scholarship encouraged critical engagement while also reinforcing the tenets of evangelicalism. Among these was Arnold J. Toynbee, an Oxford historian whose *A Study of History* described twenty-one major world civilizations that had all undergone similar patterns of rise and decline. Despite Toynbee's own ambiguous allegiance to Christianity, this grand narrative of civilizational rise and decline provided intellectual veracity to evangelical apocalyptic anticipation, and he soon earned the reputation of a prophet within these circles.[51]

In 1947, Toynbee was invited to the United States for an extensive speaking tour in which he translated his dense scholarship into a simple message: Western civilization was on the brink of collapse. In these talks, he emphasized the decline of civilizations as a spiritual problem. Decline, he argued, began with "a schism of the soul" and raised up two different kinds of saviors, one who sought to return to an idyllic past, and another who sought a utopian future.[52] Though his talks gave little indication of his trust in the Christian tradition, the prophetic tone of his conclusions prompted evangelicals to interpret them according to their own apocalyptic theologies. Warnings of moral and national decline that asserted a connection between an individual's spiritual crisis and the national crisis seemed to echo back and forth from Graham's revival tents and Toynbee's lecture halls.

Toynbee created a genealogy of civilizations, showing that Western culture was a descendant of Roman civilization. Thus, it made sense to thinkers such as Graham and Henry to focus on the fall of Rome as a portent of their own nation's trajectory. Just before their fall to external forces, the Romans had abandoned self-discipline and given themselves over to sins of the flesh. Even before the barbarians invaded, Rome was teetering on the brink of disintegration, allowing its subjects to pursue their natural inclinations without concern for the consequences. Twentieth-century fundamentalist leaders recognized a similar pattern of events within American society. The increase in sexual promiscuity, juvenile delinquency, and atheism indicated to them that the United States had itself abandoned self-discipline and would soon be in cultural schism, a signifier of a civilization's decline.

Toynbee's writings wound a substantial narrative around his basic assertion that human history had witnessed the rise and fall of twenty-one major civilizations. His self-appointed task was to examine the shape of these arcs in order to determine the universal laws that characterized this process. The basic schema he discovered was fourfold: the genesis of a civilization, followed by its growth, decline, and disintegration. The curious and controversial aspect of Toynbee's thought that endeared him to fundamentalist readers was his evidence, which included mythological and biblical texts. For example, his final example of a blow, or setback to expansion, which precipitates disintegration, comes from the New Testament. When Christ's disciples witness him ascending into heaven, they perceive this as a loss, or a blow to their work. However, Toynbee explains, Christ's command to baptize and make disciples in all lands served as psychological preparation for Pentecost, the stimulus for the expansion of Christianity and eventual Christianization of Rome.[53] Though many viewed his scholarship as a Christian witness to the world, he spoke openly about his lack of belief, calling his own Christian identity an "accident of my having been born in a country where the local religion has been Christianity." Many of his personal beliefs about love, meaning, and purpose in life grew from his understanding of Christianity, yet, he warned against any form of religious exclusivity in the conclusion to his contributions to Edward R. Morrow's *This I Believe*:

> To imagine one's own church, civilization, nation, or family as the chosen people is, I believe, as wrong as it would be for me to imagine that I myself am God. I agree with Symmachus, the pagan philosopher who put the case for toleration to a victorious Christian church, and I will end by quoting his words: "The universe is too great a mystery for there to be only one single approach to it." Love situated Christianity as just one of the great religions.[54]

Despite, or perhaps because of, his enormous popularity, Toynbee was not without his critics. Primary charges against him included criticism of the foundational elements of his thinking. The simplicity of a genesis-growth-decline-disintegration cycle seemed far too convenient to some of his peers, who considered it artificial. Others called him out for placing too much emphasis on dogmatism, determinism, and doom—the same qualities of his work that fundamentalists would find endearing. Still others found his work to be more aligned with the genre of prophecy than with history. One critic wrote, "Toynbee is a new Jeremiah, thundering against the vices of his fellows. But he is also, despite his denials, a new St. Augustine, bidding us flee an earthy city of destruction for a heavenly city of God."[55]

Kenneth Gangel, an evangelical scholar who held posts at both Trinity Evangelical Divinity School and the fundamentalist flagship institution Dallas Theological Seminary, brought his own criticism to Toynbee's claims. Writing in 1977, Gangel was quite familiar with Toynbee's popularity and, though he did not share many of the criticisms of his secular colleagues, he still found it necessary to break the spell Toynbee's work had cast over many Christians. While he acknowledged that Toynbee depicted Christianity in a favorable light, he chastened those who assumed that Toynbee made the kind of exclusive claims that characterize evangelicalism. Christianity was among the great religions, and, though it may have been the greatest of the great, Toynbee did not assert it as the only path to salvation. Moreover, Toynbee's work was not consistent with a Christian view of history, which recognizes the past not as a series of accidents and coincidences but as the hand of God working in the world. Finally, Gangel pointed out that Toynbee denied the uniqueness of Christianity, misunderstood the historical role of the Jews, and rejected the divinity of Christ. Gangel did not set out to discredit Toynbee as a historian—just the opposite. He called Toynbee's career marvelous and his methodology painstaking. Neither did Gangel participate in the debates seeking to establish Toynbee as either the greatest mind of the century or a prophetic maniac.[56] Gangel's reading audience was made up of fellow believers who he believed had been led astray by a historian who had been mistaken for an evangelical Christian. While his scholarship may have been worthy of serious engagement, Gangel held, Toynbee's work did not address the complementarity of natural and special revelation. Even more grave, Gangel claimed, Toynbee was a relativist, unlike evangelical Christians, who "constantly commit themselves to the absolute truth of special revelations."[57]

Had evangelical Christians not found Toynbee's history so compelling and consistent with their own historical and theological presuppositions, Gangel would not have found cause to reveal Toynbee's non-Christian tendencies. Nevertheless, at the height of Toynbee's popularity in the postwar era, Billy Graham and Carl Henry counted Toynbee among their cohort of evangelical-friendly intellectuals. Graham, already caught up in anticommunist revival fervor—along with Henry, whose own career as a public theologian was equally instrumental in shaping the neoevangelical movement—found in Toynbee the intellectual veracity they sought for their prophetic teachings.

Carl Henry and the Decline of American Civilization

One of the most formative theologians of twentieth-century fundamentalism, Carl F. H. Henry sought to pull fundamentalism from its protective posture after the public humiliation of the Scopes "monkey" trial. As a young adult convert to Christianity, Henry felt that American society desperately needed to be transformed by Christian social values, a task that was difficult when his fellow believers refused to engage mainstream culture. His first book, *Remaking the Modern Mind* (1948), encouraged his coreligionists to adopt a more intellectually and culturally engaged stance and criticized those who retreated behind dispensationalist theologies. As a working journalist, Henry could not leave behind his interest in the world beyond faith. He became, according to historian Joel Carpenter, the leading advocate of a "new evangelicalism"[58] by seeking a balance between temporal relevance and the apocalyptic anticipation of fundamentalist theology. He did not subscribe to the belief that collecting souls for God through church-based evangelism was believers' paramount duty. Rather, Henry spent his career as a professional theologian, receiving his doctorate from Boston University. Nor did he abandon his earlier career as a journalist. As an academic and a journalist, Henry founded two of the most significant evangelical institutions of the twentieth century: Fuller Theological Seminary and the magazine *Christianity Today*.

Henry's writings span five decades and utilize Arnold Toynbee's theory of twenty-one civilizations in order to establish his own views of moral decline in American society. For Henry, the fall of Rome stood as an omen of national decay for his own country, whose citizens he witnessed cavorting with sex and immorality in a fashion he thought similar to Romans' pagan practices. To achieve restoration, Henry called upon the country to reestablish itself according to God's commands, which he believed held absolute authority for all people in all times. Yet, for Henry, even the most faithful of Christian communities could never achieve true righteousness within the confines of this mortal coil.

Like Toynbee, Henry was highly critical of any ideology that loaded human progress with promises of social evolution and the inevitable advancement of human civilizations. In *Remaking the Modern Mind*, Henry called fundamentalists to a newfound social responsibility, not because their efforts could change the course of history, but because only their righteousness could preserve American civilization from the chaos of moral relativism: "The modern man stands amidst the ruins of twenty-one civilizations, each terminating in chaos and despair." Toynbee suggested that all of human history demonstrates that "the wages of sin is death." Among those twenty-one civilizations, fourteen have "perished in a night so black only the archaeologist's spade has disclosed them to us." The remaining seven civilizations fared no better, because their naïve reliance upon science and capitalism rendered them even more vulnerable to the kind of moral decay that causes empires to crumble.[59]

Henry used both biblical and historical evidence to chart the decline of human civilization. The key underlying cause of decay was the abandonment of an "unchanging moral order." The healthy and thriving civilization bowed to the truth, beauty, and goodness that are beyond human explanation. It recognized that moral order is a sacred order established as a design of an all-powerful creator. Christianity, the Bible in particular, was the purveyor of the divine commands that contained the universal moral principles incumbent upon all human beings.[60]

Neglect of these universal principles was an invitation to chaos and destruction. Even the towering empire of ancient Rome could not withstand a similar gestalt of immorality that Henry believed was festering just beneath the surface of American society. For further substantiation, Henry turned to the New Testament book of Romans, written by Paul, the persecutor of Christians who became a global evangelist. Paul opens his letter to the church in Rome with a rather salacious and accusatory list of un-Christian behaviors: unrighteousness, sexual immorality, wickedness, covetousness, maliciousness, envy, murder, strife, deceit, and evil-mindedness. The sexual dimensions of Paul's accusations are most salient, since he finds ample evidence of both men and women abandoning their natural desire for heterosexuality in exchange for homosexual relations.[61] These behaviors, according to Henry, are characteristic of a civilization battling a pagan insurgence. The rejection of monogamous marriage, the accommodation of divorce, the legitimization of homosexuality—all in evidence as Rome fought for its survival—were now commonplace within American civilization.[62]

Even more alarming from Henry's perspective was that these behaviors were not confined to the pagans beyond the city walls. Writing in 1988, he recognized that many young evangelicals were increasingly influenced by secular culture's preoccupation with physical satisfactions, namely premarital sex. Many had redefined sin in order to discount premarital sexuality as an offense against God. Henry bemoaned the lack of church discipline and its institutions' increasing tolerance of divorce and remarriage even among the clergy.[63]

Responding to evangelicals' lax approach toward pre- and extramarital sexuality, Henry's apocalyptic imagination shaped an end-of-times narrative in which sexual immorality played a key role:

When the great meltdown comes, where will you be? Trapped in Sodom? In the bleak twilight of a decadent culture, where will you be? Overtaken, like Lot, looking back at the citadels of sin? American culture is sinking toward the sunset.[64]

The consequences for the individual and the nation alike were dire. While the United States could never be ruled as the ancient Israelites were, with God's commandments, Henry claimed that the social commands implied in Hebraic law were fundamental for stabilizing a society.[65] Ignoring those commands, as nation-states were free to do, would be fruitless, because "the book of Revelation climaxes in a crescendo in which God who gave the moral law calls nations that mollify it to a final judgment."[66] Regardless of any human effort, Christian, pagan, or otherwise, Henry affirms that it is the providential whim of the almighty that will have the final say over human history and all of its great civilizations.

Sexual Deviance and the Decline of American Civilization

Like Henry's, Graham's historical theology was deeply informed by Toynbee. According to Graham's reading of Toynbee, Jesus Christ was the culmination of all human history. As civilizations bent on their own destruction gave way to the inertia of immorality, Jesus remained the solitary, lasting figure at the end of history.[67] Graham even employed Toynbee in his own anticommunist rhetoric. Christianity, according to Toynbee, was the one hope that could fight "man-worship, materialism, and collectivism"—all (alleged) attributes of Marxist ideology.[68] Graham predicted that as communism and the Soviet regime increasingly threatened US sovereignty, eschatological concerns would rise among churchgoers, for he himself saw the signs that indicated that "the climactic point of history is about to be reached."[69]

As with his earliest sermons for YFC audiences, Graham continued to label sexual immorality as a sign of national decay and the coming apocalypse. In one sermon during his 1958 Charlotte Evangelistic Campaign, he decried the sexual proclivities of famous actresses, the use of pornographic literature, and the increasing number of people who found these behaviors acceptable. To further his claim, Graham drew upon the research of sociologist Pitirim Sorokin, author of *The American Sex Revolution*, whose findings established heterosexual family life's central role in national vitality. Sorokin's argument began with the assumption that marriage was the culmination of an individual's physical, mental, emotional, spiritual, and civic development. Nonmarital sexual relations, therefore, were evidence of the opposite and should, in fact, be viewed as sins, crimes, and symptoms of moral and social degeneration of the individual. The greatest threat, a decline in premarital virginity, led to the possible decline of monogamous marriage and created a gateway to communal pseudomarriages. Though Sorokin found this improbable in the United States, he noted that such relationships had already occurred in his homeland, Soviet Russia.[70]

Reaffirming Toynbee, Sorokin argued that when the well-being of the individual was threatened by sexual disorder, so, too, was the nation-state. The more individuals' physical, mental, spiritual, and civic health is undermined by sexual immorality, the weaker the nation-state is rendered. A civilization comprised of individuals who are sexually disordered along with those who accommodate sexual disorder is ill-equipped to fight off threats to the nation-state, including military invasion, internal revolution, and economic competition.[71] Sorokin's own views of history also echoed Toynbee's theories of rise and decline: the society that restricts sexual freedom increases cultural creativity, while the society that permits disordered and illegitimate sex contributes to the decline of creativity. The vitality of creativity, according to Toynbee, signified a civilization's ascent, while its loss of creativity is a sign of its breakdown and pending disintegration. Likewise, Sorokin points to several civilizations—Babylonian, Persian, Macedonian, Mongol, Greek, and Roman—that, he said, all exhibited the same symptoms of advance and decline. Those civilizations that restricted sexual practices by enforcing premarital sexual chastity and monogamous marriage reached the highest level of civilized life, while those that relaxed their moral codes, as all eventually did, found themselves in cultural decline after three generations.

How Sorokin, whose book contains no footnotes or bibliography, settled on three generations remains unknown. However, given the consistency between his assertions and those of Toynbee, it seems likely that the historian had provided Sorokin with yet another piece of his argument. According to Toynbee, human civilizations emerge due to successful responses to particular challenges. This pattern of challenge and response allows a civilization to thrive for a time. However, after three repetitions—or generations—of this pattern, the civilization begins its descent toward disintegration. For Sorokin, sexual anarchy was a challenge faced by ancient civilizations, and their survival was dependent upon a successful response to that challenge.

Like many other adherents of Toynbee's theory, Sorokin turned to the precedent of ancient Rome, one civilization that almost successfully overcame its sexual and sociopolitical disorders. Christianity, one such successful response, was able to curb the incursion of sexual, marital, and familial chaos. The early Christian movement, according to Sorokin, banned lust in thought and deed, declared all nonmarital sexual relations to be sinful, valorized sexual chastity, and permitted sexual intercourse only in the context of socially sanctioned marriage. Thus, Christianity in ancient Rome was able to restore the sanctity of marriage, bolster family, and preserve normal and lawful forms of sexual activity.[72] However, after continual assault from pagan proclivities, even the bulwark of Christianity could not save Rome from its eventual demise.

In the US context, Sorokin influenced evangelists such as Graham to view this sexual revolution (not to be confused with the later sexual revolution—he was writing in 1958) as a threat to the United States. Though Graham stressed the threat of communism and socialist revolution in his sermons, Sorokin convinced him that the increased sexual freedoms enjoyed by many American citizens constituted a more imminent threat to national security. Graham encouraged his audiences to read Sorokin's book and adopt his argument that sexual revolution was the most potent twentieth-century upheaval on American soil and would fell US sovereignty long before communist incursion would. Furthermore, Graham urged his listeners to mark this revolution as more than a national threat: it was a sign of the end.[73]

However, Graham himself did not view sexual immorality and communist incursion as separate threats. Concurrent with Graham's rise to national prominence was a federal antigay initiative that presumed male homosexuals to be an imminent threat to national security. Lawmakers and government officials set about crafting a program that would remove all sexual deviants from federal positions. Numerous leaders believed that not only was homosexuality an acceptable practice under the Soviet regime, as were other forms of sexual anarchy; they also thought that American homosexuals were susceptible to blackmail by communist spies. By 1950, over ninety-one individuals discovered to be homosexual were fired from the State Department, while Senate investigations claimed to know of 4,000 others concurrently working throughout the government.[74] In the context of the Cold War, sexual deviance—and homosexuality in particular—became synonymous with anti-American activities, not because homosexuality and communism were inherently compatible, but because of the unfounded belief that individuals with nonnormative sexual practices were morally lax, susceptible to temptation, and therefore able to be turned into communist assets.[75]

Graham's sermons were mired in anticommunist rhetoric; he fully supported Joseph McCarthy's obsessive initiative, which he believed was crucial to "exposing the pinks, the lavenders, and the reds who have sought refuge beneath the wings of the American eagle."[76] He frequently used the threat of communism as a sermon illustration and always as a preface for the need for religious revival. In his sermons, Graham wove convincing narratives of a holy war between Christian America and atheist Russia in which Satan himself controlled the fate of the Soviet Union.[77] Cities such as Los Angeles were havens of sin, crime, and immorality, making them targets for nuclear attack and communist takeover. Graham's slippage between the rhetoric of national security and apocalyptic anticipation further cemented the Cold War as a supernatural battle between good and evil:

> God is giving us a desperate choice, a choice of either revival or judgment. There is no alternative! The world is divided into two camps! On the one side we see communism, which has declared war against God, against Christ, against the Bible, and against all religion! Unless the Western world has an old-fashioned revival, we cannot last![78]

Though Graham would later retract much of his anticommunist vitriol in order to open up evangelistic opportunities behind the Iron Curtain, his later writings were equally concerned with the decay of civilizations, marked primarily by the increase in sexual immorality. In 1965, he wrote that sexual obsession had always been a mark of decaying civilizations. Citing an unnamed historian whose assertion resonated unsurprisingly with both Toynbee and Sorokin, Graham warned that moral deterioration would extinguish Western civilization by the year 2000, if the communists had not yet achieved their goal of world domination.[79] Graham's *World Aflame* was a prophetic call to Americans, whose own sexual gluttony was destroying the soul of the nation. Like the biblical peoples reprimanded by Hosea or the apathetic contemporaries of Noah, US citizens were naïve to believe that their moral decadence would escape divine judgment:

> This we do know, our decaying morals do not surprise God. They add to the pile of inflammable tinder that shall someday be ignited by the fires of God's judgment . . . if ever a generation was bequeathed that knowledge of God, we were. Yet we are throwing away this glorious heritage on our lust and passions.[80]

At the end of its imperial reign, Graham thought, Rome abandoned its moral standards, suffered the disintegration of family life, accepted divorce, and accommodated immorality.[81] This behavior was not only duplicated but also exacerbated, in Graham's estimation, by contemporary American norms, both within and without the church. While the laity accommodated the "moral bingeing" of pleasure and abuse of God's gift, clergy were declaring that premarital sexuality should not be resolutely condemned.[82]

Conclusion

Graham's extensive career as an evangelist, writer, and presidential counselor cannot easily be encapsulated by his premillennialist theology, anticommunist vitriol, and condemnation of sexual immorality. However, these themes took on a cohesive function in Graham's rhetoric that marked adolescent sexuality with nationalistic and apocalyptic implication. The fear of sexuality prevalent in Graham's later writings is not simply a concern for the individual whose personal health and well-being could be toppled by a few wrong choices. Prompted by the nationalist homophobia of the Cold War, evangelicals adopted Graham's notion that sexual morality was a crucial aspect of national security, a fear that was reinforced by Sorokin's observations of the sexual revolution. For those expecting Christ to return and draw his believers into eternal glory, the dual threats of nuclear attack and moral decay piqued apocalyptic anticipations. Evangelicals and fundamentalists nurtured amid this Cold War rhetoric of sexual fear did not break stride with the fall of the Berlin Wall in 1990. Rather, the rhetoric of sexual fear that exploited evangelical anxieties continued to fester, even as a new generation was launching campaigns to reinstate the moral value of sexual purity.

Cold War fundamentalists offered historical and theological explanations for contemporary anxieties. They were not necessarily concerned with quieting national anxiety, but wanted to create a narrative that decried human progress, asserted divine sovereignty over human history, and declared communism an imminent satanic threat. These leaders offered a host of prophecies that marked moral relativism as a sign of national decline. The abandonment of moral absolutes, namely those that monitor sexual behavior, was consistently cited in their work as a grave human error that would render the United States more vulnerable to internal decay and external attack. With careers spanning most of the twentieth century, Henry and Graham crafted a rhetoric of sexual fear that linked sexual immorality, national decline, and pending apocalypse—a discourse that would remain highly relevant within evangelical circles and serve as the architectural foundation for later sexual purity campaigns.

Chapter Three

Making Family Values

AS DEMONSTRATED IN the previous chapter, Cold War–era religion, politics, and morality were shaped by fears of national decline and pending nuclear apocalypse. Politicians, religious leaders, and academics framed problems of sexual deviance and juvenile delinquency as national security issues.[1] Historian Jason Bivins provides a helpful term for framing this particular form of religiosity: *a religion of fear*. Though Bivins situates this phenomenon later in the twentieth century, it is an apt descriptor of what occurred in the postwar era. For Bivins, the religion of fear developed in response to the decline of postwar evangelicalism and the emergence of the cultural revolutions. However, the linkages between personal morality and national decline made by fear-based religion were already well established during the Cold War. As a political religion, the religion of fear grew out of a conflict between evangelical imaginings of a Christian America and a growing resistance to religion in modern politics, a formulation that borrowed heavily from religiopolitical alliances that imagined the Cold War as a spiritual battle between a Christian America and godless communism.[2]

As an outgrowth of a particular cultural moment in which evangelicals viewed themselves as victims of a secular regime, the religion of fear promoted a theology of ultimate good and evil. The religion of fear sought to discomfort its adherents by demonstrating the tenuous boundary between salvation and condemnation, a moral system which they believed mirrored a larger cosmic battle.

At midcentury, fundamentalists' ability to explain global crises with theological certainty offered them unparalleled evangelistic opportunities and access to political power.[3] In Bivins's narrative, the decline of evangelical political influence during the 1960s precipitated a new status for evangelicals, who felt relegated to the margins of American political life. In response to a political culture that no longer favored them, evangelicals developed a fear-based religious rhetoric that helped them to establish protective boundaries away from the chaos and excesses of the cultural revolutions. However, it was their subcultural status, not the religion of fear, that was new to evangelical identity.

In times of cultural turbulence that threatened evangelical identity, the religion of fear provided a rallying point for evangelicals. Both the Cold War and the cultural revolutions of the 1960s piqued these fears, though, in the former case, those fears were shared by an entire nation; in the latter, evangelicals struggled to ensure their values were represented in the mainstream.

The work of evangelicals to create a religion of fear remained strikingly similar in both eras. In both cases, evangelicals asserted axiomatic ties between personal morality and national security, and in both cases, they advanced moral absolutes in response to their own anxieties. In the late twentieth century, the religion of fear was promoted through sophisticated media representations that portrayed a downward trajectory of American morality since the 1960s. Despite feeling politically sidelined, evangelicals sought other avenues for cultural impact and easily found them in retail merchandising and lifestyle media. Throughout the 1970s, evangelical print, television, and radio media were their primary loci of transmission for ideas about raising children, adolescent sexuality, and national politics. The accommodation of modern technology by evangelicals had been a longstanding practice ever since nineteenth-century revivalists turned theaters into churches. However, evangelical use of media in the late twentieth century was less concerned with the creation of new evangelicals than with the maintenance of evangelical identity.[4]

The evangelical embrace of popular media and retail culture was just one example of the complicated relationship evangelicals developed toward the countercultural and consumerist values of the 1960s and 1970s. Sociologist Donald Miller described this relationship as a new form of American Protestantism, or a new paradigm. New paradigm churches quickly replaced mainline denominational congregations because of their willingness to accommodate the tastes, preferences, and discomforts of reluctant churchgoers. These large, suburban places of worship more often than not resembled corporate, shopping, or athletic facilities. Trying to explain how these temples to consumerism and modern suburbia replaced neighborhood churches as the driving force of American Protestantism, Miller described their ideological core as an outgrowth of values of the 1960s counterculture: individualism, self-transformation, and antiestablishmentarianism.[5] The shift wrought by the counterculture downgraded the value of theological and denominational tradition and elevated the status of personal religious experience, a change indicating that the cultural influence of religion was no longer in the hands of the older generation, but determined by younger evangelicals wrestling with identity and belonging. Furthermore, survivors of the counterculture held deep sway over trends in personal spirituality and political activism while injecting a strong dose of activism into youth culture. At the same moment, broader trends in American political discourse sought and found new sources of authority for cultural critique rooted in personal experience.[6]

In contrast to the religion of fear that shaped evangelical political culture during the midcentury, the new paradigm churches provided their consumers with a religion of accommodation. The religion of fear worked to maintain boundaries—between the United States and the USSR, between Christianity and communism, between sexual morality and sexual deviance. Theologically, the orientation was an attempt to demonstrate the radical chasm between holy and unholy. Conversely, the religion of accommodation sought to overcome these divisions and worked to quiet any unease with contemporary culture. It drew upon secular therapeutic discourses to create a morality based primarily upon the well-being of the individual. In the same way, it utilized popular media culture in order to establish itself as culturally relevant. As Donald Miller demonstrated, new paradigm churches embraced media culture (both its content and its technology) in order to find more effective means of communication with prospective audiences. These churches sought to appeal to the church-wary with their willingness to dissolve the boundaries between religious and nonreligious cultures.[7]

The changes in evangelicalism during the cultural revolutions set the stage for numerous later developments, most significantly the behaviors and definitions that would come to be called "family values." Several studies have explored the political mobilizing that occurred on behalf of initiatives to save the American family, and each provides some insight into the shaping of an adolescent evangelical culture in which the young and their families were increasingly positioned as markers of cultural stability or decline.[8] Not surprisingly, evangelicals rallied around experts who helped them make sense of adolescent experiences and provided advice for securing a godly family life. With the aid of a media market saturated with self-help and lifestyle media, Christian psychology quickly became both a resource for and an advocate of the evangelical family. The emergence of

Focus on the Family, led by James Dobson, was and remains the most prominent example of evangelicals' willingness to accommodate secular discourses to their own moral frameworks.

The introduction of a religion of accommodation into evangelical theology did not ultimately displace separatist theologies, and in many cases, fear and accommodation worked in tandem to open and close boundaries and moral structures that maintained evangelical identity. But the changes to evangelicalism wrought by the cultural revolutions are significant nonetheless, as they help us understand how it transformed itself into a therapeutic subculture.[9]

Toward Accommodation

Conservative evangelical encounters with the radical counterculture of the 1960s and 1970s are traditionally portrayed as defensive strategies.[10] Contemporary evangelicals and many scholars mark this era as a downward turn for the United States, as it exemplified challenges to established authorities and moral order. However, the evangelical encounter with the cultural revolutions was initially not antagonistic but syncretistic. The shifts in late-century evangelicalism were in large part the result of accommodations to the aesthetics, activist strategies, and spiritualities of the youth-based counterculture. This accommodation process led to the invigoration of an activist youth culture by repackaging traditional values as revolutionary. Conservative activists worked strategically to recruit these young people and demarcated cultural threats that young activists could cut their newly politicized teeth on. It was this process, both an outgrowth and contributor to the cultural revolutions, that formed the foundation for the ideology of family values and the New Christian Right.[11]

Secular countercultural youth movements of this era bore a striking resemblance to many of the populist values of revivalist Christianity. An emphasis on personal spiritual awakening, transcendence, and ecstatic expression were all hallmarks of a new spirituality that replaced more traditional forms of religious affiliation and theological orthodoxy.[12] The decline of denominationalism and the emergence of informal church structures and religious communes indicated to the older generations that young people were emboldened to advocate for their own spiritual preferences. Opting for religious experiences that reinforced their individual needs and concerns, the spiritual questing of this generation transformed Cold War denominationalism into a de-established spiritual marketplace.[13]

The close resemblance of revivalist Christianity and the countercul-ture provided evangelicals with numerous adaptive strategies. The pre-eminence of the individual spiritual quest drew young people seeking personal fulfillment and spiritual ecstasy to Haight-Ashbury, communes, Eastern spirituality, and hallucinogenic drugs. Many of these quests ended at the doors of Chuck Smith, a Hawaiian-shirt-wearing, fundamen-talist preacher from southern California who helped former drug users shift their hope for transcendence from LSD onto Jesus Christ. Known for his laid-back preaching style and for conducting baptisms in the Pacific Ocean, Smith recognized that the hippie generation, with its penchant for political and cultural protest, was ripe for religious conversion.[14] A vast number of young people, burnt out on free love and psychedelic drugs, found a home at Calvary Chapel, one of the first new paradigm churches that combined cultural relevance with biblical fundamentals. The young people drawn to churches like Smith's were called Jesus freaks, hippies who turned on to Jesus and embraced a spirit-filled movement that per-mitted their generation to rebel against rebellion and yet retain the mar-ginal identity that characterized the counterculture. In their conversion, they left behind many of the destructive behaviors, but very few of the values, that had come to shape their personal morality. Coupled with the fervency of Christian fundamentalism, the countercultural ideals of per-sonal freedom, self-expression, and cultural rebellion eventually found their way into mainstream evangelicalism.

The Jesus People Movement as it was called, appealed to the aesthetics of the hippies, whose dress, hairstyles, music, and art all exhibited a care-free disposition toward spirituality and personal expression. Comprising populists and antiestablishmentarians who rejected denominationalism in favor of revivalist Christianity, these youthful, free-spirits sought salva-tion through an intimate relationship with Jesus Christ. The shift from religion to spirituality accompanied the prioritizing of the individual. Sal-vation was not collective, except through the individual's own pious ac-tions and commitments.[15] The accessibility of its music, populist theology, and the moral absolutes of scripture proved to be the mainstays of the movement's belief system.[16]

The counterculture provided the Jesus Movement with new opportu-nities for evangelism and cultural transformation. Since evangelicals shared cultural markers with popular media, that became their market-ing avenue; they especially favored music. The emergence of a Christian music industry at a time when talk of spirituality was commonplace exemplified the syncretism of the movement and reflected the desire to reinvigorate Christianity with the enthusiasm and creativity of a youth movement.[17] Barry McGuire was one of many musicians who converted to Christianity after embracing the hippie lifestyle and experimenting with Eastern mysticism. For McGuire, the hippie life was a genuine search for truth that required freedom from material goods. Like many, he was disgusted by the constraints of organized religion but developed a deep affinity for the teachings of Jesus Christ.[18]

By adopting the trends and tastes of the counterculture, the Jesus generation established what Darren Dochuk has called "a creative conservatism" that reinvigorated evangelical Christianity and expanded its cultural influence.[19] Jesus People also recognized that the cultural and political activism of the counterculture was easily mapped onto evangelistic strategies. The idea that personal commitment and moral persuasion had a place in politics gave young evangelicals new entrées into political life. The notions of rebellion and revolution shaped a new kind of Christian identity, one headed by a man—Jesus Christ—who rejected cultural conformity and was popularly acknowledged as an outlaw. Not only did these adaptations provide new arenas for Christian proselytizing; they created a new religious identity for young Christians, one that connected personal faith, moral accountability, and youth protest.[20]

The revolution in morals and manners that characterized the counterculture anchored a new identity for evangelicals. But it also provided ample opportunity for evangelicals to remind themselves of the moral codes that distinguished them from secular culture. The women's movement, gay liberation, and civil rights all threatened the cultural and political relevance and prominence that evangelicals had enjoyed during the Cold War. In two decades, evangelicals witnessed the rapid decline of their value system, and, with it, their own political power and cultural influence. Significant court decisions on school prayer, racial desegregation, and abortion indicated that evangelicals were increasingly on the margins of America life.[21]

The upheaval of moral authority during the cultural revolutions frightened many social conservatives. As with the changing sexual and social mores of the early twentieth century, the sexual revolution and the feminist movement spurred a substantial political and cultural backlash from religious conservatives. However, evangelicals were not yet lockstep with the conservative political agenda. Throughout the 1960s and into the 1970s, many remained in favor of legal abortion and gender equality, concerned more about the immorality of racism and poverty than sexuality.[22] But the new evangelicalism was heavily influenced by the personalized politics of the cultural revolution, strategic political organizing by conservative activists, and the emergence of an evangelical therapeutic culture. It was these elements that galvanized a politically and theologically diverse religious culture into an activist voting block whose primary concern was for the survival of an increasingly besieged cultural institution: the nuclear family.

Though radical and antiestablishment in appearance and manners, this young generation of evangelical activists was guided by the same moral absolutism of their parents' Cold War religiosity. An emphasis on biblical literalism, apocalypticism, and strict moral codes distinguished this group from more left-leaning evangelicals who continued to work against racism and poverty. But more important was their distinction from secular youth, whose outrageous behavior seemed rooted in a desire for antinomian chaos. The movement's emphasis on spiritual and physical wholeness appealed to a group of young people who were adrift in moral relativism. Fundamentalist theology provided strict moral guidelines as aids so that individuals could manage and assess their own moral actions. The discipline of fundamentalist theology that posited a hierarchically created order fed directly into a conservative worldview that valued personal responsibility, self-sufficiency, and the traditional family, which, to them, was the foundational unit of social stability.[23]

Conservative Evangelical Activism

Throughout the 1960s and 1970s, conservative evangelicals developed a growing unease with a new moral climate in which premarital sex, homosexuality, divorce, and abortion were becoming normative. The ability to map these concerns onto a political platform was a new idea for many evangelicals, who had previously been discouraged from political participation. But the activist innovations of the counterculture not only provided a model for social action based on personal principles, but invigorated a young generation of new voters who were ready to put their principles into practice.[24]

While the New Left provided new expressive forms for neophyte activists, the Jesus People translated concerns for race, poverty, and war into a concern for national stability. When they learned that sexual impurity, divorce, and homosexuality were equally grave threats to the nation's well-being, they directed their work toward those issues as well. Though hard-line fundamentalists like those who affiliated with the anticommunist John Birch Society lost influence by the end of the 1960s, the apocalyptic rhetoric that often accompanied anticommunist campaigns found a new constellation of issues.[25] With renewed confidence in their ability to impact national politics, conservative evangelicals worked on the grassroots level to maintain the values they believed were the foundation of America's strength. One of the earliest efforts was in 1969, when conservatives sought to challenge new sex-education programs instituted by the Sexuality Information and Education Council of the United States (SIECUS). Some parents addressed the issue by sending their kids to private schools, while others challenged public-school policy outright. Roman Catholics and evangelicals feared that the SIECUS program was "godless, pornographic, and an affront to family privacy."[26] Opponents portrayed the program as a plot by secular humanists to undermine the traditional authority of the family. In fact, SIECUS encouraged young people to discuss and determine their sexual boundaries, which threatened parental oversight. Most significantly, the program indicated to conservatives that the nation's educational institutions had adapted a new morality that jettisoned a clear demarcation between right and wrong. A challenge to the new curriculum in California's Anaheim Union High School District proved successful, and its advocates eventually won a majority on the school board. Though previous opposition to sex education was rooted in a fear of communist incursion, the rhetoric of the Anaheim case simply replaced the godlessness of the Soviet Union with the godlessness of humanism.[27]

Evangelicals who worked to reestablish traditional values in the face of what they saw as an increasingly oppositional secular culture believed themselves to be working in the best interest of the nation. Moral codes derived from the Bible were a functional map for a secure and thriving nation. The hierarchy and obedience that characterized God's relationship with human beings was an archetype for all human relations. Patterned after this structure, the ideal American family was the locus of national life—as the family goes, so goes the nation. In this formulation, youth took on greater significance, because they held the greatest promise for civic renewal. With the passage of the Twenty-Fourth Amendment, which lowered the voting age to eighteen, conservative leaders worked to recruit young evangelicals, who they believed held the balance of political power.[28] At the same time, evangelicals positioned the young as the most vulnerable citizens, whose innocence and promise of moral fortitude could be usurped by premarital sex or homosexuals who preyed upon the young.[29]

One of the key players in the transformation of young believers into evangelical activists was Francis Schaeffer, an expat intellectual who spent most of his adult life in Switzerland hosting visitors who sought out the leader for his unique combination of cultural engagement, intellectual acumen, and fundamentalist biblical principles. At L'Abri, the community started by Schaeffer and his wife, Edith, curious young intellectuals and spiritual seekers of all stripes were welcomed into an open conversation about faith and intellectual life that many found lacking in their weekly churchgoing experiences. Schaeffer was especially sympathetic to the revolutionary desires of young people, and his assessment highlighted the syncretism of countercultural values of antimaterialism and the strict moral codes of evangelical Christianity.

> The young people had been right in their analysis, though wrong in their solution. How much worse when many gave up hope and simply accepted the same values as their parents—personal peace and affluence. Now drugs remain, but only in parallel to the older generation's alcohol, and an excessive use of alcohol has become a problem among the young people as well. Promiscuous sex and bisexuality remain, but only in parallel to the older generation's adultery. In other words, as the young people revolted against their parents, they came around in a big circle—and often ended an inch lower—with only the same two impoverished values: their own kind of personal peace and their own kind of affluence.[30]

Schaeffer held up the sexual practices of youth (and their parents' permissiveness) as an example of secular humanism's impact on human behavior. Because the United States had embraced an ideology that rejected the notion of a sovereign God and the revealed truth of the Bible, the behaviors of its citizens would follow suit, giving themselves over to lives of decadence and selfish indulgence.[31]

Schaeffer's popularity grew with a series of lectures that directly engaged the canon of Western thought and took him to Harvard University, the Massachusetts Institute of Technology, and Wheaton and Westmont Colleges. Evangelical college students were especially excited by his work, because it gave them a new permission to think and learn outside the parameters of what qualified as "Christian" thought. Just as Christian rock exemplified a cultural syncretism between secular music and the good news of Christianity, Schaeffer's intellectual syncretism gave young evangelicals another avenue toward cultural relevance. He was adept at teaching Christians how to engage history, art, literature, and architecture with equal degrees of skepticism and appreciation.[32] He wanted Christians to interact with classical texts and other hallmarks of Western civilization in order to participate in learned conversations and insert a Christian perspective into those discussion. For Schaeffer, this meant engaging the humanities with the presupposition that all human creations are limited and corrupt. His book *How Should We Then Live* chronicled the rise and decline of great Western civilizations in order to demonstrate the corrosive impact of secular humanism. Without the ultimate truths of the Bible, civilization no longer had the ability to withstand assaults on human dignity and creativity.[33]

As an outsider to his own country of origin, Schaeffer crafted a Christian identity that appealed to the young and alienated. His view was that Christians were no longer welcome in the United States, a country overrun by secular humanism, an ideology not shy about its hostility toward God. Schaeffer popularized humanism as the ultimate foe of Christianity and at the same time drew lines of comparison between that ideology and political-economic collectivism. Communism, Schaeffer contended, was the absolute rule of no absolutes, a trend that he thought evident in the Supreme Court's decision to legalize abortion.[34] But rather than encouraging cultural separatism and the development of their own institutions and schools of thought, Schaeffer urged young evangelicals to engage the secular world. He encouraged evangelicals to articulate a uniquely Christian worldview, on the premise that well-crafted intellectual formulations rooted in biblical authority could have a transformative impact on the world.

By the late 1970s, Schaeffer would exchange his intellectual pursuits for more concerted political action, bringing a whole generation of culturally astute evangelicals with him. Garnering a reputation as the philosophical correspondent of the New Christian Right, Schaeffer's work took on a fresh political tone.[35] Like many conservative evangelicals, Schaeffer believed that secular humanism was the cause of the nation's moral decay and that the United States desperately needed to return to its supposedly Christian foundations. The most striking example of the expulsion of Christian values was thought to be the legalization of abortion. In *Whatever Happened to the Human Race?*, cowritten with future US Surgeon

General C. Everett Koop, Schaeffer traced the genocidal implications of a worldview that replaced moral absolutes with moral relativism.[36]

Schaeffer's concern for national decline and moral decay revived the Cold War tropes made popular by Billy Graham and Carl F. H. Henry. He believed that evangelicals felt a deep discomfort with the norms of late-century American life but needed help articulating what was wrong.[37] Using Edward Gibbon's *The History of the Decline and Fall of the Roman Empire*, Schaeffer demonstrated how the loss of moral absolutes contributed to the fall of great civilizations. Without knowledge of God and an absolute moral structure, a culture becomes "degenerate, decadent, depraved, and violent," as the Roman Empire did just prior to its fall.[38] Felling Rome, he contended, was easy work for the invading barbarians, because the moral infrastructure of the civilization had already weakened from within.[39] He pointed to the same signifiers present in modern America. These included economic disparity, the creation of a welfare state, "freakishness in the arts," and an obsession with sex.[40] A civilization that neglected its biblical origins (as Schaeffer believed the United States had done) was ruled by an arbitrary amorality resulting in the extraction of sexual morality from biblical purposes.[41] He criticized the sexologist Alfred Kinsey, whose research prioritized real practices over ideal practices. Kinsey had popularized the idea that sexual morality was established by what people do, not by what they should do, providing Schaeffer with more evidence that Americans had given themselves over to secular humanism, an ideological foe as destructive as communism.[42]

Apocalypse in the Making

What is most curious about evangelicalism in the 1970s is that, even as countercultural adaptations transformed the tradition into a distinct branch of American therapeutic culture, the apocalyptic imagination of believers and nonbelievers remained as prevalent as ever. The prophetic claims of Cold War fundamentalists helped people to situate the global crisis within a providential view of history and provided some relief from the imminent fears of nuclear war. But by the 1970s, the evangelical Cold War warriors, most prominently Billy Graham, had shifted their attention from communist threats, nuclear war, and prophetic warnings, toward the domestic concerns of family, parenting, and sexuality.[43] And yet, the popular evangelical imagination was spellbound by narratives of the apocalypse, especially Hal Lindsey's *The Late, Great Planet Earth*, one of the best-selling books of the decade. Lindsey, a staff member for Campus Crusade for Christ and a Korean War veteran, received his theological training at Dallas Theological Seminary, a flagship institution for dispensationalist theologies. Lindsey eventually left Campus Crusade in order to concentrate his ministerial work solely on prophecy teachings.[44] *The Late, Great Planet Earth* systematized prophetic claims for the present day, providing explanation of how current geopolitical events, including the Cold War and Israeli-Palestinian hostilities in the Holy Land, had been foretold in biblical writings. As Lindsey told it, the remaining events that would precipitate the return of Christ were not only plausible but also imminent.[45]

Tensions between modes of millennialism and understanding human history were long-standing within evangelicalism, to such a degree that the tradition needs to be approached as a pluralistic, rather than monolithic, system of belief. Premillennial dispensationalism—the sort espoused by Lindsey—first entered American Protestantism in the late nineteenth century, when influential evangelicals encountered the thought of Irish theologian John Nelson Darby. Millennialism, post- and pre-, were two strains of an apocalyptic theology that diverged in their views of human progress. Postmillennialism, which had characterized evangelicalism from the early American republic through the Civil War, asserted that human beings participated in the perfection of civilization. Utopian communities and progressive movements such as the social purity movement, the focus of chapter one, flourished in this era because Protestant evangelicals believed their efforts could help establish a period of peace and harmony that would beckon Christ back to earth.[46] Premillennialists did not ascribe to the high anthropology of postmillennialism, viewing human history as a slow decline into chaos and destruction. By the end of World War I, premillennialism and the pessimism of human progress were firmly ensconced in fundamentalist theology. In fact, the shift from post- to premillennialism marked the emergence of fundamentalism in the early twentieth century.

Darby introduced the notion of dispensationalism, which can be briefly explained as the trajectory of divinely planned human history plotted through his careful exegesis of the biblical books of Daniel and Revelation. Dispensationalism divided history into several ages, or dispensations, each characterized by a particular divine-human interaction but following the same narrative framework: God offers salvation, humans reject salvation, God punishes humans.[47] According to the prophecies Darby deciphered from the books of Daniel and Revelation, human history had been in its final dispensation since Christ's first appearing on earth. Numerous prophecies were set to be fulfilled in this era as signs of Christ's second coming. These signs include the appearance of the Antichrist, a tyrannical church leader who is often identified as the Roman Catholic pope, and a political despot, known as the beast, who will unite ten nations that emerged from the Roman Empire. It also involved the extensive persecution of the Jews and their return to Jerusalem. Seven years prior to Christ's return, faithful believers would be taken to Christ in secret rapture, sparing them the torment of a final battle. Upon his return, Christ will lead an army against the Antichrist and the beast, soon defeating them in the Near Eastern region known as Armageddon. Christ's victory will reinstate his reign over the holy city of Jerusalem, restoring the Jews to nationhood.[48]

Throughout the Cold War and into the cultural revolutions, evangelicals who anticipated the return of Christ prioritized evangelism and sought reassurance that they and their loved ones would be saved from any form of tribulation, even if they were uncertain of what that will entail. Given their uncertainty, evangelicals were not wholly defined by their desire to offer and seek salvation for the next life; instead, they found numerous temporal causes, practices, and beliefs that allowed them to cultivate full and righteous lives in this world.

Lindsey's version of the end times reflected the rampant pessimism of the younger generation and utilized the vernacular of the Jesus generation to engage his readers.[49] He helped college-age students make sense of global and local events and trends fraught with violence and confusion. His efforts were supported by the growing Christian-rock industry, whose most prominent artist, Larry Norman, had long been concerned with the end times and whose songs chronicled a culture in decline and anticipated large-scale destruction. Though crafted to elicit fear and despair, the apocalyptic message shared by Lindsey and Norman situated the signs of a world in decline as part of a divine plan. Just as Cold War fundamentalism offered prophetic explanations for the rise of the Soviet Union, Lindsey offered young evangelicals a way to cope with the violence and disruption of the 1970s. Lindsey's fear-based prophecies exploited already heightened fears. In a new age of spiritual seekers, he popularized the idea of the rapture by giving people a way to comprehend an incomprehensible future.[50]

Lindsey's apocalyptic predictions for the 1970s were eventually disproven, but his ability to recognize and tap into the apocalyptic expectations of the decade help illuminate the discordant strains contending for the evangelical imagination. The massive popularity of *The Late, Great Planet Earth* reinforced a belief among evangelicals that the ability to address widespread political crises was the key to maintaining their political salience. At the same time that evangelicals were embracing therapeutic practices that enhanced their experiences in this life, they continued to seek theological formulations to help prepare them for the next.

From the End Times to Family Time

At least one historian has challenged the presumably ubiquitous presence of prophecy and dispensationalism during the 1970s. David Harrington Watt contends that 1970s interest in end times lagged behind that of earlier decades. Other scholars who maintain its prevalence during that ten-year span rely upon popular sources—the publications and music of people like Lindsey and Norman. Watt's premise, on the other hand, comes from his analysis of evangelical magazines that indicated the marginalization of apocalypticism within mainstream evangelical theology. He contends that evangelical skepticism about the end times emerged at the same time that evangelical attention shifted away from the millennium and toward a new source of hope: the family.[51]

The purpose of raising this debate isn't to ultimately determine the degree to which apocalypticism infiltrated mainstream America or maintained its relevance within evangelicalism. Rather, it exemplifies the complex relationship between the theology of fear left over from the Cold War era and the theology of accommodation newly emerged from the counterculture. The convergence of fear and accommodation within evangelical belief was aided in large part by the establishment of Christian psychology and the development of an evangelical therapeutic culture.

The politicization of American family life by late-century evangelicals is best understood as an attempt to return to Victorian ideals of domestic piety. Domestic ideologies of the nineteenth century fostered a direct correlation between the well-being of the nation-state and the health of the family. Domestic ideologies imagined the nation as a home with foreign bodies, actual and ideological, always presenting a potential threat. Nationalistic tropes of colonialism and the project of civilization were mapped onto expectations of home and family life, situating the future of the nation squarely within the domestic realm. The white, middle-class family, free of relational strife and other consequences of immoral behaviors, represented the hopes for a nation that likewise sought to vanquish the moral and social threats to its stability and flourishing.[52]

This connection between domestic stability and national security emerged as a mainstay of evangelical rhetoric in the 1970s. More than ever before, the American family was at the center of American political life, because calls for the family unit's restoration created new allies between Republican politicians and evangelical leaders. As a political strategy among conservative evangelicals, domestic ideology has been well documented by numerous historians of the Christian Right.[53] It blended the new therapeutic values that were helping young churches grow at exponential rates and lingering Cold War anxieties that cast a shadow over significant political events. Political strategists were instrumental and deliberate about constructing the ideology of family values. But the more significant and long-lasting contribution was the development of a therapeutic evangelical culture led by experts in the area of parenting, family life, and adolescent psychology. This development, more than anything, created a new mode of evangelical faith practice and a new kind of evangelical leader, the Christian psychologist, whose expertise provided families with biblically based advice for securing a faithful home life and a godly nation.

Evangelicals on the Couch

To numerous observers of the movement, evangelicalism had undergone a radical reversal in its embrace of psychotherapy and its accompanying rhetoric. Fundamentalists in the early twentieth century opposed modern psychology, which they perceived as promoting a secular-humanist agenda by emphasizing the optimization of selfhood. For these Christians, the nature of the self, mired in sin, required extreme self-denial and self-discipline for adequate rehabilitation, a spiritual process that psychology rendered irrelevant. Psychological theories rejected the notion of sin and explained morality with the presumption that individuals were less responsible for their action. The solution to harmful (not immoral) behavior wasn't spiritual but medical.[54] But, during the 1950s, an increasing number of evangelicals found therapeutic language not only compatible with conservative Christianity but also aptly descriptive of the kind of healing and wholeness only available through the gospel message.

Among these was Clyde Narramore, one of the earliest evangelicals to present Christianity using the language and frameworks of psychological discourse.[55] Narramore, who was not a psychologist by training, became popular for a radio show that dispensed biblically based advice for whole and healthful living. He alleviated fears that counseling was inconsistent with the Christian faith and shared his belief that "the talking cure" was a biblical concept endorsed by Jesus himself.[56] By 1965, Fuller Theological Seminary, the most prominent evangelical seminary in the country, had established a school of psychology in Pasadena, California, and, with it, the means to produce its own form of Bible-based psychology.[57] Along with Fuller and the graduate psychology program that Narramore established nearby (now a part of Biola University), other evangelical schools began developing both undergraduate and graduate programs in the field of Christian psychology. Field specific journals such as *Psychology and Theology* and the *Journal of Psychology and Christianity* along with the creation of the Christian Association of Psychological Studies (CAPS) provided professional resources and networks to its members, who were comfortable adapting the behaviorist and psychoanalytic practices they had learned in their secular training programs.[58]

Evangelical psychology distinguished itself from secular therapy and from the already established field of pastoral counseling. Liberal Protestants adopted psychology and psychoanalysis much more quickly than did evangelicals. With little opposition to new medical and academic practices, liberal Protestants had already developed the practice and study of pastoral care that taught clergy how to use current findings in the field to benefit their own ministerial work. These clergy were influenced by situational ethics that advised pastors that morality was contextual and that absolute principles of right and wrong were unhelpful when serving parishioners in need. Christian counselors, on the other hand, were not clergy but practicing therapists who sought to integrate established psychological practices with the evangelical beliefs in a personal relationship with Jesus Christ and in the authority of scripture. They were critical of pastoral care, because they felt that it, like secular psychologies, was not ultimately rooted in the authority of scripture. Biblical authority provided Christian counselors with a moral absolutism that other forays into psychological work did not provide. Though the science and practice of psychology could address some issues of human distress, they could not ultimately replace the revealed truths of scripture.[59]

By the 1970s, therapeutic rhetoric had renegotiated the way most individuals perceived themselves in relationship to their work, careers, and families. Gone were the days of extreme personal sacrifice and ascetic living. For those entering the middle class—a transitioning group that included many evangelicals—self-enhancement and quality-of-life issues became prominent in shaping individual spirituality. This gave rise to a therapeutic rhetoric that integrated the disciplinary language of psychology with a traditional theological orientation that asserted an inherent spiritual root for every personal problem, a result of the fall of man as narrated in the book of Genesis. Thus, the only true solution was a restoration of one's faith in Jesus Christ.[60]

The relationship between Christianity and psychology was debated throughout the 1970s, even as evangelicals made their mark on American therapeutic culture. Evangelicals maintained their suspicion of secular institutions yet worked to incorporate the psychological establishments' findings into their own practices. The shift toward individuals and self-care that was inherent in psychological practices and increasingly common within new paradigm evangelical spirituality unnerved some, who remained concerned about the boundaries between evangelicals the rest of the world—demarcations arguably foundational to evangelical identity. One of the concerned was Carl F. H. Henry, whose work throughout the late twentieth century warned of a diminished visibility of a distinctive evangelical culture. In Henry's estimation, the therapeutic culture embraced by Christian psychologists shifted the nature of authority away from the Bible and to the self. Notions of goodness no longer centered on obedience to and the cultivation of moral absolutes; instead, goodness derived from personal fulfillment, an idea that for Henry was one step away from secular humanism. In an obverse refrain of his early work, Henry viewed evangelical therapeutic culture as evidence that Christians had become far too engaged in the culture they had set out to transform according to biblical truths. Indulging in self-help and personal fulfillment had encouraged evangelicals to define sin not as disobedience but as anything that kept an individual from achieving personal fulfillment. And, in an echo of Francis Schaeffer and the Jesus People, Henry used countercultural language to call evangelicals back from a life of hedonism.[61]

Regardless of criticism, psychological practices and therapeutic discourses became part and parcel of evangelical faith practice. By 1987, when James Davison Hunter studied the impact of this shift, 12 percent of evangelical publishing was devoted to Christian psychology or self-development, and the membership of CAPS had increased to 2,350 members, an 85 percent increase since the 1970s.[62] Hunter determined in the same study that college students with evangelical commitments were highly influenced by therapeutic rhetoric and talked frequently of self-understanding, self-improvement, and self-fulfillment—to the same degree as their nonevangelical peers did.[63] However, these students described their quest within the context of a relationship to God, believing that attention to self-development assisted one's spiritual maturation.[64] This orientation toward the self *in relation to God* continued to persist among young evangelicals and their spiritual leaders, who learned to incorporate therapeutic processes and rhetoric into their biblical beliefs, signaling another moment of evangelicalism's cultural accommodation.[65]

Making Family Values

The culmination of evangelicalism's therapeutic pulse and its direct confrontation with the "new morality" of secular humanism was best exemplified in the work of James Dobson and Focus on the Family. Unlike more politicized brands of conservative evangelicalism, Dobson's evangelical consciousness grew out of work as a caregiver and advisor, offering support to families weathering the stresses of contemporary life. His work as one of America's premier popular psychologists and parental experts reshaped evangelical self-understanding by creating an institution that manifested evangelicalism's ability to thrive at the confluence of cultural accommodation and cultural resistance.

Even more than the political efforts by other family-values advocates, Dobson's work confirmed for evangelicals the significance of family life to national stability by providing everyday people with common-sense advice for dealing with the challenges of married and parenting life. With a background as a child psychologist and a fierce commitment to biblical authority, Dobson shaped a rhetoric of the family that situated it on the front lines of what he viewed as an all-out war between the godly family, on one hand, and antifamily forces, on the other.[66] His work was most instrumental in laying the groundwork for late-twentieth-century purity movements.

Dobson defined family well-being according to the strength of the partnership between husband and wife; sex outside of marriage was an early indication that this partnership was unsound. Beyond that, his writings on adolescence and parenting reinforced the notion of a created order—that God created all things to function according to a particular design. Sexual practices that did not respect that design consequently weakened the mechanics of human relationality and, in doing so, jeopardized the human-divine relationship. Unlike later purity organizations, Focus on the Family advocated abstinence before marriage as part of a more expansive plan for a godly family life. But, like earlier claims on sexual purity, Dobson's position was supported by theories of civilizations' rise and decline to connect the well-being of the American family with the thriving American nation-state.

Encouraged by Narramore to pursue Christian psychology, Dobson began his professional career at the University of Southern California, where he earned a doctorate in child psychology. While working as a professor of pediatrics at USC Medical School, he became concerned with newer trends in parenting that disregarded the importance of discipline and obedience. Benjamin Spock, the most well-regarded child psychologist of the time, was advising parents to allow their children freedom of expression, accompanied by positive reinforcement. Spock did not present parents with particular guidelines for parenting success, but encouraged them to recognize their own innate abilities to understand their child's developmental needs. From Dobson's perspective, the outcome of this parenting trend was a generation of undisciplined children and beleaguered parents struggling to understand their children's out-of-control behavior. The problem, as Dobson diagnosed it, was a lack of discipline and an inability to recognize the human condition. Children, according to Dobson's theological understanding of original sin, were born into depraved selves that required strict training in order to acquire the traits necessary for appropriate human development and spiritual maturity. As opposed to Dr. Spock's permissive parenting approach, Dobson emphasized the importance of authority and obedience in the parent-child relationship. Spiritual, not personal, development was the goal of parenting for Dobson because it was the primary mechanism by which children learned to accept the authority of God in their lives.[67]

Dobson initially rose to prominence as a parenting expert on the lecture circuit, but he was dismayed by how much time it subtracted from his own family life. To address this concern, he created video recordings of his lectures and made them available for purchase. According to one account, over ten million people viewed this series in the first three years of its availability. In these one-hour lectures, Dobson developed what would become his signature approach to advice-giving: an accessible and authoritative combination of research findings, his professional expertise, and anecdotes from his own family life.[68]

Between 1977 and 1978, Dobson published his first book, *Dare to Discipline*, at the request of Tyndale Publishers and established his family-centered ministry, Focus on the Family, with a grant of $35,000, also from a Christian publishing house. In the late 1970s, evangelicals were quickly establishing a vast network of publishing houses, booksellers, and retail merchandisers, aided by the burgeoning market for self-help literature. Dobson and Focus on the Family emerged at this opportune moment, helping along the mutually assured success of his organization and the Christian retail industry.[69]

Focus on the Family became known for its advocacy of a domestic ideology that reflected a desire to return to family life and gender roles that closely resembled the ideals of nineteenth-century white, middle-class America. For Dobson, these ideals were more than a historical legacy: they amounted to an act of obedience to the order of creation established by God in the book of Genesis. Dobson translated his biblical lessons into an accessible formulation clearly demarcating gendered behaviors and relations. Men and women, he asserted, were created with different but complementary traits that, together, fulfilled God's design for human relationships. Dobson's gender complementarianism was rooted in the physiology of sex. The physical bodies of men and women and the ability of those bodies to copulate and procreate indicated to Dobson a deeper emotional and social bonding that was only possible in the context of marriage. Though Dobson did not use hierarchical language to describe marriage to the degree that he used it to describe the parent-child relationship, his insistence on gender complementarianism reinforced a divine order.

Explaining this in *Love for a Lifetime*, he wrote, "[God] put greater toughness and aggressiveness in the man and more softness and nurturance in the woman—and suited them to one another's needs. And in their relationship He symbolized the mystical bond between the believer and Christ, Himself."[70] The marriage union, as Dobson imagined, signified the union between the human and the divine. Followers of Focus on the Family understood that family stability was an indicator of religious piety. Disordered and chaotic family life did not raise red flags just because it created an unsuitable parenting environment; it indicated a rupture in the human-divine relationship.

At the foundation of Dobson's family ideology were the natural and essential distinctions between men and women that he believed were at risk of dissolution. Just as parenting depended on the hierarchy of parent and child, marriage depended on the proper ordering of the sexes. In the desire to develop and maintain self-esteem, women sought love, romance, security, and a harmonious home life. Men, on the other hand, achieved self-esteem through respect and sexual congress and professional achievement.[71] According to Dobson, feminism inverted this order by claiming that gender differentiation was a construct of a male-dominated culture that needed dismantling, causing confusion for men who based their self-esteem upon traditional expressions of masculinity. The increased sexual and professional freedom advocated by the women's movement threatened to confuse these roles, leaving men uncertain about their gender identity.[72] As a movement intent on usurping male privilege and freeing women from the cultural mandates of marriage and motherhood, feminism threatened the gendered order that Dobson believed was biblically mandated.[73]

Dobson's concern for the development of boys into men is also reflective of nineteenth-century efforts to remasculinize Christianity. Evangelical leaders and child psychologists of earlier eras expressed similar fears about the development of young boys, fears that were related to the increases in women's social and political power. For Dobson, the feminist movement created a crisis of masculinity presumably because it sanctioned women's participation in traditionally masculine roles. Without the exclusive right to leadership and authority, men floundered. Echoing the concerns of G. Stanley Hall, Dobson recommended that boys, who were often raised in highly feminized environments, needed opportunities to express their physical aggression through play in order to learn how to be masculine. Despite his insistence on the gender determinism of human biology, Dobson's fears reflected his underlying belief that gender roles were not innate but learned through processes of socialization. The gendered order of family life was crucial, because children needed to learn from their parents what it meant to be boys and girls. Without proper instruction, children were at risk for a crisis of sexual identity.[74] This process of gender socialization proceeded alongside a child's moral and spiritual development—as children learned to address their sinful nature, they also learned to distinguish between male and female. Dobson argued that the result of confused gender roles in the family encouraged a child to displace his or her sexual feelings onto the same-sex parent. As an explanation for homosexuality, disordered gender family life impeded a child's ability to leave the homosociality of childhood and embrace the heterosociality and -sexuality of normal adolescence.[75]

Dobson advocated for gender instruction throughout his career at Focus on the Family. Both boys and girls needed guidance and instruction for proper sexual development, again presuming that heterosexuality, like gender, was not a fixed notion but a tenuous prospect that required careful cultivation. Along with endorsing outlets for boys' aggression, Dobson encouraged the idea of "daddy-daughter dating," in which fathers and daughters set aside time and special activities to engage in together. The practice encouraged girls at a young age (six years or earlier) to develop romanticized attachments to the opposite sex and learn how to nurture a heterosexual partnership.[76]

Developing these respective skills assured young boys' and girls' psychological, spiritual, relational, and sexual maturation. Girls became women by learning how to develop and maintain a romantic partnership that captured and held the attention of a man, who in turn would be willing to curb his aggressive tendencies and enter into a domestic partnership. This dynamic was foundational for a successful marriage, according to Dobson's family ideology. Marriage was the cornerstone of civilization because it put men under the influence of women, whose inclinations for domestic harmony refined men's destructive impulses.[77]

This particular formula for marriage was adapted from George Gilder's work on marriage, masculinity, and social order. Gilder, a conservative, antifeminist activist who would eventually found the Discovery Institute, the flagship institution for intelligent design, first espoused his ideas in his book *Sexual Suicide*, written in 1973 and later revised and reissued in 1992 under the title *Men and Marriage*. Encouraged by his own father's reading of Gilder, Dobson came to recognize Gilder's *Sexual Suicide* as the most important book for addressing the implications of disordered gender roles.

According to Gilder, human beings have always sought to ritualize sexual difference in order to establish self-identity and create a balanced social order. As Dobson explained it, the natural inclinations of men and women must be harnessed within a marriage relationship. A man's natural tendency for conquest, while helpful in environments that require a competitive edge, can easily be displaced in destructive ways. Dobson contended that it is unmarried men who are the most likely to commit crimes and exhibit social pathologies. Left to their own devices, men's destructive instincts dominate their behavior. Women, on the other hand, are drawn not to conquest but to long-term stability.[78] Though Dobson does not moralize on these distinctions, Gilder argues that women do not fully understand the moral authority that they wield over men. Referring to young men and boys as barbarians, Gilder insists that many men are simply unfit for citizenship without the emotional and relational demands of married life. Women, though, have the ability to live cooperatively for the long term and the common good, but not the competitive and aggressive nature required to obtain financial stability.[79]

Gilder's analysis of gender and social order rests upon older notions of women's moral authority and ability to refine men's behavior according to the expectations of higher civilization. As explained in chapter one, these were traits first endorsed by nineteenth-century feminists, who deployed their moral authority and civilization work to expand their realm of influence. But the expansion of women's influence throughout the twentieth century, especially over their own sexuality and reproductive rights, alarmed Gilder, Dobson, and others who felt that American economic and political life depended upon the willingness of women to socialize men into rational, interdependent social participants. This is only possible if women accept the expectations of their own sexual restraint, since they can't possibly control men's sexuality if they are unable to contain their own. More emotionally and socially stable, women are able to harness men's aggressive energy for the purposes of creating a viable civilization. In his updated text, *Men and Marriage*, Gilder wrote,

> In creating civilization, women transform male lust into love; channel male wanderlust into jobs, homes, and families; link men to specific children; rear children into citizens; change hunters into fathers; divert male will to power into a drive to create. Women conceive the future that men tend to flee; they feed the children that men ignore.[80]

In Gilder's estimation, and therefore Dobson's, women are the primary party responsible for the cultivation and maintenance of civilization and social order. Unsurprisingly, Gilder and Dobson viewed second-wave feminism, which sought to release women from the confining implications of these expectations, as a threat not only to family stability but also to national strength.

Adolescent Sexuality and American Civilization

The project of family values was not merely a reinstatement of Victorian gender roles, but a new articulation of American identity. Dobson's body of work evidenced the same influence of theories of civilizational rise and decline that had substantiated evangelicals' beliefs of a causal relationship between sexual immorality and national instability. Like purity reformers, child psychologists, and Cold War fundamentalists before him, Dobson deployed tropes of sexual morality and national stability in order to make claims about personal morality and citizenship. The cultural shifts of the 1960s and 1970s wrought a new brand of therapeutic evangelicalism that allowed Dobson to make his claims about family life, parenting, and sexuality in the name of self-fulfillment and personal well-being. It was Dobson who reframed the Victorian ideology of family that connected religious piety with family life in the individualist mode of therapeutic culture: he promoted and supported a concept of family that was self-sufficient in that it provided for all the needs of its members. In nineteenth-century formulations of domestic piety, families were self-sufficient either because of economic status, or social services that compensated for economic status. But the turn toward individualism allowed Dobson to prescribe a family life that provided emotional, spiritual, and economic stability and, if correctly constituted, would produce self-sufficient, law-abiding citizens.

To some, it seemed the therapeutic culture of evangelicalism provided a veil for Dobson's more overt political claims. Even as Paul Weyrich constructed the architecture for the Moral Majority and as Jerry Falwell mobilized conservative evangelicals, people were drawn to Dobson, the counselor whose caring tone offered an attractive mixture of correction and comfort. Through Dobson, earlier tropes of sexual morality and national stability became neutralized to the point of seeming apolitical—after all, a stable family life was primarily about personal well-being and self-fulfillment. Some observers and even Dobson have asserted that Focus on the Family was almost entirely apolitical.[81] But the organization's establishment of the Family Research Council in 1983 after the collaborative efforts of Dobson and the Reagan administration indicated a new political life for social conservatives.[82] A hallmark of his work was a consistent demonstration of the well-traveled rhetoric of sexual fear and national decline.

Dobson's attention to issues of gender and sexuality within family life offered him numerous opportunities to connect sexual morality with national stability. Most known for explaining the transitional age of adolescence both to parents and to teenagers, Dobson popularized new ideas about youth to help prepare them and their parents for the front lines of the "Civil War of Values." Dobson recognized and accepted the storm and stress of adolescent life and encouraged parents who were anxious about the erratic behaviors of their teenagers. He reminded parents and teenagers that sexual urges were natural and that the intense desire for sex experienced by young people was not cause for alarm. He assured his readers that all teenagers struggled to understand their sexuality in the midst of a culture that no longer valued virginity and overwhelmed them with decadent promises of sexual gratification.[83]

As with children, adolescents required strict boundaries and regulations to assist them through the turbulent years between childhood and adulthood. Like G. Stanley Hall, who first articulated a theory of adolescence, Dobson believed that these years were fraught with dangers that could derail the sexual and spiritual development of an individual. Unlike Hall, however, Dobson was contending with what he understood to be the excesses of a sexual revolution. Because of advances in birth control, premarital sex was no longer the taboo it used to be. Students were educated and learning how to talk about sex, something Dobson was in favor of, except when those lessons compromised biblical morality. In his first publication, *Dare to Discipline*, Dobson warned that "sexual sophistication without sexual responsibility is a sexual disaster." That is, young people needed to learn about sex, but in a value-laden context. Adolescents required moral guidance in their sexual lives, for their own safety. Not surprisingly, the demarcation between responsible and irresponsible sex education was whether or not it tolerated homosexuality and premarital sex. The legacy of the sexual revolution bequeathed to the younger generation an era of sexual decadence and irresponsibility. New sexual mores indicated to Dobson that youth had greater sexual opportunity than ever before, leading to the demise of the institution of marriage.[84]

As an advocate of premarital virginity, Dobson's attention to adolescent sexual purity predated the emergence of a nationwide purity movement. According to Dobson, before the sexual revolution, premarital abstinence was normative and teenagers thrived under social constraints that helped them navigate their strong sexual urges.[85] Postrevolution adolescents were caught in a civil war of values, between those who advocated for the accessibility of contraception and those who retaliated with calls for sexual purity. Dobson characterized adolescent sexuality as a natural yet dangerous force that required careful handling. At the same time, he used alarmist language to describe his ideological opponents, who he believed were poised to usurp parental authority and indoctrinate young people with secular-humanist values that would ultimately destroy the parent-child relationship. In *Children at Risk,* coauthored with Gary Bauer, Dobson laid out the opposition's strategy:

> Secular humanists, particularly the more radical activists, have a specific objective in mind for the future. They hope to accomplish that goal primarily by isolating children from their parents, as they did so effectively with the parental consent issue. It will then be relatively easy to "reorient" and indoctrinate the next generation of Americans. This strategy explains why their most bitter campaigns are being waged over school curricula and other issues that involved our kids. Children are the key to the future. Let me put it another way. Children are the prize to the winners of the second great civil war. Those who control what young people are taught and what they experience—what they see, hear, think, and believe—will determine the future course for the nation. Given that influence, the predominant value system of an entire culture can be overhauled in one generation, or certainly in two, by those with unlimited access to children.[86]

In Dobson's understanding of the culture wars, which was heavily influenced by Francis Schaeffer's critique of secular humanism, young people were positioned on the front lines of the battle. Their sexual morals were the last line of defense against the rampant moral relativism that threatened family stability. In Dobson's mind, secular humanists had chosen to target adolescent sexuality, because teaching teenagers ideas about sex that their parents did not agree with threatened the parent-child relationship. Even better, or worse from Dobson's perspective, evangelical adolescents who became sexually active were more likely to leave their faith tradition. Dobson asserted that premarital virginity was the hallmark of all major religions, and that to undercut it was to undermine the young people who were attempting to navigate their sexual desires in the context of their faith tradition.[87]

Not surprisingly, Dobson recognized that teaching youth about sexuality and sexual responsibility was a precarious endeavor. Reminding parents that adolescent heterosexual development could be derailed, Dobson often returned to his less-alarmist tone to describe sex as a wonderful gift, though one not easily opened. Like any important developmental moment in the life of a person, sexual fulfillment required discipline and restraint. The forces working against a fulfilling sexual life were powerful. Sexual gratification was portrayed by the media (which were believed to be under that thrall of secular humanism) as readily available to teenagers. These circumstances created expectations for sexual fulfillment that were not feasible. Even for young people who waited until their wedding night for sexual intercourse, the pleasures of sex were not always apparent. In *Love for a Lifetime*, Dobson kindly explains that sex can be disappointing, especially the first time around. And if expectations are too high, that disappointment can be destructive to a young marriage.[88]

Dobson outlined numerous threats to young marriages, many of which could be sidestepped by maintaining one's virginity and choosing a virgin as a marriage partner:

> This mutual purity gives special meaning to sex in marriage. No other human being has invaded the secret world that the two of you share, because you reserved yourselves exclusively for one another's pleasure and love. By following the Biblical plan, you also protect the production systems from new viruses, bacteria, and fungi transmitted during casual intercourse. It is now known that when you sleep with a promiscuous partner, you are having sex with every person that individual has slept with in the past ten years! Virginity before marriage is by far the healthiest approach.[89]

By 1987, when Dobson wrote this piece of advice, conservative fears of unbridled sexuality had been realized with the AIDS crisis. Purity advocates had physical evidence that the sexual revolution was a destructive historical moment and that, more than ever, Americans needed to embrace sexual traditionalism. In the early years of the purity movement, Dobson noted the thousands of youth seeking refuge from an oversexualized world. Upon his ten-year-old daughter's own commitment to purity, Dobson had provided her with a gold key on a chain that she wore to symbolize her virginity—and he heartily encouraged other parents to do the same.[90]

The sexual differences between boys and girls were especially relevant to Dobson's purity rhetoric. As a Christian counselor working with a therapeutic framework, Dobson frequently used the language of self-esteem and self-care to talk about adolescent sexuality. For girls, especially, sex was a means to power and respect. Dobson referred to it as their "basis of exchange." Together, marriage and courtship were an elaborate ritual in which women offered sexuality for male security. Without her own offering, a young woman would lose not only her self-respect but her ability to barter for an emotionally advantageous marriage relationship.[91]

What was most compelling about Dobson's use of purity rhetoric was his ability to revitalize old tropes of sexual immorality and national decay. George Gilder gave Dobson the language to reassert the relevance of personal sexuality to national well-being. As noted earlier, Gilder's view of gender and marriage supported Dobson's assertion that sex differences were God-ordained and foundational for raising children into sexually healthy adolescents. Gilder provided for Dobson what Toynbee and Sorokin did for Graham and Henry: a rational, intellectual argument that reinforced biblical mandates by providing historical and sociological evidence for the causal relationship between a stable family life and a secure nation-state.

Using data from the controversial Moynihan Report, which described the destitution of black family life, and armed with a series of consequences that emerged from the sexual revolution, Gilder's work connected family stability (i.e., self-sufficiency) with a prosperous capitalistic economy that, for Gilder, existed at one of the higher stages of civilizational advancement. Harnessing sexual energy into family life, he contended, fostered creativity and economic growth that benefited the common good. The sexual revolution, therefore, by releasing sexuality from traditional social constructs, undermined the nation's economy. Gilder used familial and economic language interchangeably to demonstrate the inherent ties between heterosexual family life and a thriving economy. In *Men and Marriage,* he wrote,

> Parents are the ultimate entrepreneurs, and, as with all entrepreneurs, the odds are against them. But all human progress—of businesses and families as well as societies—depends on an entrepreneurial willingness to defy the odds. It is in the nuclear family that the most crucial process of capitalized defiance and faith is centered.[92]

Economic prosperity was an outgrowth of the family order that Gilder prescribed, but it teetered on the edge of the sexual freedoms made available—to women especially. Women's ability to redirect men's aggressive energy toward the development of cultural institutions that facilitate the market economy was key to sustaining a nation's stability. This is what civilizational advancement required of them. Thus, a woman's choice not to bear children or establish a household threatened civilization itself. In Gilder's words, "The fact is that there is no way that women can escape their supreme responsibilities in civilized society without endangering civilization itself."[93]

Gilder's assertion about women and civilization shed some light on Dobson's insistence on premarital virginity, especially for girls and women. Dobson described female sexuality as a commodity that reached the height of its value on the wedding day. By maintaining her virginity, a woman retains her moral authority over her husband, and, with it, her ability to constrain his baser instincts. A successful marriage is one in which the woman is able to civilize the destructive tendencies of masculinity in exchange for protection and the economic stability provided by her newly industrious husband.[94] What is curious about this proposition is that both Gilder and Dobson resisted connecting these ideas with the concept of the sexual double standard. Yet, the Victorian purity activists who sought the end of the double standard (notably for the sake of civilizational progress) recognized that it was rooted in the unbalanced moral expectations of men and women. If women behaved like men by embracing sexual freedom, then no one would hold men accountable for their failure to channel their sexual energy into productive work. Gilder thought that "in a world where women do not say no," men are unable to contribute to civilizational progress.[95] Women, then, are responsible for men's behavior and the party primarily accountable for a nation's civilizational advancement.

Even more prominent in Dobson's work is the thought of J. D. Unwin, a British anthropologist whose lecture "Sexual Regulations and Human Culture" was reissued in 1969 and circulated among conservative activists in Southern California throughout the 1970s. According to Unwin's study of eighty human civilizations, the restriction of sexuality to monogamous marriage was necessary for a culture to flourish and establish permanence. Without using gendered language, Unwin made the case that sexual abstinence created an "expansive energy" for civilizations that used the momentum to expand their territory and establish dominance over other cultures (i.e., colonialism).[96]

Unwin produced a formula for explaining the benefits of sexual re-straint for cultural advancement. He was able to determine that a cul-ture's development was directly correlated with the group's willingness to restrict its sexual behaviors. And because social evolution worked both regressively and progressively, sexual permissiveness led to social decline. In short, Unwin demonstrated that human civilization and progress were built on the sacrifice of sexual gratification.[97]

Not surprisingly, Unwin's work appeared in Pitirim Sorokin's 1956 study *The American Sex Revolution*. As detailed in the previous chapter, Sorokin's book furthered the particular claim that a decline in premarital virginity and other forms of sexual containment weakened the nation-state. Billy Graham and Carl F.H. Henry popularized this ideology for the particular purpose of framing sexual morality as an asset in America's confrontation with the Soviet Union. Though Dobson's work shows no evidence of Sorokin's influence, his earliest writings drew directly from Unwin's theories of civilizational rise and decline.[98] As a way of rebuking the sexual revolution, Dobson repeated Unwin's claims about the causal relationship between sexual permissiveness and social decline.

Unwin provided Dobson with a historical taxonomy of a civilization's process of advancement and decline, along with the accompanying sexual habits. He contended that civilizations and societies are first established through their members' willingness to redirect their sexual energy toward the creation of a social infrastructure. However, once social stability is secured, the members of the group become frustrated by sexual restric-tions and thus begin their descent into self-destruction. Drawing on both Unwin and Gilder, Dobson asserted that the proper use of sexual energy allows a nation to maintain its economic and geopolitical status. Ameri-ca's rejection of biblical views of family and sexuality, which prescribed sexual restraint, Dobson concluded, was responsible for "the weakening of America's financial position."[99] Dobson goes on in *Dare to Discipline* to connect sexual restraint with financial responsibility and the success of capitalism. Unlike socialism, which offered no incentives for hard work, capitalism motivated people to submit their baser instincts to the common good. As natural forces, both capital and sex provided incentive and moti-vation that propelled human creativity and flourishing.[100]

By articulating this link between a capitalist economy and sexual re-straint, Dobson revealed the underlying economic mandate of the family-values project. As the Cold War faded from view and Americans no longer lived with the imminent threat of a nuclear apocalypse, the new challenge was to secure a thriving economy, which, in the financial crisis of the 1970s, appeared difficult. By linking Unwin and Gilder, Dobson translated the formula for preventing national decay into economic terms.

But Dobson was not quick to relinquish the rhetorical power of the Cold War. In *Children at Risk*, published four years after the fall of the Berlin Wall, Dobson and Bauer articulated a theory of civilization that reflected the same Cold War tropes of sexual fear and national decline made popular by Billy Graham:

> It follows, then, that stability in society is dependent on the healthy expression of our sexual nature. If this energy within us is siphoned off in the pursuit of pleasure; if it is squandered in nonexclusive relationships; if it is perverted in same-sex activities, then the culture is deprived of the working, saving, sacrificing, caring, building, growing, reproducing units known as families. Robbed of sexual standards, society will unravel like a ball of twine. That is the lesson of history. That is the legacy of Rome and more than two thousand civilizations that have come and gone on this earth. This family is the basic unit of society on which all human activity rests. If you tamper with the sexual nature of familial relationships, you necessarily threaten the entire superstructure. Indeed, ours is swaying like a drunken sailor from the folly of our cultural engineers.[101]

Like previous purity reformers and evangelical activists, Dobson drew upon the precedent of ancient Rome as evidence for the correlation and causation of sexual immorality (homosexuality in particular) and the decline of the nation-state.[102] Dobson's use of military and nuclear metaphors provides even stronger evidence of his lingering Cold War preoccupation. Using Unwin's idea of sexual energy, Dobson conveyed his belief that this energy could be as destructive as a nuclear bomb. Marriage provided the structure needed to balance the powerful elements of sexuality, but its dissolution or fission was understood to release a destructive force whose impact is felt far beyond the initial unit of containment.[103]

The sober and compassionate tone that many of Dobson's listeners encountered on their radios was never able to fully disguise the urgency of Focus on the Family's moral crusade, especially when it came to adolescence and sexuality. Already in 1975, before abortion and homosexuality dominated the evangelical moral agenda, Dobson was alarmed by the prevalence of premarital sex:

> I have never considered myself to be a prophet of doom, but I am admittedly alarmed by statistical evidence of this nature. I view these trends with fear and trepidation, seeing in them the potential death of our society and our way of life.[104]

Since that time, Dobson claims that his views on family, adolescence, and sexuality have remained consistent, even if his metaphors no longer invoke the same degree of alarm, especially in a young generation who never had to learn to "duck and cover."[105] What emerged in Dobson's rhetoric was a new articulation of ideas almost as old as the country itself. With the assistance of a new therapeutic pulse within evangelicalism, Dobson highlighted the intersection between self-preservation and national security and successfully transmitted the moral codes of an older generation into a psychology of adolescence. By constructing a nationalistic moral agenda that positioned adolescents on the forefront of the battle lines, Dobson primed a new generation of evangelicals for cultural and political activism.

Chapter Four

New Purity Revolution

IN LATE JULY 1994, over 20,000 adolescents descended upon the National Mall, despite the rain and humidity, and found themselves caught in the thrall of a sweaty, rock-'n'-roll-induced fervor. With loud musical performances, big crowds, and multimedia excitement, the evening's events, according to its widespread media coverage, suggested a tone of adolescent, reckless abandon.[1] However, these youth were not the wayward slackers of Generation X, but evangelical Christian teenagers poised to take a public stance on a very personal matter: sexual purity. In fact, these teenagers were into the third day of a national youth conference sponsored by Youth for Christ, the evangelical organization committed to showing teenagers that following Jesus isn't about boring sermons, stuffy church music, and quiet contemplation of one's misdeeds. But, even as Christian pop music helped to lift the shared burden of social disaffiliation often carried by evangelical adolescents, a nearby public display stood as a stark reminder of these young people's distinction from their nonreligious peers.[2]

Earlier that morning, a large cohort of these young people staked 211,163 pastel-colored cards into the lawn like tiny crosses. On each card were these words:

> Believing that True Love Waits, I make a commitment to God, my family, my friends, my future spouse and my future children to live a lifetime of purity including sexual abstinence from this day until I enter a biblical marriage relationship.

The True Love Waits (TLW) pledge was first uttered only sixteen months prior by fifty-six teenagers at Tulip Grove Baptist Church in Hermitage, Tennessee. These teens were the first to take the pledge, a publicly spoken commitment regarding sexual abstinence until marriage.[3] By the weekend of the Youth for Christ event, the pledge had made its way from a small town in

Tennessee to the Southern Baptist National Convention in Orlando, Florida, and into numerous local churches nationwide, where pledgers each signed two cards—one for themselves and one to send back to TLW headquarters in Nashville. Though short of the goal of 500,000 signed pledge cards, the expansion of the pledge was impressive in its ability to captivate adolescent evangelicals and garner support from dozens of other Christian denominations and parachurch organizations.

Though not the first of its large-scale displays, the True Love Waits rally, held in conjunction with Youth for Christ's DC '94, introduced the nation to young people who boldly and publicly declared their virginity and saw their sexual status as a witness to the transformative power of Jesus Christ. But, unlike previous gatherings of the Southern Baptist Convention (SBC), this event marked a new ambition for the young people—to stand as exemplars of social renewal in a nation whose future was threatened by the legacy of the sexual revolution. To this end, 150 white-ribboned purity activists attended the week's pinnacle event: a special session with President Bill Clinton. Though two years later the president would sign a bill into law providing unprecedented government funding for abstinence education, his remarks that day elicited disappointment, as he commented upon the limitations of government to influence sexual behavior. Though he lauded their commitments, the president's lack of formal backing prompted the movement to seek other venues for its social and political goals.

Just twenty years prior, young people of a different generation were known for publicly declaring their right to sexual freedom. The new 1990s young evangelicals, schooled in the destructive consequences of sexual excess, likewise found themselves fueled with political and spiritual fervor and able to find a national stage—including an audience with the president, no less—for their cause. Why, given that evangelical Christians were already convinced of the emotional, physical, and spiritual hardships resulting from premarital sexual activity, did they feel the need to publicly declare an already accepted value of their religious subculture?

For this first wave of publicly declared purity advocates, personal faith commitment and political activism went hand in hand, a strategy first made politically viable due to the feminist assertion, rooted in 1960s counterculture, that personal choice, self-expression, and point of view are more than sturdy platforms for political involvement. In their stance, these young evangelicals employed the same political and cultural strategies that buoyed the antiestablishmentarianism of the baby boom generation. With the resurgence of Christian fundamentalism, young evangelicals found a politicized evangelical culture that was both appealing and accessible. At the same time, they also found themselves the beneficiaries of an evangelical-Republican alliance forged in the late 1970s that created a political landscape highly amenable to the social concerns of conservative evangelicals. Together, these two factors explain the rapid expansion of the purity movement when it officially emerged in the form of the first church-based national abstinence organization.

True Love Waits was founded in 1993 by Southern Baptist youth minister Richard Ross as a Christian sex-education program with the sole purpose of promoting premarital sexual abstinence.[4] Influenced by surveys that indicated religious devotion was not a deterrent for adolescents engaging in sexual activity, TLW set out to challenge youth to a higher standard. The hallmarks of TLW are its public displays of signed pledge cards—DC '94 was only the first of these. In February 1996, the group displayed 360,000 pledged cards stacked on top of each other at its "Thru the Roof" event at the Georgia Dome. In 2004, the group displayed over 460,000 cards from twenty different countries during the 2004 Summer Olympics in Athens, Greece. Beyond these events, the organization makes available for purchase plentiful Bible-study materials (including its own *True Love Waits Bible*), event guides and planners, the use of its logo, and purity rings for churches, communities, and other organizations that wish to participate in any of TLW's detailed initiatives. Though founded in conjunction with the Southern Baptist church, TLW quickly established itself as a nondenominational program that transcended the theological and liturgical distinctions of socially conservative, churchgoing Americans.

Unlike TLW, the second abstinence group with national ambitions that emerged in the mid-1990s did not seek political endorsement at its inception. Initially concerned with their own county's rate of teenage pregnancy, Denny and Amy Pattyn, youth ministers from Yuma, Arizona, began a local program that encouraged churchgoing youth to adopt abstinence until marriage as a tenet central to their Christian faith commitment. Amy even traveled to Mexico to purchase silver rings for the young people to wear as a sign of their commitment.

In its nascent stages, Silver Ring Thing (SRT) was hesitant to accept government funding: the organization began in 1993, after Denny Pattyn eschewed public funding that expected him to downplay the role of faith

in his abstinence teachings. He was disgusted by the government's insistence that his abstinence work be devoid of all religious content. This directly contradicted his belief that the promotion of sexual abstinence was
a ministry and, as such, held no substance without reference to religious
belief.[5]

However, by the time the Pattyns moved their organization, along
with their ambitions for a national audience, to Pittsburgh, Pennsylva-
nia, in 2000, the political climate had changed in favor of faith-based
groups seeking federal funding. Under the new guidelines, Pattyn felt
encouraged rather then constrained by the possibility of federal funding
and contacted his senator, Rick Santorum (R-PA), to help him apply to
the Maternal and Child Health Special Programs of Regional and National Significance (SPRANS) block grant.[6] SRT was awarded the grant
and received $700,000 for 2003. The grant was renewed the following
two years, with SRT receiving total federal funding in the amount of
$1,400,000.

The emergence of the contemporary purity movement would not have
been possible without federal initiatives that brought sexual abstinence into
mainstream political discourse. The first abstinence funding, introduced
in 1981, sparked a controversy that was not resolved until 1996, during
which time evangelical leaders chose to move beyond political means to
develop church-based programs addressing the cultural crises associated
with premarital sex. After the fits and starts of the Clinton administration,
which only responded to calls for federally supported abstinence education
as they converged with larger economic concerns, the abstinence movement garnered a huge boost with the election of George W. Bush. With the
newly extended faith-based initiatives funding policy, religious-abstinence
organizations enjoyed newfound access to federal resources.

Still wary of the fickle nature of government policy and their own mer-
curial relationship with Washington, evangelicals in the 1990s sought
other avenues for social transformation. Because of leaders like James
Dobson, evangelicals established both political and therapeutic approaches to restoring moral order to America. While some fought for
moral restoration over the body with political and moral persuasion, contemporary purity advocates sought transformation *through* the body, believing that the transformed bodies of sexually pure adolescents held
promise of a similarly transformed society.

Leaders and youth of the evangelical purity movement shared the
goal of large-scale moral and spiritual transformation, which required

numerous strategies drawing upon the rhetoric of personal sexual rights, the therapeutic discourse of personal well-being, and the cultivation of an activist youth movement adept at cultural criticism.[7] For the purity movement, the main obstacle to national moral restoration remains sexual immorality, and sexual abstinence becomes the catalyst for course correction. Asserting this, the movement positions sexual purity, and the adolescents who embody it, as an embattled sexual minority poised to save America from the repercussions of its own moral turpitude.

Government-Sponsored Sexual Purity

In the landscape of sexual purity, True Love Waits and Silver Ring Thing emerged as the clear frontrunners of a movement that encompassed hundreds of smaller community organizations, churches, schools, crisis pregnancy centers, and nonprofit agencies. Unlike other groups, these well-known organizations successfully transcended religious, organizational, and national boundaries to introduce the mandate of sexual purity onto both the national and international stages. Though the contemporary sexual purity movement, like its nineteenth-century counterpart, is comprised of numerous groups working on a variety of initiatives, TLW and SRT have been the groups most successful at situating purity work and rhetoric firmly within the American mainstream. In practical terms, these organizations found their legs because of the political efficacy of the evangelical-Republican alliance established in the late 1970s. Ideologically, they represent the aftermath of the same rhetoric of sexual fear that helped to propel the religious right into power.

In 1981, President Reagan signed into law the Adolescent Family Life Act (AFLA), which addressed concern for the escalating rates of teenage pregnancy.[8] This bill, sponsored by senators Orrin Hatch (R-UT) and Jeremiah Denton (R-AL), was a direct attempt to shift federal funding away from comprehensive sex education that provided information on contraception—an approach that conservatives like Hatch and Denton believed was responsible for escalating rates of sexual promiscuity, teenage pregnancy, and abortion.[9] By allowing two-thirds of the funding to support already pregnant teenagers while the other third provided funding for abstinence education, the bill gained support among Democrats who did not share Hatch and Denton's views.[10] In truth, the bill passed as a result of a political deal in which liberals agreed to support the AFLA in exchange for conservative support of funding for family-planning clinics.[11]

Despite the seemingly conservative bent of the 1980s, the controversy pitting safe sex against abstinence-only education, which would eventually become a hallmark of political discourse, began with a compromise.

Still, controversy was quick to follow, and from an unlikely source. In 1983, a group of federal taxpayers, clergymen, and the American Jewish Congress filed the first lawsuit through the American Civil Liberties Union, claiming that the AFLA's funding of religious organizations that promoted abstinence violated the First Amendment's insistence on religious disestablishment. Though the clergy initially won their case, the Supreme Court overturned the ruling in 1988, prompting the ACLU to proceed with its own appeal. Finally, in 1993, an out-of-court settlement determined that religious organizations that received funding for abstinence education must abide by the following stipulations: abstinence education must not include religious references, must be medically accurate, must respect the "principle of self-determination" regarding contraceptive referral for teenagers, and must not allow grantees to use church sanctuaries for their programs or to give presentations in parochial schools during school hours.[12]

That same year, the Southern Baptist church officially launched its True Love Waits initiative at Tulip Grove Baptist Church in Tennessee. Though it has never received federal funding, the organization has been integral to maintaining the relevance of sexual abstinence within political discourse, primarily through the public displays such as the National Mall demonstration. Despite their disappointing meeting with President Clinton during DC '94, Richard Ross and TLW gained support among a Republican-controlled Congress just two years later, when they found themselves instrumental in the creation of a little-noticed provision in the Personal Responsibility and Work Opportunity Reconciliation Act (PRWORA) of 1996.

In 1996, clergyman a support coordinator for True Love Waits, testified at a Senate Appropriations Committee chaired by Senator Arlen Specter (R-PA). He provided a brief mission statement and history of the organization and submitted a fact sheet that chronicled the explosive growth of and increasing media interest in True Love Waits. His testimony challenged abstinence efforts that focused solely on lowering pregnancy rates and limiting the spread of sexually transmitted diseases. He claimed, on behalf of the True Love Waits organization, that this approach neglects the negative emotional and moral consequences of premarital sexual activity and sends the message to youth that premarital sex is okay as long as one practices safe sex. These negative consequences were the focus of the organization he represented and were in fact the impetus for its founding.[13] Though numerous other groups were represented during the hearings, the particular concerns of Turner and True Love Waits reemerged later that same year in the context of the highly anticipated PRWORA.

Debates surrounding the act while it was still a bill intensified with the publication of Charles Murray's *Wall Street Journal* editorial "The Coming White Underclass." Though not particularly concerned with the issue of government-funded abstinence-only education, the language of Murray's essay and the values of the purity movement together heavily influenced the welfare reform policies soon to be instituted.

In his essay, Murray argued that rates of illegitimacy among white women were escalating to such a degree that the white middle class was in danger of falling to the same economic level as the black underclass. Though out-of-wedlock births had long been frequent among African Americans, Murray quickly dismissed the phenomenon as old news and turned to, in his opinion, a more pressing concern: the demise of the white family and white social and economic status. Murray blamed the failure of social policy for this demise.

> But the white illegitimacy rate is approaching that same problematic 25% region at a time when social policy is more comprehensively wrongheaded than it was in the mid-1960s, and the cultural and sexual norms are still more degraded.[14]

Murray's suggestions for federal and social adjustments were based on his belief that women should not raise children that they cannot support and that the government should not be responsible for providing them assistance, such as subsidized housing and food stamps.

That year, with a Republican Congress and a Democratic administration, the Personal Responsibility and Work Opportunity Reconciliation Act accommodated both Murray's suggestions and the cause célèbre of True Love Waits with a key addition to the bill: a little-noticed provision regarding abstinence education. Unlike the AFLA of 1981, this provision limited funding to abstinence-only programming: sex-education programs that promoted abstinence as the only assurance against unwanted pregnancy and sexually transmitted diseases and did not provide information regarding contraceptive use.

By joining the concerns of social welfare and abstinence-only educa-tion, the federal government acquiesced to Murray's assumption that single parenting was tantamount to economic decline, an argument he supported with evidence from the black underclass. For Murray, the crisis was not the economic standing of blacks, who he assumed already suffered from economic decline due to the prevalence of single mother-hood, but the risk that whites would soon fall to this same level. Thus, the federal government, unwittingly or not, imported Murray's racist views into public law when it approved a bill that asserted out-of-wedlock births as a major cause of economic decline. With the federal institution of abstinence-only education and unprecedented opportunities for fund-ing, the purity movement was launched onto the national stage at the same time that Murray was raising concerns regarding the loss of white economic and social status. By constructing welfare reform based on lan-guage from both Murray and True Love Waits, the US government helped to mobilize a faith-based abstinence movement on the premise of racial-ized, class anxieties.

During the Bush administration, when funding for abstinence-only education reached its peak, organizations could apply for funding from three different sources, including the Special Projects of Regional and National Significance, or SPRANS, which provided funds for groups pro-moting abstinence-only-until-marriage sex education to adolescents aged twelve through nineteen. Administered through the Administration for Children and Families (ACF), SPRANS provided funding through a com-petitive grant process to community-based organizations committed to creating a supportive environment for adolescents committed to sexual abstinence.[15] After its inaugural year, when thirty-three groups received $20 million in federal grant monies, the community-based program in-creased its funding dramatically, providing $104 million to over 100 orga-nizations by 2005. The most prominent among these recipients was Silver Ring Thing, which, as mentioned at the opening of this chapter, received almost $1.5 million over the course of three years beginning in 2003.[16]

Even with this funding, Denny Pattyn remained wary, having wit-nessed other organizations lose their religious focus when tied to govern-ment regulations. He hoped to avoid financial dependence upon the federal government and refused to accept funding if it meant being unable to proselytize. However, the federally required adjustments to his organi-zation proved insignificant, and Pattyn accepted the funds, allowing the group to establish its nonprofit status. The organization made its best effort to comply with federal regulations, but soon found itself at the center of a lawsuit brought by the ACLU, whose complaint toward the Department of Health and Human Services accused the government office of neglecting to "sufficiently monitor or audit the use of funds" by a faith-based group.[17] Though SRT had been providing an alternative secular event for students not wishing to attend the faith-based part of a show it produced, the ACLU claimed the provisions separating the faith-based portions of the show from the secular components were insufficient. Furthermore, the ACLU's own research contended that Silver Ring Thing utilized abstinence education as an evangelistic tool, the funding of which would be a clear breach of the Constitution's establishment clause. The claim was supported by SRT's IRS filings, which were listed under the name of another organization: the John Guest Evangelistic Team.[18]

Despite these setbacks, SRT made several attempts to prove its compliance with federal law shortly after the legal complaint was filed. Regardless, in August 2005, a letter from Harry Wilson, assistant commissioner for the Administration on Children, Youth and Families and one of the defendants in the case, alerted the organization that its funding had been suspended. Pattyn and colleagues displayed a lack of concern at this injunction and announced to the media that this lawsuit had in fact aided the organization by generating enough private donations to offset any eventual loss of federal funds.[19]

The election of President Barack Obama in 2008 caused a significant shift in the federal government's participation in abstinence-only education. A liberal Democrat, Obama took the executive office with little faith in abstinence-only education and promised to defund the programs that the previous administration had so ardently supported. But as with Clinton's welfare reform bill, abstinence-only education reappeared during the negotiations for the Patient Protection and Affordable Care Act (PPACA). Though it's unclear what negotiations transpired, the Affordable Care Act was eventually signed into law with a section that included the restoration of funding for abstinence education. At present, only thirty-one programs have been approved for funding, and only three take an abstinence-only approach: Heritage Keepers Abstinence Education, Making a Difference!, and Promoting Health Among Teens! Abstinence Only Intervention.[20] Only Heritage Keepers offers abstinence education to high school students, and the choice to include that organization on the list of evidence-based programs raised a great deal of criticism from advocates of safe-sex education, who claimed that its inclusion was a political ploy to placate conservatives.[21] Despite some acquiescence to abstinence-only advocates, the Obama administration has shifted political favor away from support for abstinence-only education. Though many conservative activists find this deeply troubling, many evangelical leaders within the purity movement recognized the folly of tying goals for social transformation to the political climate.

The New Sexual Revolution

The first wave of purity activism emerged as part of an evangelical youth culture increasingly engaged in political and cultural activism. The ideological descendants of the Jesus People, who, twenty-five years earlier, successfully integrated the rhetoric and aesthetic of the counterculture with the hardline moralism of Christian fundamentalism, young purity advocates willingly stepped into the role of moral exemplars.[22] The use of countercultural rhetoric allowed them to defy mainstream mores of sexual freedom and promiscuity, and to assert a traditional sexual identity as the avant-garde of the sexual revolution. Claiming to be a sexual minority, sexually pure adolescents positioned themselves as new sexual revolutionaries owed personal respect and a political voice.

"So many of us are coming out of the closet," seventeen-year-old Lara McCalman told the *New York Times* on June 21, 1993. "I have had so much fun saying no. I'm a virgin and proud of it." In the first months of True Love Waits's activity, public proclamations such as McCalman's were not uncommon. Capitalizing on a revolutionary rhetoric that praised young people's defiance of certain cultural and moral norms, leaders of the purity movement sanctioned their own forms of counterculturalism that proved highly appealing to the increasingly activist evangelical youth culture. Headlines such as "Abstinence with an Attitude, Why Virgin Is No Longer a Dirty Word," "Baptist Youth Wage Their Own Sexual Revolution," "A Revolt against Casual Sex," and "Rebels with a Cause" helped further establish the purity movement as both a direct descendant and hostile critic of the 1960s counterculture that championed youth rebellion and free love.

Downplaying their commitment as a form of religious obedience, numerous young people portrayed themselves as defiant, independently minded individuals seeking personal fulfillment and the right to self-expression. The *St. Petersburg Times*, for example, reported that fourteen-year-old Monica Schoenthaler believed engaging in sexual activity was a type of social conformity that stunted her personal identity: "I think, why go with the flow? Be an individualist. You can be like everybody else, but why do that when you can be yourself?"[23] Schoenthaler's call to sexual and personal empowerment did not prioritize any particular religious or moral belief, but relied solely upon the values of individualism, self-fulfillment, and personal development. Likewise, the *Baptist Press*, a media outlet supported by the Southern Baptist Convention, reran a *Newsweek* article that portrayed eighteen-year-old Alice Kunce as a "regular churchgoer, Sunday school teacher and feminist" whose political, not religious, commitments inspired her to commit to sexual abstinence: "One of the empowering things about the feminist movement is that we're able to assert ourselves, to say no to sex and not feel pressured about it."[24] Though Kunce's views were initially printed in a mainstream publication, it is telling that the *Baptist Press* picked up the story, indicating evangelicals' concern for connecting sexual abstinence with a form of self-empowerment reminiscent of feminist assertions of women's autonomy.

Other reports indicated the influence of queer activism: sexual purity was cast as the latest minority sexual status in search of cultural affirmation and political voice. Like McCalman, David Medrod proclaimed his virginity to the *New York Times* as a "coming out." Said Medrod, "It's awesome to be a virgin. I want to give that as a gift to my wife. I want it to be special, not something I do just to fit in. I feel there's a lot of people that are virgins, but they're afraid to come out."[25]

As members of a religious subculture that situates itself on the margins of a perceived inhospitable mainstream, evangelical adolescents understand their pledge not as a choice but as the expression of a sexual identity. They assert this identity in the face of ridicule and pressure to conform to accepted standards of sexual behavior. As Heather Rachelle White describes it, the pledge has "positioned them as cultural outsiders hiding a despised sexual secret."[26] By invoking the metaphor of the closet, Medrod and McCalman stake a claim rather similar to queer identity politics. Like queerness, sexual purity is transgressive in the sense that it defies cultural and social norms. And, like queer identities, purity is transformative—even prophetic, to use theological language—in that it is a sexual orientation that witnesses to a new way of being that has the ability to transform the world.[27]

In 1994, *Washington Post* editorialist Colman McCarthy aided the movement's reputation as a counterculture initiative in his August 20 editorial, which discussed the then-recent True Love Waits rally in Washington,

DC. While many young people enjoyed live music and socializing, a small group of "sexual revolutionaries," as McCarthy called them, made their way to the White House. His piece lauded their efforts by referring to the sexually abstinent young people as courageous, even rebellious, individuals moving against the tide of social expectations. By his words, McCarthy helped the movement in its quest to reappropriate the rhetoric of sexual revolution,

> If that sounds as though debauchery were the agenda, it's only because such notions of sexual liberation have come to be equated with reckless hedonism. A current and growing revolution differs from the conventional one: Its goal is abstinence, for teenagers to be liberated from peer and commercial pressures that push or cajole the young into premarital sex.[28]

Within a year of its founding, the purity activists of True Love Waits had successfully outlined the latest chapter of the sexual revolution and reframed the entire 1960s counterculture according to the moral parameters of evangelical Christianity.

The Therapeutic Impulse of Sexual Purity

As with many aspects of contemporary evangelicalism, the purity movement is highly indebted to a therapeutic rhetoric that fuses psychological language of self-care, self-development, and self-improvement with the spiritual message that authentic personal transformation is only possible with the assistance of Jesus Christ. Heather Hendershot's study of True Love Waits and the chastity literature that accompanies the movement is especially helpful for establishing how the purity culture articulates its particular form of this rhetoric.[29]

Like most evangelical therapeutic discourse, the chastity literature that Hendershot examined is heavily indebted to so-called secular definitions of the therapeutic and asserts a taxonomy of rehabilitation described in three stages: the eruption of the problem; the confession and diagnosis of the problem; and, finally, the solution or cure for the problem.[30] However, given evangelical understandings of sin, which is viewed not as a problem to be cured but a state to be endured, the third phase of this taxonomy poses some challenges. Thus, the best that chastity advocates can hope for is to help teens learn to manage their sexual desire (the problem that needs solving) without providing any assurance that this problem will cease to exist.[31] Hendershot describes the therapeutic discourse of this body of literature as a "melding of health and religious language" in which chaste youth are encouraged to use words such as "purity, sin, health, recovery, redemption and temptation"—language that clearly denotes a high level of comfort with the blending of the spiritual and the psychological to create a therapeutic rhetoric that is distinctly evangelical.[32] A close analysis of this rhetoric reveals a variety of concerns that shape the therapeutic impulse of the movement, most of which focus on the desire to avoid the negative consequences of premarital sex. This generates a therapeutic rhetoric that asserts the physical, emotional, and spiritual consequences of premarital sexual activity.

This threefold framework, however, has not always been as prominent within the purity culture's therapeutic rhetoric. In fact, early iterations of the therapeutic rhetoric, found in True Love Waits media and literature, focused primarily on the spiritual consequences of premarital sexual activity. Though some references to health issues such as pregnancy and sexually transmitted diseases are in evidence, True Love Waits initially sought to position sexuality (and sexual transgression) within the trajectory of adolescent spiritual development, with less concern for the physical and emotional consequences of premarital sexual activity. For its part, Silver Ring Thing has worked for over two decades to perfect a live performance that effectively and efficiently presents the organization's therapeutic process in less than two and a half hours. The SRT event presents skits, videos, and testimonials that lay out a spectrum of seemingly inevitable emotional, physical, and spiritual consequences that result from premarital sexual activity. The majority of an SRT evening is spent convincing the audience that the problem is severe enough to merit a behavior reversal.

In order to pinpoint causes for the "eruption of the problem," SRT strategically places its most attention-getting sketch in the first half hour of its live performance in order to clarify that premarital sexual activity is, indeed, a problem in need of a solution. Just after introducing SRT's high-tech, multimedia program, the evening's emcee, Matt Webster, retrieves four volunteers from the audience: three young women and one young man.[33] With humor, sincerity, and enthusiasm, he offers the young man a board on which was painted half a heart. He explains that this board represents the young man's emotional life. He then motions to each young woman and explains that, throughout the course of his life, the young man had engaged in premarital, sexual activity with each of them. Matt then places the young man's heart-board into a vise, asks the volunteers to step aside, and retreats backstage. Seconds later, pyrotechnics explode, lights flash, music thunders, and Matt reemerges, sporting a hockey mask and operating a live chainsaw. As the audience screams and the volunteers fall to the floor, Matt hacks the heart-board into pieces. As the noise subsides and the volunteers catch their breath, Matt explains once again that due to the young man's intimate relationships with each of these young women, they will now each carry a piece of him for the rest of their lives. After Matt gives the pieces of the young man's heart-board to the three women, he holds up the piece of heart that remained. "This is what you will take with you when you get married," Matt says as he displays the remaining heart-board, reduced to a jagged-edged splinter of wood. This sketch asserts that premarital sex causes a significant spiritual and emotional rupture. Like jagged splinters of wood, sexually active youth tragically move from one relationship to the next, leaving pieces of themselves like worthless debris. The remaining core of the self, the soul, is left weakened, incapable of genuine intimacy, and less fortified against the challenges of married life.

"But tonight we're gonna give you the chance to start over and right now I'm gonna give you a whole new heart": Webster's promise is not to the young man alone, but to anyone in the audience ready to remake his or her fractured soul into one suitable for Christian marriage. This is just one of the many ways, though certainly the most effective one, in which SRT marks adolescent premarital sex as a problem in need of a solution. Following the establishment of this problem, abstinence advocates must move onto the second stage of therapeutic discourse: confession and diagnosis.

The confessional stage is quite effective, because even adolescents who have not broken their pledge continually monitor themselves according to the well-established confessionalism embedded in the movement. Students who have attended SRT events indicated in a survey conducted in 2006–2007 that many held themselves accountable not only to physical abstinence but to sexual purity, a more spiritually holistic concept that monitors behavioral, verbal, imaginative, and emotional boundaries. Upon betraying these boundaries, the students were quick to acknowledge their transgressions and identify the causes for their misdeeds. Julie Breyer, a student at Midwestern Christian College, maintained her pledge yet still felt the consequences of an intense emotional connection that she described as giving "pieces of my heart to a guy I dated."[34] Her classmate, Jonathan Pierce, also noted struggles with lust and sexual temptation, "Even though I have physically kept myself pure, I know my thoughts have been tainted for a long time and it is a daily struggle to repent of that."[35] Still another, Walter Newsome, was even more frank about his own struggles:

> I have not yet had sexual activity/intercourse (of any variety) and do not intend to do so before marriage. However, as a teenage male, I have certainly not been free from the ever-present and almost cyclical (as they sometimes seem) temptations of pornography and masturbation.[36]

This continual self-monitoring allows students to diagnose and rediagnose their particular challenges and assess how they are faring according to the expectations of sexual purity established during their SRT experience. That sense of self-accountability has become a natural outgrowth of the therapeutic rhetoric of the abstinence movement. It is important to note that individuals who have moved through these stages have not necessarily done so in a linear fashion. As indicated above, the practice of self-accountability presumed that students were not cured permanently but, rather, were given tools to negotiate setbacks more effectively.[37] Thus, the final stage, the cure, is often presented as a point at which to start over, rather than an achievable end point.

Sexual Purity and Adolescent Spiritual Formation

The therapeutic rhetoric of contemporary evangelicalism compels believers to understand their personal spiritual commitments in light of their individual well-being and self-development. For the purity movement, this means cultivating narratives that demonstrate the indistinctiveness of spiritual awakening and personal care. One such narrative appeared in a Silver Ring Thing newsletter and tells the story of Anna, who had lost her virginity at the age of fifteen and only slowly came to realize the repercussions. By the time she started feeling remorse for her sexual choices, she also began to recognize that she felt dirty, weak, and burdened. In short, Anna had sinned, and had done so so badly, she no longer had the ability to resist further temptation. Anna was already an active member in her church youth group, but her sexual activity marred her Christian commitment and her reputation among her peers. When Anna and her youth group attended an abstinence event hosted by SRT, she heard a story very similar to her own, but with a very different ending.[38]

As an evangelical Christian organization, SRT situates sexual delinquency within a traditional conversion narrative that begins with the act of sin, followed by the conviction and repentance of sin, and culminates in the acceptance of Jesus Christ and obedience to God's will. Sexual sin is central to the salvation history of humanity and, according to most evangelical leaders, begins the metacycle of sin and redemption that frames all of human existence. Groups like Silver Ring Thing have modified this formula only slightly with revival-like events at which students like Anna are called forward to an altar that offers both personal salvation and sexual purification.

With sex as sin and purity as salvation, audiences are offered the gift of a new birth, an idea that revivalist Jonathan Edwards popularized during the Puritan awakenings of the eighteenth century. A new birth, of course, means a new body, and for Anna, whose "body had been tarnished by the fingerprints of others," this was a transformative moment. Anna's story followed the narrative formula of conversion testimony, except that her salvation was not only a recommitment to obey God but a renewed hope that she would meet the man "whom God has set aside for me."[39]

Anna's testimony exemplifies the relationship between sexual purity, marital ambitions, and personal salvation, a formula that the contemporary purity movement has found highly motivating for adolescents. The careful construction of sexual behavior as religious practice is as old as the Christian tradition itself. But the work to identify sexual purity as a central practice of Christian faith commitment is unique to the twentieth century because of its particular concern for the spiritual formation of adolescent believers. The evangelical purity culture has grown up around attempts to elevate sexual purity from moral code to Christian creed. For evangelicals who focus more on personal spirituality than theological tradition for the formation of Christian spiritual life, private, sexual acts, rather than doctrinal statements, are sites for reinforcing orthodoxy, especially during the formative years of adolescence.

The Bible as text and as object of personal devotion plays a central role for evangelical purity advocates. Creating a seamless relationship between sexual purity and personal salvation happens almost effortlessly, since, from their perspective, sexual purity is upheld by the Bible's narrative of sin and salvation. The production and marketing of Bibles whose titles and parabiblical commentary center on themes of abstinence, sexual temptation, and purity further reinforce the connections between biblical authority and sexual purity.

Compelled by the idea of new beginnings, especially after defilement and destruction, purity advocates turn to scripture to help adolescents understand the creation of sexuality, its strictures, and the consequences for defying those strictures. When purity speaker and author Doug Herman writes for his younger audiences he encourages them to regard the Bible as the ultimate authority for sexual behavior. He asserts that the Bible incontrovertibly condemns premarital sex and helps readers recognize where and how the scriptures define appropriate sex. Most notably, he highlights the sexual metatext of the creation story, in which the first humans defy God's command to abstain from eating the fruit of a particular tree. In his retelling of the story, Herman exchanges the word *apple*—the object of desire and source of delinquency in this story—for the word *sex*, and in doing so shows his readers that "anything outside of God's plan brings death."[40]

Purity is an inherently theological concept for Herman, who subscribes to the Calvinist doctrine of total depravity. To be human is to be impure and unclean, a state all are born into and can only escape with superhuman intervention. Though purity codes, especially in the Hebrew scriptures, address far more than sexual matters, the purity movement has elevated the value of sexual purity to such a degree that other ways of approaching the theological value of purity have become obsolete. Sexual purity began in *the* beginning, with Adam and Eve, whose complete acceptance of one another was a physical, spiritual, and emotional union. Herman's readers learn that "this is the spiritual and physical foundation of our sexuality."[41] Sexual purity for evangelicals is a new beginning, a sign of a new creation, and a chance to restore humans' relationship with God and return to the original paradise.

Evangelicals who insist on purity as a biblical mandate are not solely reliant upon textual evidence. The two most prominent purity organizations, True Love Waits and Silver Ring Thing, produce and distribute abstinence-themed Bibles that affirm the mandate both materially and visually. Whereas Broadman and Holman Publishers created and marketed the *True Love Waits Bible*, Silver Ring Thing produced its very own and thus provides a more accurate representation of how the purity movement utilizes bibles.

The *Abstinence Study Bible,* developed especially for SRT, is the most critical resource the organization provides its audiences. This Bible is only available to students who attend the SRT show and purchase a purity ring or make a public commitment to Jesus Christ. Tracy Webster, the SRT staff member who guided the Bible project and created much of its content, believes that a commitment to sexual purity is futile unless that commitment is rooted in "the Word of God." For SRT, that word is best spoken through the New Living Translation (NLT), so SRT president Denny Pattyn and Webster adapted a structure for the scriptures that would highlight the significant role of sexual abstinence to one's Christian faith practice. To do this, they organized two sets of reading plans: one for new believers and another for confirmed believers needing support in their abstinence commitment. New believers can utilize a section, entitled "First Steps for New Believers," that provides an introductory reading plan to the Bible itself. Webster found the commentary provided by evangelical minister Greg Laurie in the NLT to be a useful tool for explaining the central tenets of Christianity and responding to questions asked by new converts. These questions included: Why did Jesus have to die for me? Who is God? Who is Satan? What does God say about marriage?[42]

The SRT portions of the Bible, located both before and throughout the actual scriptures, offer resources to young people, including dating advice such as "always go out in groups," "keep the lights on," "avoid the horizontal," and "keep your clothes on, in, zipped and buttoned."[43] More important, SRT connects this set of advice to particular scripture passages that reinforce the primacy of sexual abstinence in the Christian faith. The primary text used by the organization is from the New Testament epistle 1 Thessalonians. When I interviewed her, Tracy Webster recited the passage without hesitation: "This is the will of God through sanctification that you should avoid sexual immorality that each one of you should learn to control your bodies in a way that is honorable." The NLT translation reads more directly: "God wants you to be holy, so you should keep clear of all sexual sin. Then each of you will control your body and live in holiness and honor." The most interesting aspect of this text is the note regarding the clause, "then each of you will control your body." The note provides an alternative translation for "control your body" that reads, "or *will know how to take a wife for himself.*" The Greek translation, also noted in the NLT, provides the missing link between these differing interpretations: "*will know how to possess his own vessel.*" The evolution of this passage reveals a striking undercurrent to the quest for sexual purity. According to the initial note, there is a direct correlation between refraining from sexual immorality and taking a wife. Though SRT never addresses this underlying message of the text directly, the organization performs the subtext perfectly by asserting that God blesses people who wait to have sex before marriage. In our discussion of this particular text, Webster noted,

> And we really believe that God blesses people who wait until they are married to have sex in a ton of different ways. And so it's not just the fear-based thing of like "God's gonna strike you down if you have sex." But more in the sense of you get so many blessings and good positive things when you do things God's way and you wait until you're married. Whether it's a first time commitment or even a recommitment. That this is all huge. So that's the main verse that we really focus on.[44]

Webster further explains that abstaining from sex before marriage is only part of her organization's campaign. SRT, like TLW, emphasizes sexual purity, a concept that expects adolescents to learn to control their bodies. In this sense, Webster argues, sexual purity, or control of one's body, is practiced and learned; it is not simply the automatic result of one's commitment. It is this practice of bodily control that requires a personal commitment to Jesus Christ.

According to Denny Pattyn, one of the most pressing challenges for someone ministering to adolescents is verifying the authenticity of a person's spiritual transformation. He considers the difficulty of this transformation especially for students who, as was his experience while a young person, do not have the support of a Christian family and thus are more likely to fail in their commitment. Some of his students, he recognizes, make a commitment and never follow through, while others "mess up a couple of times" and then find their way back and get serious about their commitment. As a student who "messed up" more than once, Pattyn is not quick to give up on an adolescent who strays. But he is concerned with differentiating between those who are authentic and those who are not. Pattyn's own wisdom advises him to notice an adolescent's use of scripture. Students indicate an authentic spiritual transformation, according to Pattyn, when they are regularly reading the Bible and finding inspiration for their lives.

This type of inspiration is best understood in evangelical parlance as "the work of the Holy Spirit." For Pattyn and his organization, the third person of the Trinity is not merely concerned with the creation of a born-again identity. This same inspiration or work of the spirit is central to a successful abstinence commitment. According to Pattyn,

> When you have the Holy Spirit living in you and you're in the backseat of a car . . . what you really need is a voice within you that says "not with this guy, not with this girl, get out of there." That voice, that's very important to the process of what we're all trying to do, which is help kids wait.[45]

In making sexual decisions, adolescents, Pattyn believes, are not likely to turn to medical descriptions of STDs or to the conclusions of social scientific studies for encouragement. Instead, Pattyn argues, a silver ring with a biblical inscription helps remind them of a commitment to God and their future spouse. This biblical inspiration is a sign of the Holy Spirit working in the lives of teenagers, a sign that a student has been transformed both spiritually and sexually.

Conclusion

As is evident from the careful construction of the *Abstinence Study Bible*, purity groups hold a high regard for the spiritual development of adolescence. As a relatively new stage of human development, at least in terms of the historical arc of Christian history, adolescence provides a unique challenge for adults. Even a brief excursion into the work of purity advocates demonstrates that the idea of sexual purity presumes an inherent link between sexuality and spiritual development, a link made more coherent through the use of therapeutic discourses. However, this linkage did not originate with contemporary conceptualizations of sexual purity. As chapter one demonstrates, the notion of adolescence as established within the field of developmental psychology was defined by the natural conflict between sexual desire and religious duty. In this formulation, Christian conversion became the mark of religion's triumph over sexual desire in order for the individual to properly mature from childhood to adulthood. In the 1970s, when evangelicals like James Dobson were articulating adolescent sexuality and spirituality within a new therapeutic framework, these developments were reimagined as highly individualized processes, but as processes that held implications for the welfare of the nation-state. With the emergence of the contemporary evangelical purity movement, adolescent spiritual formations and sexual desire became co-belligerents in the task of raising a young generation of evangelicals who would stake their bodies and souls on claims of evangelical truth.[46]

Chapter Five

Performing Sexual Purity
in the Media Age

ON ANY GIVEN weekend throughout the United States, hundreds of churchgoing youth are sitting in a darkened sanctuary, eyes glued to a video screen, and soaking in all-too-familiar images of bikini-clad women and bare-chested men bracing themselves for the dramatic entanglements that only reality television can offer. Excerpts from previously aired episodes of *Survivor, Big Brother,* and *Temptation Island* entice the teenage viewers to abandon all cares and indulge in the hedonistic pleasures that the shows offer the contestants and their voyeurs. The industry of reality television has revolutionized media production and consumption, but to the producers and consumers of this particular promotional piece, that matters very little. What does matter is that these viewers recognize the images of sweaty, fleshy bodies groping one another as unclean, dangerous, and out of control. Announced by a deeply resonant voiceover, "the pregnancies, the diseases, the emotions" mark the experiences show contestants have to look forward to on the new season of *Infection Island.*

In fact, this is not a screening for the Fox network's latest reality show offering, but a parody of such shows produced and presented by Silver Ring Thing (SRT). Since the mid-1990s, Silver Ring Thing has been traveling the country, as well as making numerous trips abroad, to present a live performance described as a "2–2.5 hour stage performance [that] incorporates high energy music, special effects, fast-paced video, personal testimonies, and comedy all delivered in a concert-style approach with which teenagers can respond and relate."[1] Indeed, an evening with the Silver Ring Thing is a delight to adolescents who strongly identify with popular culture and multimedia extravagance. As an organization that proudly claims the label "culturally relevant," SRT uses its media and cultural resources together as a strategic device to address the needs, desires, and collective identity of its adolescent audiences.

Contemporary nondenominational churches target prospective members, referred to as "seekers"; SRT adopts the same strategy. Seeker-friendly services like the SRT live event prioritize the comfort level of their audiences and provide familiar environments, narratives, and images that are explicitly nonreligious so as to avoid invoking any misgivings a prospective member may harbor about organized religion. Not surprisingly, many of SRT's shows are sponsored by churches whose worship spaces betray little of their religious purpose.

As a church-based movement using seeker-friendly tactics, SRT situates itself within a "commodity culture of the media sphere,"[2] which allows its leaders to utilize the promotional strategies that their audiences of adolescent media consumers recognize and eagerly respond to. By doing so, the organization communicates to its audiences that they are known—their desires, interests, and means of expression are recognized as legitimate and are addressed with great sophistication. In short, SRT recognizes its audiences to comprise individuals whose agency is best displayed by their practices of media consumption.

Religiously based themes mediated through television, film, and other popular venues participate in the creation of identities that are in constant search of transcendent experiences. In fact, media stimulate the creation of "spiritual omnivores" who continuously seek moments of connection, understanding, and self-revelation.[3] Furthermore, media offer an unending series of these moments as the viewer-self seeks to negotiate her or his identity in relationship to the circumstances and characters being depicted. Recent scholarship of religion, media, and marketing asserts that this strategy is not merely about creating consumers of a particular religious product, but about utilizing postmodern theories of destabilized identities that can be shaped and reshaped according to particular mandates.[4]

Rather than dismiss popular and media culture altogether, SRT utilizes media's ability to render identities malleable and therefore open to transformation. Abstinence advocates first gain the trust of their adolescent audiences by acknowledging them as consumers of popular culture and mainstream media, and then offer an alternative media discourse. This counterdiscourse, portrayed through a series of skits, videos, and testimonials, highlights the moral discrepancies between audience members' past transgressions and future desires, discrepancies only resolved by present action in the form of a commitment to sexual abstinence. Through the counterdiscourse, the organization establishes a moral economy that represents an unbroachable gap between themselves and the value system of the very same popular media used to gain the audience's trust initially.

Considering the extensive historical collaborations between evangelicals and consumer culture, it is no surprise that the media utilized by the group reflects the mainstream or worldly values that the organization opposes.[5] As an organization intent on promoting a countercultural message of sexual abstinence through the use of culturally relevant media, Silver Ring Thing employs a number of strategies for adapting popular culture into its abstinence presentation. The first assault against worldly value systems is to parody popular media and reveal the inferiority of mainstream value systems that permit and even encourage sexual promiscuity. The revelatory effects of parody allow the group to directly challenge any contending morality systems that do not actively define sexuality within the confines of the evangelical purity culture. And yet the success of moral and media parody is dependent on the audience's familiarity with these worldly technologies and meaning systems.

Similarly, the organization has adopted a brand of Christianity that endorses both media and material consumption. As with product branding, religious branding allows a group to transform a collection of individuals whose autonomy is best demonstrated by their ability to consume into a cohesive collective with a shared identity marker. The use of media allows the organization to pitch a religious product that appears to have grown organically from the same earth that produces consumers' favorite late-night TV shows. Branding Christianity with the theme of sexual purity, SRT transforms adolescent consumers into moral agents capable of choosing between right and wrong.

The numerous paradoxes presented in this strategic formulation require some examination in order to determine just how abstinence advocates utilize popular media to construct their own moral economy—an apt descriptor of the goals of purity work for two reasons. First, "moral economy" implies an arrangement of morality in which behavior and ideology create a system of exchange as a prerequisite for participation.[6] Second, the close connection between morality and economic systems helps to further locate an organization like SRT within the discursive structures that help us explain the phenomenon of religious marketing, branding, and consumption. The construction of the moral economy is highly dependent upon temporal trappings of mainstream media culture, but it is controlled in such a way that it fails to displace the transcendent values of the evangelical purity culture. The way in which SRT utilizes media is especially interesting for understanding how evangelicals maintain a balance between worldly and otherworldly values, what Christian Smith has called an orientation of "engagement with distinction." For SRT, the engagement with popular culture and consumerism is made distinct from secular formulations by situating it within a moral economy structured by ultimate forms of good and evil.

One Ring to Rule Them All

The audiences attending the Silver Ring Thing are introduced to a hybrid of popular media culture and original media that portray the foolishness and dire consequences of premarital sexual behavior.[7] As a series of progressively serious skits, videos, and testimonials laying out a spectrum of seemingly inevitable consequences that result from premarital sexual activity, the SRT live event encourages audiences to recognize the correlation, or eventual correlation, between their own experiences, past or future, and the tragedies dramatized for them. The audience members are required to negotiate their own meaning-making processes and identity formation in relationship to these messages of shame, abandonment, disappointment, and heartbreak. These narratives not only attempt to evoke past memories and the feelings associated with them, but also warn against a future reality haunted by disappointment and emotional turmoil.

The live event is strategically organized, beginning with a series of skits and videos conceived of as "light and funny." During the first half of the performance, audiences enter into the familiar yet strange worlds of Middle-earth, the game show *Jeopardy!*, and television advertising. These are just three examples of the organization's use of parodic play that develops a cache of cultural capital that SRT hopes audiences will invest in. Tracy Webster, a former program coordinator for the group, explains further:

> We like to use just enough popular media to make the students comfortable, especially the ones who haven't ever gone to church or heard the gospel message. If we can get them laughing at the beginning and give them points to connect on they can say, "Oh *Austin Powers*, yeah, I saw that movie." Or anything along those lines where they can say, "Oh, these people do get where I'm coming from, they know what kind of culture I live in." It makes them more likely to receive the message throughout the rest of the show.[8]

The use of media, and parody in particular, is employed to cultivate social identification among the adolescents, to help them recognize SRT as a grouping of peers who share their vernacular, interests, and desires. The group selects films, celebrities, narratives, and tropes that create a short-hand for interpersonal intimacy. In doing so, SRT begins to develop their moral economy by inverting familiar meanings while maintaining the original meaning-making devices.

Early in the SRT live event, audiences are transported into the Tolkien-ian realm of Middle-earth, where two new elves have joined the Fellow-ship of the Ring at their meeting in Rivendell. These new elves, Justin and Chris, are SRT evangelists expertly spliced into a scene from Peter Jack-son's film trilogy, creating a parody version that inserts an unfortunate miscommunication into the original narrative, along with small bits of humor for levity. Chris, one of the few nonwhites who has worked for Silver Ring Thing, is introduced to the delighted audience as "the first black elf of Middle-earth." The humor of this moniker is multilayered, for it acknowledges the lack of diversity among the characters in the film, while inadvertently acknowledging SRT's own lack of racial diversity.[9]

Tolkien's adventure is posed as a natural ally to the cause of sexual purity, because both value systems embrace a classical narrative trajectory where innocence, friendship, and goodness triumph over the forces of confusion, manipulation, and evil. This battle is hard-won by Frodo, the unlikely Hobbit hero, who must face ultimate danger, isolation, and his own evil inclinations on an arduous journey to destroy a ring so powerful it corrupts innocence. Such a task is easily mapped onto the autobiogra-phy of any abstinence pledger. And yet the organization makes the un-likely choice to create a parody of the story that does not play upon these commensurate attributes. Rather, SRT uses the film to begin developing for the audience a moral economy rooted in the presumably natural antag-onism between the value systems of popular culture and the evangelical purity culture.

In the parodic reinterpretation, Chris and Justin convince Elven ruler Elrond and the others to help them take the ring to all of Middle-earth, teaching people about sexual responsibility and self-respect. Frodo, of course, bravely accepts the task and begins the journey, accompanied by the two SRT elves. To the dismay of Justin and Chris, however, Frodo ends their journey by destroying the ring—a conclusion that traditionally reas-sures Tolkien fans that good has overcome evil. However, the SRT version rescripts the conclusion as one of disappointment and frustration: Justin and Chris realize that their goal to spread the message of the silver ring has been thwarted.

This video, by design, makes only an initial contribution to the moral economy SRT intends to develop throughout the evening. Its primary goal is to convince the audience of the organization's cultural capital—or, in this case, its popular-cultural capital. By illustrating its concern for and attention to the adolescent imagination, SRT hopes audiences will soon find the countermessage compelling. This is the first step in shifting the young viewers' trust away from the worldly values represented by popular media and toward the transcendent values of Silver Ring Thing.

In the course of the *Lord of the Rings* parody video, SRT only hints at its intentions to intervene in the meaning-making processes employed by adolescents. At this earliest stage, SRT seeks just to establish its people as members of an in-group and the guardians of something worth desiring—though what that something is has yet to be fully revealed. The thematic tensions of good versus evil, companionship versus isolation, and innocence versus manipulation are expertly tagged by the producers of this particular piece of media, in that they are able to construct an insider-outsider dynamic. However, the creation of a new text—SRT's own version of the Tolkien scene—asserts an interpretive framework all its own.

Media-studies theorist Jonathan Gray notes the significance of *The Lord of the Rings* as quest films, a genre so powerful that it is replicated in the seven hours of documentary material that accompanies the DVD collection of the films. In these extras—or paratexts, as Gray calls them— the filmmaking process itself is recast as an epic journey, the cast members come to embody the qualities of their characters, and the group often refers to off-camera relationships as a fellowship. In short, the making of the film comes to represent a feat of personal trust, risk, and endurance—the same qualities that characterize Frodo's quest to destroy the ring.[10] Thus, these paratexts offer viewers another meaning-making technology with which to engage Peter Jackson's retelling of the story.

In the same way, SRT has created its own paratext, one that at the very beginning of the live event draws upon the heightened drama of the quest genre and will eventually spin off into its own tale of good and evil. Rather than creating a text that moves parallel to the original, this narrative asserts a competing moral: Frodo's quest is to destroy the ring, while Justin and Chris's is to take the ring far and wide, accompanied by the message of sexual purity. By portraying this conflict, SRT has established a counterdiscourse that will frame the entire evening, one in which the organization posits itself as the sole arbiter of truth over and against all other value systems. In the hands of SRT, one of the most beloved and trusted protagonists in literary history is recast as an untrustworthy antagonist.

This competitive framework allows SRT to position itself as the countercultural underdog poised to challenge mainstream culture, a site from which many evangelicals stake their claim to truth. Evangelical Christians are most actively and effectively engaged when embattled by conflicting cultural forces. They compete in the marketplace of ideas by asserting a subcultural identity that is neither disengaged with nor assimilated to mainstream culture, thus developing a creative tension in which evangelical activism thrives.[11] SRT's parody of *The Lord of the Rings* exemplifies this very pattern and marks out one of the organization's most effective tactics: creating familiar yet distinct media portrayals that capture the adolescent imagination. This recasting allows the group to chart the plot of a new and more significant narrative, one in which the conflict between sexual purity and sexual promiscuity is mapped onto a cosmic battle between the godly and the worldly.

The Gospel According to Paris Hilton: Creating a Moral Economy

As the evening progresses, SRT incrementally shifts the tone of the performance, moving deftly away from Middle-earth and toward narratives that bring into clearer view the moral economy the group represents. Even at this stage, humor and parody work to further establish a competition between the increasingly questionable values of the "world" and the stalwart forces of sexual purity. Almost an hour into the show, almost no mention of God, Jesus Christ, or faith has passed between presenters and audience: a delightful homage to the oeuvre of Will Farrell, yes; any mention of the transformative power of Jesus Christ, no. Again drawing upon seeker-friendly strategies, SRT first develops an argument based solely upon criticisms of celebrity culture and mainstream sexual values, without any mention of the value system proposed as a replacement.

The first stage of developing a moral economy rooted in evangelical purity culture is revealing the failures of the mainstream value systems that adolescents easily recognize from popular media. The use of parody allows SRT to deconstruct the transmission of a particular value set by certain figures, narratives, and symbols. It also allows the group to recode the values of immediate gratification, sexual freedom, and casual relationships as selfish, foolish, and ultimately dangerous behavior. According to Jonathan Gray's analysis of television parody as a tool for teaching media literacy, parody is the optimal mechanism by which to reveal how media promotes particular ideologies that are proffered as normative, even natural.[12]

The parodic strategy comes to the fore in a live sketch performed by young SRT evangelists who attempt to destabilize the authority of the values espoused by popular media and their influence over young media consumers. However, in order to utilize parody at all, the group must depend on the cachet of the very same media sources. The device used in this instance is the game show *Jeopardy!*, but it is no ordinary game: it is a celebrity version with the contestants Johnny Depp, Paris Hilton, and Jack Black. On top of that, the characterizations of the hosts and contestants reveal that this is not merely a parody of the game show, but a parody of a parody—*Jeopardy!* as known to fans of *Saturday Night Live*. The insults that Alex Trebek hurls at the players indicate a low degree of respect for their intelligence and lifestyles. In this sketch, Trebek is the arbiter of moral values—a role he plays with relish by insulting the intellectual, interpersonal, and sexual failings of each of his guests. In this role, the actor playing Trebek is showing little derivation from the *SNL* depiction. The portrayals of Depp, Black, and Hilton also indicate little change from the late-night formula. It is not until the contestants begin fielding questions—rather, *answers*—that another layer of meaning becomes evident. Alex Trebek mocks his absent, vain, and inane guests for their inability to answer simple questions regarding not great works of literature, architecture, or art, but sexually transmitted diseases.

Here, SRT has constructed a scenario in which popular culture is put on trial and found lacking in a number of ways. The dearth of knowledge is not an indictment of mental acuity alone but of a culture whose exemplars display little awareness of and concern for the excesses of sexual promiscuity. These celebrities represent everything that SRT does not advocate: self-indulgence, irresponsible living, and the sexual ennui that allegedly intoxicates popular media.

Of course, as a parody of a parody, the success of this sketch rests upon the audience's familiarity with the game show, its sketch-comedy version, and its three celebrity contestants. Within this sketch, several messages compete for dominance: the influence of celebrity, the tolerance of sexual irresponsibility, and the unwise "jeopardy" of promiscuous sexuality. With little effort, the sketch is able to use parody to portray the foolishness of the first two options, leaving the third as the only viable interpretation. The antipromiscuity message, delivered under the guise of caustic humor, sarcasm, and insult, further develops a competitive framework in which the losing argument is clearly demarcated. And yet this sketch would not be successful without the use of an easily recognizable context and its trio of megastars that provides a level of familiarity and comfort for the audience.

The goal of this sketch is to further establish the moral economy promoted by Silver Ring Thing. By setting up cultural exemplars as strawman caricatures, the organization depicts mainstream cultural values as inherently dimwitted and narcissistic—features that leave the individual with few resources for self-protection. Jonathan Gray describes parody as a useful tool for media literacy that allows viewers to deconstruct the production and consumption of media messages to reveal the underlying ideologies of those apparatus.[13] Though Gray's pedagogical intention is far from that of any abstinence advocate, his model helps demonstrate SRT's own use of media parody. Rather than media literacy, SRT uses parody to establish a moral literacy whereby adolescents learn to deconstruct the amoral codes of mainstream culture and to see them as unnatural and dangerous.

According to SRT's own account, the live performances are successful on paper: almost half a million people have attended events, and over 200,000 adolescents have each made a commitment to sexual purity in the group's seventeen-year existence.[14] However, the organization makes little effort to track the sustained fidelity of purity pledgers, making its long-term impact rather hard to evidence.[15] Unlike other abstinence groups, SRT uses parody, but this puts the organization's message in a precarious position. Parody by definition is limited because of its dependence upon previous iterations of a narrative, image, or theme. A parody is successful only to the degree that it maintains the recognizable qualities of that which was initially represented. This dependence creates a paradox, for the unveiling of ideology that parody performs is authorized by the ideological norm itself. Thus, while parody may deconstruct a value system, it does not destroy it. Rather, the power of parody exists to the degree that its antagonist continues to thrive.[16]

The authority of SRT's moral economy is predicated upon its inversion of mainstream values that the organization perceives to endorse sexual libertarianism and moral laxity. Parodies of those values and the technologies that produce them are only temporary—they do not ultimately displace the first iteration, because the new argument would not exist without it. SRT simultaneously valorizes and critiques popular media, expecting its audiences to reject the meaning of popular culture and yet not expecting them to reject the meaning-making devices that create and promote those meanings.

Such an arrangement would not be problematic, except that the group's efficacy rests upon its ability to portray popular culture and its values of sexual freedom and casual relationships as culturally and intellectually inferior and morally bankrupt. The *Jeopardy!* sketch further deepens the competitive framework first hinted at in the *Lord of the Rings* video. The creation of a counternarrative began by recasting Frodo as an untrustworthy antagonist. In the *Jeopardy!* sketch, the antagonists are quickly revealed because the narrative itself already presumes a competitive framework between the celebrity guests and the intellectually and morally superior Trebek. These two media presentations together help SRT to define the parameters of a moral economy in which the countercultural narrative of sexual purity seeks ascendancy over a mainstream narrative of sexual freedom.

The use of parody to develop this moral economy is inconsistent, to say the least—unless, of course, Silver Ring Thing is only using popular media as a diversionary tactic and an attempt to garner good standing with its audiences. If such is the case, the organization offers little guidance for decoding that same media. If SRT's core organizers are accurate in their assumption that their adolescent audiences have no interest in decoding the amoral messages of popular culture and simply find themselves swayed by media as a substitute for interpersonal connection, SRT is spared the paradox of parody. However, given the fluidity of media and the identities it constructs, the organization has little to no power to predict the impact of its parodic media.

As a decoding process, parody reveals the ideological assumptions of mainstream culture, yet it also reveals that ideological assumptions of Silver Ring Thing are rooted in the creation of a moral economy that privileges religious proselytization over the sexual and physical well-being of adolescents. During official events as well as outside interviews, the founder, Denny Pattyn, asserts sexual abstinence as a form of obedience to God. Practicing safe sex or any form of premarital sex is dangerous, he claims, not because of infections or disease, unwanted pregnancy, or thwarted future ambitions, but because it is an act displeasing to God. Sex outside of marriage creates a barrier between God and the believer, thus the goal of his work is not the physical protection of adolescent evangelicals but the confirmation of their personal salvation.[17] Perhaps this is why, then, as the live performance grows more serious, the organization relies less upon popular media and more on original media, personal testimonies, and other traditional evangelistic methods to clearly draw the boundaries of a new moral economy.

Put a Ring on It: Branding Christianity

Despite the seemingly stark distinctions between purity and impurity that permeate abstinence discourse, it is not the ascendancy of the sacred over the secular, the spiritual over the material, and the eternal over the temporal that ultimately shape the moral economy of the movement. Rather, like evangelicals before them, abstinence evangelists exploit the tensions between the worldly and otherworldly in order to procure for themselves a distinctive brand of Christianity that appeals to the wireless generation, a group that values autonomy without disconnection and brand allegiance without crass consumption.

While most attendees at purity events are already part of the evangelical subculture, leaders recognize that the battle between sexuality and spirituality raging within adolescents is not easily won. Some may have become sexually active and some may have become less committed to their faith, while a few others may never have made any commitment. Silver Ring Thing provides one means of continued transformation by asking audiences to recite the following prayer:

> Dear Lord Jesus, I truly am sorry for what I've been doing. I truly am sorry for all sins in my life. And I want you to forgive me. So right now Lord Jesus I ask you please forgive me for all the garbage all the sin that's in my life. And Lord Jesus I ask you now to come into my life, to take over my life, to be the Lord of my life. So now Lord Jesus I ask you to please come into my life. Thank you for coming in. Now Lord I need your help. I need you to give me guidance and direction for this incredible decision I'm making here today. So Lord help me and lead me. I pray in your name. Amen.[18]

Faith-based purity organizations impress upon their audiences that a commitment to sexual abstinence is fruitless unless accompanied by a personal relationship to Jesus Christ. Young people who feel moved to commit to sexual purity are also expected to embrace the belief system of evangelical Christianity, if they have not done so already. The exclusive claims of evangelical Christians to sexual purity furthers an ideology that only Christians are capable of sexual morality and marital happiness. And given the historical connections between sexual morality and national identity, sexually pure Christians stand as the exemplar of national integrity and security.

Incongruously, these claims became most evident in a court case in the United Kingdom that emerged shortly after Silver Ring Thing toured the region in 2004. Lydia Playfoot, the teenaged daughter of SRT leaders in England, began wearing her silver ring to a school that held strict policies against jewelry. Exceptions to this rule included bracelets and headscarves, which Sikh and Muslim girls are required to wear in their respective religious traditions. Playfoot and her friends, believing their rings held equal significance, felt entitled to wear a symbol of their religious faith. The school, however, refused to accept this view and began disciplining the girls for breaking the school's dress code.[19]

Playfoot and her parents were troubled at the school's behavior, especially at what they perceived to be a religious double standard. Playfoot and the other ring wearers continued to assert their right to wear something that signified a practice central to their Christian belief. Heather Playfoot, Lydia's mother, remarked that purity rings had a long history within the Christian church and were often worn by nuns. Lydia herself articulated the importance of her ring this way:

> My ring is a symbol of my religious faith. I think, as a Christian, it says we should keep ourselves pure from sexual sinfulness and wearing the ring is a good way of making a stand.[20]

Though Lydia eventually stopped wearing her ring so she could complete her studies, she and her parents chose to pursue the issue through legal action. After two years of dispute with the school, the Playfoot family formally initiated a lawsuit, one that echoed previous suits brought by Muslim girls seeking the right to wear headscarves to school.[21] In June 2007, the British High Court heard Playfoot's case, in which she charged her school with denying her human rights by refusing her the expression of her religious beliefs. In her statement to the British High Court, she asserted that "the real reason for the extreme hostility to the wearing of the SRT purity ring is the dislike of the message of sexual restraint, which is 'countercultural' and contrary to societal and government policy."²² Paul Diamind, a human rights lawyer, argued Playfoot's case by asserting that secular school authorities were not entitled to determine religious beliefs or practices on Playfoot's behalf. He charged the school with violating Playfoot's right to "freedom of thought, conscience, and religion" as articulated in Article 9.1 of the European Convention on Human Rights.²³ Leon Nettley, headmaster of the Millais School, defended his institution's actions by arguing that the ring "is not a Christian symbol, and is not required to be worn by any branch within Christianity."²⁴ The British High Court agreed with Mr. Nettley and declared that the Millais School had not unjustly banned the purity ring. The court found that because neither Lydia's religion nor her commitment to sexual abstinence before marriage required her to wear the ring, the school had not infringed upon her right to religious expression.

The court's decision was based upon the determination of whether or not Lydia's wearing of a purity ring constituted a religious practice. Therefore, in order to rule upon Lydia's case, the court had to assert a legal definition of religious practice. Based on precedents from two previous cases regarding Muslim headscarves, the court utilized a definition of religious practice in which the practitioner was obligated by her religion to practice such behavior.²⁵ Any nonobligatory practice done in service to religious beliefs, the court ruled, was not "intimately linked" to the religion or to the practice of that religion.²⁶

The Playfoot case brings numerous issues to the fore, revealing that the faith-based abstinence movement is far more complex than just a revivalist group inspiring young people with rituals and romantic promises. In both the United States and the United Kingdom, SRT is embroiled in a heated debate over the role of religion, and religious views of sexuality in the public sphere. This conflict was apparent in media accounts of the case from both sides. Leon Nettley, Lydia's headmaster, raised concerns in the *Daily Mail* (London) that Lydia and her parents were using the case to gain publicity for SRT.²⁷ Terry Sanderson of the National Secular Society told the *Times* (London) that the suit was a deliberate attempt to impose a particular view of sexual morality onto the school.²⁸ For their part, Playfoot and her family viewed the court's decision as a move to marginalize from public discourse Christian belief in sexual abstinence before marriage. Lydia told the *Times* that the ruling meant that "slowly over time people such as school governors, employers, political organizations and others will be allowed to stop Christians from publicly expressing and practicing their faith."²⁹

By situating the Playfoot case in the context of the US culture wars, the British and domestic media revealed that the purity movement is seeking to establish sexual abstinence before marriage as a religious practice that is owed legal protection. Though England and the United States share similar statistics for unwed pregnancies and sexually transmitted diseases, the differences in the nature of public religious expression helped uncover the purity movement's larger goals: to establish sexual abstinence before marriage as a legally recognized tenet of Christianity. In the same way that wedding rings symbolize both a legal and relational commitment, SRT hopes that purity rings will mark their wearers' sexuality as pure, and that "pure" sexuality will become a marker of authentic Christian practice.[30] Playfoot was hailed as a hero by the organization for standing up to governing officials who refused to recognize her abstinence decision as religious practice.

The silver ring, the piece of jewelry sold to participants of the Silver Ring Thing event, is inscribed both physically and metaphorically with scriptures and meanings that serve contemporary evangelical purposes. The accompanying pledge recited by pledgers reads,

> In making this covenant before God Almighty, I agree to wear a silver ring as a sign of my pledge to abstain from sexual behavior that is inconsistent with Biblical standards. On my wedding day, I will present my silver ring to my spouse, representing my faithful commitment to the marriage covenant.[31]

The silver ring is imbued with sacred status as a sign of the pledger's commitment to oneself, God, and one's future spouse, and it symbolizes the wearer's sexual and spiritual transformation. Beyond its ritual significance, adolescents who purchase a ring at an SRT event are provided with care instructions in the *Abstinence Study Bible*: how to clean the jewelry, what to do if one needs a new size, and how to handle losing a ring. Beyond these practical instructions, this introductory section of the Bible implores the wearer to wear the ring every day: "Wear this ring like you'll wear your wedding ring—it is a promise to the person you will marry."[32] After participating in the ritual, students are also advised on what to do if they are tempted to break their promise. One of the SRT evangelists ends the live evening by instructing the audience to flush the ring down the toilet if they do indeed break their promise.

Despite its moniker, Silver Ring Thing did not originate the idea of the purity ring. Neither does True Love Waits, the organization that popularized the purity ring, take credit for its invention. Richard Ross, founder of True Love Waits (TLW), explained that they were simply picking up on a trend that was already occurring among church families:

> Parents might take a 12-year-old to a nice restaurant, give a gentle nudge toward purity, and then present the ring. As True Love Waits emerged, it made more sense to most parents to present the ring after making the promise—often in a beautiful church ceremony.[33]

As an extension of a family-based ritual, True Love Waits became the first organization to mark a commitment to sexual purity with a purity ring ceremony. Started in 1992 as a sex-education program for Southern Baptist youth, True Love Waits formally launched its campaign in Tennessee when fifty-one teenagers participated in the first purity ring ceremony at Tulip Grove Baptist Church.[34] Ross presided at the event intended to encourage already chaste young people by providing them with peer support and a symbol that reminded them of their commitment to sexual abstinence before marriage. Unlike Silver Ring Thing, True Love Waits does not focus its energies on a live performance. As an organization, TLW has launched numerous campaigns focusing on church, family, school, and neighborhood involvement. In each of these contexts, hundreds of thousands of students have participated in purity ring ceremonies that vary according to the creative outlets at their disposal. True Love Waits assists in these events only to the degree that they provide a template for the purity ring ceremony that can be downloaded from the organization's website. TLW also provides a detailed set of instructions for before and after the ceremony.

Though SRT specializes in large concert-style events, the smaller TLW ceremonies convey much the same message in a more family-based setting. TLW encourages leaders to include the entire family or to provide a "significant adult" for those whose families will not be involved. Adults are responsible for purchasing rings for the youth to bring to the event. In some cases, churches commission rings for the group. The ceremony itself begins with a prayer and continues with a responsive litany in which students, parents, adults, and the ceremony leaders read responses proclaiming their rejection of corruption and commitment to purity.[35]

Churches and other groups hosting TLW ring ceremonies are not ob-ligated to use these resources, often employing their own creative ener-gies to stage more unique events. Most of these ceremonies resemble weddings to some degree or another. They are held in church sanctuaries, sometimes with pledgers wearing white, and, though there is no exchange of rings or vows, the inclusion of these elements is crucial for communi-cating the importance of the event. In 2003, the youth of Greater Starlight Baptist Church in New Orleans participated in a True Love Waits debu-tante ball. Having run a True Love Waits program for three years, the church decided to create a more elaborate event to follow its twelve-week study program. Dressed in formal wear, the young people were intro-duced, made their pledges, and were presented with purity rings by their parents.[36]

Another church in Bartlett, Tennessee, displayed its ingenuity with a mock purity wedding. Instead of making vows to one another, the two young people involved made vows of purity. Playing the role of bride and groom, Courtney Magness and Jonathan Nason, accompanied by a wed-ding entourage, wore wedding attire as they received their purity rings. Following the ceremony, the attendees were invited for punch and cake to celebrate the happy occasion.[37] As this example illustrates, the purity ring ceremony is not an isolated event. Rather, it functions as a prenuptial agreement that extends the wedding ritual into a series of events that re-quire self-control and deferred gratification. The only way to participate in this extended ritualization of adolescent sexual development is to main-tain the commitment. Though not every young person who practices this extended premarital rite wears a ring to symbolize the commitment, those who do are hardly unique in the movement.

As a cultural and religious symbol, the silver ring and the accompany-ing pledge represent a brand of Christianity that advertises both a per-sonal commitment and a distinctive way of life. Considering that the ring is the central material object marking an adolescent's affiliation with this particular brand of Christianity, SRT take pains to inscribe its rings with various degrees of nonmaterial significance. In one dramatic introduc-tory video, a ring is imbued with superhero powers. In Denny Pattyn's "gospel message," it is portrayed as a moral conscience reminding stu-dents—who may find themselves "in the backseat of the car"—of their commitment.

During the live event, Justin Matthews tantalizes the audience with the promise of exciting marital sex. To prove the authority on which he speaks, he kneels down and points to his left ring finger while it is illuminated by a spotlight. Simultaneously, strains from Handel's "Hallelujah" chorus burst from the stage, indicating the sense of awe that should rightfully be bestowed upon married people. In stark contrast to the classical-music intervention, Matthews refers to his wedding ring as an "all-day free-ride pass," lest any audience member remain unconvinced that Matthews finds his marital sex life to be "awesome."

As a central symbol of an extended prenuptial agreement, the purity ring is often incorporated into wedding ceremonies. True Love Waits even provides liturgical resources that can be used in the wedding ceremony. This text tells the couple of the many benefits they will receive from their prenuptial commitment to abstinence as they approach the challenges of marriage. It honors them as a counterexample to those who demand instant gratification and blesses them for choosing to "prioritize God's ways." Though there is no way to know how many weddings incorporate the TLW liturgy, the organization's website offers one report of a couple who melted down their purity rings in order to make the bride's wedding band.[38] Other reports indicate that couples exchange purity rings at the altar, and Denny Pattyn often officiates at ceremonies in which the purity ring plays a central role in the wedding ritual. For some ring wearers, the silver circle functions as a placeholder.[39] Many students wear their rings on the left ring finger in anticipation of someday exchanging that ring for an engagement ring or wedding band.

But in order to achieve the nuptial benefits of their commitment to purity, students must first be convinced that the worldly moral codes to which they have previously been accustomed do not offer the same opportunities. For those who are uncertain of the rings efficacy, the organization provides clear instructions for caring for the ring, but also for its discarding if sexual indiscretion occurs. Rings are only available to students who attend SRT events; those who request to purchase one for an absentee friend are not allowed to do so. The exclusive policies regarding the ring help SRT maintain the ring's status as a special object to be coveted by those who do not have one and prized by those who do.

With a metal adornment, SRT brings to light its contribution to a moral economy designed to establish the boundaries between sexual purity and worldly contamination. However, in order to establish the supremacy of its value system, the organization must enter into the murky waters of Christian marketing. Like many before them, the marketers of Christian purity benefit a great deal from the blurred boundaries of sacred and secular, most noticeably in the creation of religious branding. Recognizing that religious experience often replicates marketing strategies, evangelical Christians have long sanctioned the use of secular trends to market and sell their product.[40] To suit these trends, abstinence organizations have created and marketed a brand of Christianity that addresses one's need for attachment and identification while reinforcing the autonomy of the religious consumer.

In the same way as popular media culture, groups like SRT work to reinforce the autonomy of their audiences through consumption. Showing them that they have the skills to choose meaningful material objects over mere ornamentation establishes religious consumers and potential abstinence pledgers as moral agents. Wearing the ring not only declares one's allegiance to sexual purity, but exhibits young evangelicals' ability to participate in consumer culture without being consumed by it. This ideal of participation without cooptation is portrayed with narratives and images borrowed from popular culture. One piece of media that exhibits this particular ethic is a commercial pastiche based upon the popular marketing campaign of the credit company MasterCard. This video presentation is coded by the group as transitional in that it traverses the gap between comedic portions of the event and the more serious tone of the night's conclusion. Unlike the previously featured sketches and videos, SRT does not deploy parody to challenge the rampant consumerism of the credit card industry; rather, the organization chooses to capitalize on the much-used trope and rhythm of MasterCard's well-known marketing campaign.

In this video, two young people return home from a date, accompanied by soft, comforting music on the verge of a triumphant swell. The voiceover informs viewers that this night on the town cost $55. The flower bouquet lovingly carried by the young woman: $20. The silver ring worn on the young man's finger: $15. As the young couple kisses a brief but meaningful goodnight, the narrator intones, "always knowing how the night is going to end: priceless." The young man walks triumphantly away from his date while the audience is told that "there are some things money can buy; for everything else, there's a silver ring."

The kind of relationship that SRT idealizes is so pure that it is entirely exempt from the pressures and expectations of a consumer society, even if the couple in question is participating in the consumer market in the process of their courtship. Money can buy adolescents the accoutrements of a good date, but only the silver ring can ensure a godly romance. While

sexually pure relationships may be postconsumerist, the silver ring functions within a religious marketplace that traffics in the rebranding of traditional religious ideologies and identities. Wearing the ring is not simply
a sign of a commitment to God, parents, and a future spouse, as its adherents pledge: it is about marking adolescent bodies with a particular brand
of Christianity that thrives in the creative tension between worldly and
otherworldly.

Yet even Denny Pattyn concedes that what truly transforms an individual is not a material object, but the presence of the Holy Spirit:

> If you have any hope of surviving the years of sexual temptation,
> you will need supernatural strength to do it. The strength will not
> come from your friends, parents, church, media, a vow you make or
> your silver ring on your finger. This power must come from inside,
> from the Holy Spirit operating within you and speaking to you in
> the moment of your greatest need.[41]

This distinction between material and spiritual needs and even between
temporary and permanent relationships amplifies the tension between
authentic religious belief and the consumption of religious products that
Pattyn and others must constantly negotiate. Straddling the divide between pure intentions and crass marketing of their own sexual status,
young people who choose to don rings simultaneously participate in and
critique a hypersexualized consumerist culture that values immediate
gratification over hard-won fidelity, and spiritual connection over material
worth.

Media Messages and the Negotiation of Ritual Identity

Keen on adapting images, films, songs, themes, and narratives from
mainstream media, SRT adeptly "recasts" these according to the strictures of its abstinence message. In doing so, SRT's events have accom-
plished several intended and unintended effects. First, the organization
confirmed its position within the long tradition of Protestant evangelicals who, since the nineteenth century, have utilized the most advanced
marketing and mass-media technologies to spread their gospel messages. Second, SRT further broke down the distinction between the
public and private, thus shifting the location from which Christian moral
values are transmitted. Third, the theme of sexual purity effectively

recast both religious and media images and messages. The heavily mediated sexual purity message is then transmitted via both live and recorded performances, prompting audiences to assess their own religious identities and sexual pasts.

As an evangelical organization that adapts themes from popular culture and relies upon the most up-to-date technology, Silver Ring Thing is hardly unique. Adapting, advancing, and even inventing media outlets have long been characteristic of evangelicalism's strategies for transmitting the gospel message to the widest audience possible. Historically, evangelicals have transformed technologically sophisticated theatrical venues into worship spaces and utilized mass production—they even created the prototype for the modern-day corporation. More recently, they have adapted sacred scriptures into a "culturally relevant niche Bible" marketed to teenage girls.[42] Culturally relevant niche Bibles provide a recent example of evangelical adaptation to consumer tastes and market trends. Book historian Paul Gutjahr asserts that, due to the technological shifts that occurred in the publishing industry starting in the 1980s, culturally relevant niche Bibles are now the norm for Bible publishing. By adapting to the digital revolution in secular publishing, Bible publishers can now easily add extrabiblical content to their products. They now produce endlessly diverse specialized Bibles marketed to specific readers who fall into a variety of categories: newlyweds, mothers, adolescents, dieters, single parents, and those addicted to drugs and alcohol, for example.[43]

Without a doubt, this phenomenon has aided the faith-based abstinence movement in promoting its own moral agenda. *The True Love Waits Study Bible* and *The Abstinence Study Bible* published by SRT rely strongly on the niche-Bible phenomenon to ascribe sacred status to abstinence teachings. Silver Ring Thing inserted over sixty pages of nonbiblical material written by Tracy Webster and based on the live show's content.[44] Students who purchase rings are each provided a copy of this text, developed especially for new adherents to sexual abstinence and new Christian believers. With a detailed introduction to studying the Bible and a topical reference guide, SRT's Bible readers are introduced to a form of Christianity within which sexual abstinence stands as a key tenet of the faith. In this light, the sexual abstinence movement is positioned solidly in the Protestant evangelical tradition of adapting to innovations in technological advancement while also unwittingly—but necessarily—revealing the malleability of the values and meanings of Christian belief and practice.

SRT's use of popular culture and multimedia technology illuminates more than evangelicalism's relationship to mainstream culture. It also shapes the way in which moral values are transmitted and the context in which this transmission occurs. According to Stewart Hoover, the images and narratives wrought by media entertainment are initially experienced within the domestic sphere. However, further examination reveals that media consumption actually erases the distinction between the public and private, raising questions regarding the locus of moral authority. Hoover investigates these boundaries by inquiring whether or not the "symbolic marketplace" of the media functions outside domestic boundaries, playing merely an influential role in the transmission of love, care, values, meanings, and identities. Or, he asks, does it function within these boundaries as an integral meaning-making technology? In short, Hoover is attempting to assess the impact of media on the location of moral development.[45] His analysis of the symbolic marketplace is helpful for understanding how the abstinence movement positions itself with respect to the process of adolescent moral development, which, for evangelicals at least, has traditionally resided within the domestic parameters of family life.

In response to early drafts of this project, American religious historian Amy DeRogatis noted with surprise the degree to which Silver Ring Thing, strongly rooted in the "family-values" code of morality, focuses on the actions of the adolescent individual.[46] Despite the organization's attempts to educate parents in a brief seminar aimed at them and not open to adolescents, SRT's stage show dedicated little time to the importance of family relationships and parental authority. Moreover, the SRT pledge, unlike the pledge taken at True Love Waits events, does not articulate a commitment to one's parents, nor are parents allowed to purchase official silver rings on behalf of their children, because the organization insists on selling their rings directly to the newly initiated. In this way, the organization aims to shape the behavior of adolescents directly, circumventing any parental involvement. The shift away from parental involvement is best explained by Hoover's argument regarding media consumption and the location of the transmission of values. For SRT, media consumption is not something that requires vigilant regulation. This is most evident during the SRT event, which is heavily dependent upon media entertainment to maintain the audience's attention and to gain its trust. The group attempts to transfer parental moral authority away from the domestic family unit and onto the public event. Drawing upon the boundary-crossing capabilities of the symbolic marketplace of mediated images, narratives, and themes, SRT positions itself as the arbiter of adolescent moral development. But, is it SRT's intent to expand parental-style authority, or to eradicate it altogether?

Certainly, the organization would resist any assertion that it is undermining parental authority. One of Pattyn's most severe criticisms of school-based sexual education is his belief that these programs intentionally strip parents of their decision-making rights. Thus, to conclude that SRT is not concerned with the transmission of moral values directly from parent to child would be disingenuous. Nevertheless, the ability of the symbolic marketplace to render the location for the transmission of moral values ambiguous remains a challenge to those who rely so strongly on media entertainment to elicit trust, responsibility, and compliance from their adolescent audiences.

Whether intentional or not, abstinence evangelists create and utilize adaptive meaning-making technologies that initiate a process of personal assessment. Under the influence of religious messages and media images, pledgers are asked to renegotiate their identities. The abstinence message, with its emphasis on emotional vulnerability and spiritual triumph, is especially appealing to adolescents, who are keen to experiment with new identities.

Memory and the negotiation of the self are central to the use of media in the abstinence movement. Thomas Csordas's analysis of charismatic healing in the United States is especially helpful for decoding the interplay of memory, identity, and the self in the context of the therapeutically charged, media-saturated abstinence event. As a symbol of the self, memory is a "privileged zone of communication" through which access to the sacred is granted.[47] Memory, and particularly the healing of memories, participates in the creation of the sacred self because these memories are ritually transformed according to the stipulations of the present moment. The students attending an abstinence event may have found themselves reshaping their memories according to the therapeutic tone of the evening. Even though Silver Ring Thing did not attempt to incorporate issues of sexual violence into its programming, that trauma is included in SRT's list of memories that require healing, thus equating this trauma with that of a consensual sexual experience. By presenting a cure-all for all forms of past sexual trauma, SRT reinterpreted memories to shape the present and future religious beliefs and sexual practices of its audiences.

With the assistance of a media-saturated discourse, the abstinence event collapsed the past, present, and future as the audience negotiated its own meaning-making processes. The attendees were encouraged to make decisions based not only on memories of past experiences but on the creation of a *future memory* that emerges from the ritual healing in which the sacred self is constituted.[48] For abstinence adherents, the shaping of the future self, sexual and sacred, is best exhibited in the recitation of the abstinence pledge. Silver Ring Thing, like True Love Waits, asks its audiences to commit to sexual abstinence for the sake of God and of each attendee's future spouse. By asking its pledgers to cast themselves into their future roles, the abstinence pledge constructs a future reality in which the ritualized self seeks and finds sexual and spiritual gratification.

In the same way that ritual disrupts the timeline of an individual's personal history, media images, symbols, and narratives blur other kinds of boundaries. The sacred self constituted in the ritual moment is a self that breaks down the spiritual boundaries that have traditionally characterized evangelical spirituality: public and private, sacred and secular. [49] Because of evangelicalism's acceptance of popular psychology and other mainstream cultural phenomena, the boundaries between the providential and the therapeutic are continuously blurred and redefined.[50] Practicing religion in a postmodern culture means that consumers are free to select and integrate seemingly contradictory symbols and practices, thus creating new narratives and sacred sites.[51] In particular, evangelical spirituality integrates the healing of body, mind, and soul and is increasingly comfortable acknowledging the whole person as a site for religious conversion. Historic suspicions of secular life have been suspended as contemporary evangelicals have come to embrace a world where the natural and supernatural are no longer distinct oppositions.[52] The abstinence movement is shaped extensively by secular therapeutic discourse, the focus of the next chapter. For the present purposes, it is important to note the parallel roles of the media and the construction of a ritualized self in effectively blurring the boundaries that evangelical Protestants have traditionally guarded.

Ritualized bodies unwittingly make meaning out of events by creating "strategically organized oppositions."[53] During the purity ritual, certain bodies and embodied practices are coded as oppositional: pure and impure. Oppositions come to dominate other forces controlling embodied practices and allow the ritualized body to create strategies for negotiating all other sociocultural situations by authorizing the pure to govern the impure.

This opposition effectively persuades young people to privilege the distinction between pure and impure and mark it as central to their Christian faith commitments. Marked as pure, adolescent ritualized bodies are prepared to navigate dating, courtship, and their own sexual desire according to the stipulations of their abstinence pledge. By taking the purity pledge, students create a ritualized identity that requires them to relentlessly negotiate the boundaries of purity and impurity. Though this boundary is sometimes crossed, it never ceases to exist. Thus, the ritualized body is one that must maintain these boundaries by marking itself as pure or impure depending upon its relationship to that boundary.

Through the purity ritual, students develop a ritualized identity and enter into an extended purity practice that shapes decisions regarding dating, sexual behavior, and the selection of marriage partners. As many students attest, the purity ritual is a prenuptial commitment whose performance, rhetoric, and symbols help adolescents to re-envision futures worthy of their present commitment to sexual abstinence before marriage.

Conclusion

The new paradigm spirituality that took hold of mainstream evangelicalism in the 1970s embraced the media age and created new genres of lifestyle media and Christian worship. One of new paradigm evangelicalism's tactics for reaching the unchurched was to seek greater degrees of cultural relevance. Not surprisingly, culturally relevant strategies were most adept at creating a vital youth culture: carefully calibrated tropes, images, music, and paraphernalia marked believers as a distinct American subculture. Though the marriage of Christianity and consumer culture was not a new one, religious leaders now more than ever have the ability to custom design their ministries for their target audience. The purity movement is just one of many brands of Christianity available to teenagers, though it is certainly the most successful in its ability to capture the adolescent imagination. As in the early days of evangelical youth movements, those who minister to youth recognize the extensive competition for adolescent attention. But the purity movement doesn't simply use popular media culture as a way to hook its audiences. Rather, media plays a critical role in the ritual performances of sexual purity by facilitating the creation of new identities for individuals seeking transcendence and transformation.

Conclusion

FEAR AND ACCOMMODATION IN THE CONTEMPORARY PURITY CULTURE

*America is truly the last bulwark of Christian civilization
. . . if America falls, Western culture will disintegrate.*
—BILLY GRAHAM, 1947

*Any society that goes on "do whatever you want" . . . has
been destroyed . . . and now we're experiencing the moral
decay within the civilization.*
—DENNY PATTYN, 2006

Introduction

Recent scholarship on evangelical purity culture situates the phenomenon at the individualist turn of evangelicalism, one that heightened the value of personalized beliefs and self-actualization. Organizations like the nondenominational Silver Ring Thing characterize sexual purity as a form of personal transformation and emotional fulfillment, religious values first described by Donald E. Miller's concept of the new paradigm church.[1] Most recently, Christine Gardner has portrayed the movement's rhetoric as providential assurance of relational happiness, sexual fulfillment, and emotional well-being.[2] Like Gardner's work, other studies addressing the evangelical purity movement utilize qualitative and quantitative approaches to explain either the impact of religious faith upon sexual decision-making or the effectiveness of the pledge movement.[3]

These studies provide important content and analysis for understanding the movement's impact on the lives of individual adolescents and the shaping of public and religious discourses around premarital sex. But, while they provide important insights into contemporary trends in adolescent sexual behavior and spirituality, their methodologies are confined by the therapeutic individualism of contemporary evangelicalism. The counterculture of the 1960s and 1970s reshaped US Protestantism by challenging the value of religious institutions and theological traditions. At the same time, the cultural revolutions elevated personal spiritual quests and the individual's desire for self-transformation. As participation in local congregations faltered, suburban "megachurches" expanded, offering nontraditional worship and numerous self-help programs that cemented a new paradigm in Christian spirituality and generated an individualistic turn in American evangelicalism.[4]

By defining evangelical purity culture according to this individualistic turn, recent studies fail to recognize the nationalistic themes in sexual-purity rhetoric. Since the nineteenth century, evangelical Protestants have sought cultural and political influence by asserting sexual purity in the face of national insecurity, particularly through threats of civilizational decline and race suicide. By the mid-twentieth century, themes of sexual immorality and juvenile delinquency within fundamentalist and later neoevangelical circles reinterpreted that rhetoric in the context of a global crisis: the Cold War.

During the Cold War era, religion, politics, and morality were shaped by fears of national decline and pending nuclear apocalypse. Politicians, religious leaders, and academics framed problems of sexual deviance and juvenile delinquency as national-security issues.[5] Therefore, understanding purity work in subsequent decades requires some attention to scholarship that addresses the role of fear in religious belief and practice. Jason Bivins's *Religion of Fear* provides an important starting point for explaining the political and later cultural activism that purity movements have stimulated. According to Bivins, the religion of fear developed as the boomer generation came of age, the same era in which new paradigm churches came into existence. In response to the chaos and excesses of the cultural revolutions, this generation sought to create popular cultural representations that connected "fears of damnation to a carefully identified range of sociopolitical practices and beliefs."[6]

Bivins's examples include the popular evangelical haunted-house franchise, Hell House, as well as the apocalyptic book series *Left Behind.*[7] These seemingly apolitical media play a prophetic role by calling mainstream culture to account for its failure to maintain strict moral codes. Without making overt political claims, they recall the earlier rhetoric of the Moral Majority and Anita Bryant's Save the Children campaign. The narratives of evangelical popular culture position children or adolescents as victims of the nation's failure to observe biblical prohibitions, especially those concerning sexuality. The evangelical purity culture has grown up around the belief that certain sexual practices are threatening to the nation's moral and spiritual trajectory. Parallel to Bivins's notion that the 1960s can serve as a historical marker for the religion of fear, purity culture cites the sexual revolution as the beginning of American moral descent. The goal of contemporary purity work and rhetoric is the protection of adolescents from the aftereffects of the sexual revolution.[8]

Bivins's definition of the religion of fear provides an important interpretive framework when historicizing evangelical purity culture beyond the hyperindividualism of new paradigm spirituality. But unlike Bivins, I do not locate the purity phenomenon's genesis as a response to the excesses of the 1960s. Rather, I argue that the religion of fear deployed by the purity movement, as observed in the late twentieth century, first emerged at the historical moment when mid-century fundamentalist leaders sought to regain cultural respectability, political influence, and the intellectual veracity of their theological tradition.

If we take the emergence of postwar fundamentalism, not the cultural revolutions of the 1960s and 1970s, as the genesis of the contemporary purity culture and Bivins's religion of fear, this historical scope allows us to recognize an internal tension within contemporary purity culture and evangelicalism as a whole. The impulses of the individualistic, self-transforming optimism of new paradigm spirituality and of a religion of fear stemming from Cold War fundamentalism are equally formative for the contemporary purity culture. The therapeutic mode of contemporary evangelicalism and the fear of personal and global destruction are neither equally self-evident nor equally beneficial to the purity movement. New paradigm churches have proven especially effective at translating evangelical Christianity for present-day believers and spiritual seekers who desire strict moral guidelines primarily for individual, spiritual, and psychological benefit.

While this belief system positions the new paradigm firmly within the culture wars, it does not require participants to embrace the cultural separatism of Cold War fundamentalism. As a theological mode that encourages the use and adaptation of mainstream culture, the new paradigm acts as a counterbalance to the religion of fear: a religion of accommodation. At the same time, Bivins's religion of fear helps us identify a remnant of sexual fear in contemporary purity culture that was first forged not in response to the cultural revolutions of the 1960s and 1970s but in the Cold War fundamentalism of the 1940s and 1950s. The historical origins of this rhetoric of sexual fear remain the underexamined subtext of the contemporary purity movement.

In 1904, G. Stanley Hall's *Adolescence* confirmed what many revivalists had known for decades: that the period of life between childhood and adulthood held the greatest potential for religious conversion. That age range was also accompanied by the equally great risks of newly awakened awareness of sin and sexual desire.[9] Not surprisingly, the point of entry for the reemergence of fundamentalism in the 1940s was not in the churches, seminaries, or denominational structures that fundamentalists had so carefully constructed during the post-Scopes era; instead, a youth-based movement that used adolescent vitality to promote national pride and religious commitment became the flashpoint.

Youth for Christ and Billy Graham's early ministry sought to prepare young Americans especially for the risks that threatened the nation's future. His early sermons, which addressed sexual morality, national identity, and the imminent return of Christ, allowed Graham to create a prophetic distance from mainstream adolescent culture, calling those within it to repentance. As part of a larger effort to restore the intellectual veracity of fundamentalism, Graham employed the intellectual arguments of Arnold Toynbee and Pitirim Sorokin, whom he used to craft a prophetic message linking sexual immorality and national insecurity.

The Cold War era elicited numerous apocalyptic scenarios that established the religion of fear among midcentury evangelicals. Along with its ability to explain global crisis, the religion of fear translated the nineteenth-century tropes of sexual purity and national security for the nuclear era. But as the century wore on and the threat of nuclear war declined, neofundamentalists sought to invigorate depoliticized conservatives, finding themes of nationalism and sexual delinquency motivating tools. Though Graham would distance himself from these efforts, new leaders in Christian psychology, especially James Dobson, would further reinvent the rhetoric of sexual immorality and nationalized fear in order to gain political and cultural influence through the 1980s.[10]

By the 1990s, when the evangelical purity culture emerged as an organized movement, both the Cold War and the Moral Majority had faded from popular consciousness. As a movement, purity plays upon themes of spiritual well-being and personal fulfillment that has allowed observers to mark it as an outgrowth of new paradigm spirituality. However, another look at the movement's rhetoric demonstrates a continued reliance upon older fundamentalist tropes of spiritual warfare, adolescent risk, sexual immorality, and national insecurity.

Religion of Accommodation / Religion of Fear

In contrast to the religion of fear that shaped evangelical political culture during the midcentury, contemporary purity culture reflects a religion of accommodation that came to define new paradigm churches. A religion of fear works to maintain boundaries and even a separatist stance in the face of mainstream culture and seeks to discomfort its adherents by demonstrating the radical chasm between holy and unholy. It rests upon absolute narratives of good and evil that shaped every narrative of the Cold War era, from geopolitical threats to first dates. It creates absolute moral boundaries that mirror a larger cosmic battle. Conversely, a religion of accommodation seeks to overcome these divisions and works to quiet any unease about contemporary culture. It draws on secular therapeutic discourses to create a morality based primarily upon the well-being of the individual. Similarly, it utilizes popular-media culture in order to establish itself as culturally relevant. As Donald E. Miller has demonstrated, new paradigm churches embrace media culture (both its content and its technology) in order to find more effective means of communication with their prospective audiences. These churches and organizations seek to appeal to the church-wary with their willingness to dissolve the boundaries between religious and nonreligious cultures. Not surprisingly, this strategy is most prevalent with initiatives directed toward adolescents.[11]

Traditionally, historians of religion have used the distinction between fear and accommodation in order to demonstrate the differences between evangelicals and fundamentalists. They maintain that these groups are best sorted out by degrees of frustration with or abstraction from mainstream culture.[12] The contemporary purity movement complicates this framework by deploying both cultural strategies simultaneously. The purity movement seeks to construct a moral economy, not simply a code of morality, in which the assurance of emotional, marital, and sexual fulfillment is provided in exchange for bodily control and spiritual obedience. In order for the economy to function, the purity movement relies upon the moral absolutism of the religion of fear while benefiting from the cultural and therapeutic permissions of the new paradigm.

Historian Grant Wacker described the Pentecostal tradition by juxtaposing two competing impulses among believers: primitivism and pragmatism. He argued that the kind of person drawn to Pentecostalism "displayed those traits at the same time, without compromise, in a knot of behavior patterns so tangled and matted as to be nearly inseparable." Furthermore, he utilized the idea of textual layering in order to analyze how these contrasting themes existed within the same religious tradition. Though one theological impulse served as the surface text and the other as a submerged text, the process of meaning-making depended upon the interplay of the two.[13]

This framework is especially helpful for understanding how contemporary purity culture is able to utilize a religion of fear without threatening the accessibility and optimism of new paradigm spirituality. Compared with Cold War threats of nuclear apocalypse, national insecurity, and sexual deviance, contemporary purity rhetoric emphasizes a therapeutic, sex-positive message of self-fulfillment and self-care. This is the primary narrative of today's purity culture, but it does not explain the persistence of a religion of fear that denotes sexual purity as a strategy for victory in a spiritualized battle between the ultimate forces of good and evil.

The sexual purity movement demonstrates the ability of evangelicals to utilize textual layering to maintain a complex, consistent, and historically grounded theological tradition. For the purity evangelists of the Silver Ring Thing, sex is great! But it also has the ability to destroy the entire human race. This seemingly discordant message makes sense only when contemporary purity culture is placed within a historical trajectory that marks its genesis in the fundamentalist resurgence of the 1940s, not the 1970s. By surfacing the subnarrative of sexual purity, historians are able to recognize the theological and historical continuity between evangelicalism's religion of fear and the religion of accommodation.

The moral absolutism of the purity movement cannot be conveyed without the construction of a moral economy that works alongside the larger cosmic battle between good and evil. The organization Silver Ring Thing provides a useful case for examining the collaboration of accommodation and fear within the purity movement. As one of the few organizations that presents its message to national and international audiences, SRT maintains a prominent position within the evangelical purity movement. At its live events, audiences encounter a sophisticated multimedia extravaganza that begins with irreverent and absurdist themes drawn from late-night television and ends with an invitation to eternal salvation. The arc of this spectacle reveals two distinctive narrative threads, one drawn from the religion of accommodation characteristic of new paradigm spirituality, and a second drawn from the religion of fear and the legacy of Cold War America.

The fundamentalist resurgence in the Cold War era succeeded in part because of its attention to adolescent culture. As a model for evangelical revival, Youth for Christ's practice of adapting popular cultural and media entertainment has continued among evangelical youth organizations. The resemblance, then, between Youth for Christ and the purity organization Silver Ring Thing is not surprising. Like YFC, Silver Ring Thing produces live shows across the country that entice youth away from secular entertainments by adapting popular media and technology for its own purposes. And like Youth for Christ, Silver Ring Thing is a delight to a culture of adolescents who strongly identify with popular culture and multimedia extravagance. An organization that proudly claims the label "culturally relevant," SRT uses its media and cultural resources as a strategic device to address the needs, desires, and identities of its adolescent audiences and ultimately gain their allegiance.

Audiences attending the Silver Ring Thing are introduced to a hybrid of popular and original media that portray the foolishness and dire consequences of premarital sexual behavior. As these earlier strategies succeed only by blurring sacred and secular meaning-systems, the organization must also employ media that portray a clear distinction between right and wrong, which in the rhetoric of the purity movement translates into pure and impure. Despite its initial acquiescence to popular culture and media consumption, the moral economy of sexual purity is not fully established until the organization has situated sexual purity into a larger theological narrative. As a series of progressively serious skits, videos, and testimonials lay out a spectrum of seemingly inevitable consequences, the themes of great sex and personal well-being are supplemented with the spiritualized language of sin and salvation. The performances and presentations move away from representations of parody and consumption, and the group slowly introduces themes with greater gravitational pull. The SRT live show demonstrates for its audiences a cosmological system in which the forces of good and evil are in an ever-present battle for the souls of adolescents.

Images of violence, war, and even nuclear apocalypse allow the group to reestablish the stakes in its moral economy. Sexual purity is not simply a personalized code of behavior, but an indicator of the collective moral temperature. Drawing upon theories of civilization's rise and decline, Denny Pattyn, founder of SRT, has commented in venues outside of the live performance that sexual impurity is a sign of national moral decay and, more significantly, is an indicator of pending apocalypse. Though it remains a covert element of SRT's official statement of belief, the group's public use of fear, violence, and nuclear war draw clear inferences to Cold War ideologies linking sexual immorality, national decline, and apocalyptic anticipation.

It's like Playing with a Nuclear Bomb

By their own admission, faith-based abstinence groups are ultimately concerned with the spiritual salvation of their charges. Much anxiety emerges from the fact that religious transformation is primarily a personal and internal process—one that is often not easily detected by another unless revealed explicitly. To address this challenge, many religious groups have adopted some form of bodily expression of this internal transformation. For the weight-loss evangelist Gwen Shamblin, a sign of spiritual transformation is a slim body that is marked as holy and pleasing to God.[14] For Denny Pattyn, the founder and director of Silver Ring Thing, a spiritually correct course is outwardly expressed in a sexually pure and disease-free body that is adorned with a silver ring.

Despite its efficacy, the necessary tension between engagement with popular culture and the distinctiveness of sexual purity threatens to dismantle the tightly constructed boundaries that help one establish an assurance of personal salvation. The permissive orientation toward popular culture that characterizes the early portion of the group's presentation plays a strategic role in the identity construction of SRT audiences. But once SRT has established a shared social identification with the audience, the boundaries must be restored in order for SRT's moral economy to take full shape. To compensate for this initial boundary transgression, the group must find ways to reestablish the distinctions between good and evil in such a way that adolescents are able to distinguish between other dichotomous themes—most significantly, between pure and impure. As a result, much of the media utilized during the final hour of the SRT presentation draw upon both humorous and serious conflict narratives. This allows the viewer to easily recognize the forces that battle for their allegiance.

Many forms of popular comedy make use of fictive and hyperbolic forms of violence, a trope that SRT has no problem replicating in its own original media. As such, SRT's use of violence and conflict narratives is presented in varying degrees of levity and severity. One series of videos, entitled *Laws of the Father*, narrated by a stern father figure (the voice belonging to none other than SRT's Denny Pattyn, a parent to three daughters) is presented intermittently throughout the live performance. In this series, the voice of the father speaks directly to his daughter's love interest, feigning threats of violence for comic effect. In one instance, the voice threatens, "I have a shotgun, a shovel, and five acres behind my house" in which to bury the body of the young man. In another, the father threatens to remove the eyes and hands of his daughter's date, later stating, "If you make my little girl cry, I will make you cry." Though in jest, this series positions the father as the guardian of his daughter's virtue and future happiness. The father's opinion of the young man never considers the daughter's view of her date, only that the young man is in a position to emotionally wound the daughter and that she is in need of her father's protection. The last installment of this series reveals that the father is a veteran of the Vietnam War, unable to distinguish the sound of the young man's car from military helicopters, thus inciting flashbacks and violent tendencies.[15]

In this video sequence the gender assignments come into clear relief and fit squarely into a conflict narrative that heightens audience awareness of the firm boundaries that guard purity against impurity. In this case, that boundary is guarded by a semicrazed, overprotective father who patrols his daughter's purity like a soldier on alert for enemy invaders. The need for protection is made all the more clear in the use of gender stereotypes that cast young men as voracious sexual predators and young women as sexually disinterested, vulnerable, and in need of protection.

While this particular narrative conforms to long-standing tropes of paternal control, male aggression, and female vulnerability, more often, it is adolescents as an entire group who are cast as sexually vulnerable. Silver Ring Thing insists upon portraying mainstream popular media as predators that prey upon vulnerable adolescents, both male and female, not yet mature enough to recognize the danger of attachment to material desire. SRT responds by helping teenagers to recognize sexual temptation as the work of Satan. For young men, temptation is physical and sexual desire is aroused by sight. Thus, young women are given stern warnings regarding their dress. "Don't advertise what you aren't selling," they are told. At the same moment, boys are cautioned about the ways in which they touch girls, whose romantic desires are aroused by even the most harmless of physical encounters—the example provided is a friendly high-five exchanged in a school hallway. While the source and type of desire conform to the kind of gender stereotypes that conservative evangelicals believe are both biological and God-given, the severity and solution for both is the same. While sexual impurity is mired in the confusion of gender roles and sexual desire, the path to sexual purity is a universal track that remains constant regardless of the sex of its seeker.

Gender essentialism, the notion that males and females are defined primarily by their biological instincts, is axiomatic within evangelical understandings of adolescent sexual desire. The sexual aggressiveness of boys and the sexual vulnerability of girls is normative and natural, a formulation that critics suggest demonstrates the commonalities between evangelical purity culture and a culture that perpetuates sexual assault, misogyny, and human trafficking.[16] Of course, the mandates of sexual purity require that these natural states of existence be transcended. It is these natural, God-given inclinations that attract the opposite sexes to one another, but those proclivities cannot be fully indulged outside of marriage.

Feminist criticism of the purity movement contends that its use of sexual/gender stereotypes is an outgrowth of conservative evangelicalism's animosity toward feminism and its inability to address the real concerns of girls and women.[17] But the historical trajectory of sexual purity indicates a more complex relationship with feminism than secular feminist critique would allow. Recall that the earliest purity movement was rooted in Victorian gender ideologies that also rested on the assumptions of men's and women's respective sexual aggression and disinterest. Those women social reformers used gender essentialism to assert their moral authority over men, whose baser instincts required a civilizing, feminine influence. Without this perceived advantage, nineteenth-century women had little leverage for their own claims to increased political, social, and religious involvement.

American purity culture emerged from the first wave of American feminism; thus, it comes as no surprise that female advocates for purity employ the language of female empowerment and personal choice. As explained in chapter four, the accommodation of feminist language by evangelicals is part of the 1970s counterculture's larger influence on evangelicalism. New paradigm spirituality's emphasis on individual well-being and personal transformation assumes that women's quest for these goals are equally as important as men's. Christine Gardner's analysis of one purity event led her to conclude that it is young women, not young men, who benefit the most from sexual purity. As in the nineteenth century, today's sexually pure young women are in a position of power over men's sexuality by maintaining their own moral and bodily conduct.[18] Sexual purity is a choice for female empowerment, but only within the construct of gender essentialism, where women's only option for bodily integrity is in not being sexually active and in taking responsibility for men's sexual purity. As a countercultural movement, sexual purity is only workable, then, within the gender ideology from which it emerged: that of nineteenth-century Victorian America.

However, gender is not the only construct that shapes the narrative of sexual purity. The purity seeker is a universal figure caught up in a spiritualized battle against the ultimate evil. Only supernatural assistance in the person of Jesus Christ can adequately defend a young person against sexual impurity. The moral economy of sexual purity is organized not primarily by sex/gender distinctions, but on the basis of an all-out war between the temptations of fleeting material satisfactions and the eternal reward of spiritual salvation. Rooted in this theological framework of sin and salvation, SRT's conflict-based media materials easily fit into a narrative of spiritual warfare, a genre of story that frequently places both the individual and the collective at mortal risk.

At its conclusion, the SRT live event must convince the young audience that the choice to remain sexually abstinent until marriage is paramount to one's spiritual well-being. However, that decision has implications far beyond personal spirituality and morality. A heavy reliance upon literal themes and images of violence and nuclear war easily pique the apocalyptic imagination of anyone already inclined toward millennialist theologies concerned with the return of Christ and the destruction of the material world. Though not readily apparent to the uninitiated, the overlapping interests between evangelical purity culture and rapture culture become increasingly evident. SRT's use of spiritualized conflict narratives that feature violence assert a weighty meaning: the sexual status of the adolescent population holds apocalyptic implications.

Connections between sexual immorality and millennialist theologies play a central role in the personal theology of SRT's founder and executive director. Though Denny Pattyn didn't assert a precedent for his own ideas during the course of my interview with him in 2006, his views represent the very theological systems and historical trajectories that found their expression in the crucible of the Cold War. According to Pattyn, human history has been controlled by twenty-one great civilizations, all of which have experienced strikingly similar stages of rise and decline. The penultimate stage of decline just preceding removal from power is moral decay, a category often construed in sexual terms.[19]

In an aside during our conversation, Pattyn articulated his belief that the United States is the twenty-second great civilization and is currently experiencing moral decay due to the nation's government-sanctioned moral relativism. As a result, Pattyn's descriptions of terrorism and nuclear war are fraught with biblical apocalypticism: he believes that Christ's return is imminent. "Do I believe that is true personally? Yes, I do. Do I think that I might see the end of the world in my lifetime? I absolutely do think that." The next great battle, he concludes, will be the last.

Because of evangelicalism's traditionally populist orientation, purity leaders like Pattyn are rarely required to establish theological or intellectual reference points for their own ideas. Pattyn insists that his end-times theology has little relationship to his purity work and emphasizes the physical, emotional, and spiritual benefits of sexual purity in the individual lives of adolescents. His primary concern is the personal salvation and sexual health of his audiences. His gospel message, which immediately precedes a revival-like opportunity for audience members to make a commitment to Christ and to sexual purity, focuses on biblical narratives used to point out the dangers of safe sex. Using the therapeutic language of self-protection and spiritual growth, SRT crafts a message that uses emotional conflict and relational distress as the primary narrative in lieu of the nationalistic and millennialist claims of earlier purity advocates. However, the moral economy presented to SRT audiences is not entirely dependent upon the optimistic, good feelings of new paradigm spirituality. Rather, it indicates the remnants of a more established rhetoric of sexual fear that relies upon older tropes of sexual and national risk.

"Mixed-Message Mum" is a video presentation produced by Silver Ring Thing that demonstrates how contemporary sexual purity rhetoric remains informed by Cold War fundamentalism. It draws the strongest inferences to apocalyptic and nationalistic themes by way of challenging maternal moral authority. The presentation portrays the well-intentioned mothers who believe in the efficacy of safe-sex teachings and condoms as naïve and foolhardy. This original song and video presentation narrates the story of a permissive mother who blithely responds to each of her son's dangerous plans with the same words: "Be sure and use protection." Throughout the song, the young boy of seven or eight years is permitted to engage in several dangerous and morally suspect activities. After receiving permission from his mother, the boy, with safety goggles firmly in place, attempts to construct a shelter "for illegal aliens." He next appears with blood spurting from a severed limb. He then announces that he is "creating a fire for the gods" and again is encouraged to "be sure and use protection!" Shortly after, he is engulfed in flames. As part of a video presentation created and presented by an international sexual purity organization, "Mixed-Message Mum" demonstrates the folly of safe-sex teachings that endorse condom use. Silver Ring Thing takes to task the promise that condom usage equals safety; instead, the organization portrays barrier methods of birth control as luring the sexually innocent into dangerous behaviors. But, the message goes beyond the personalized threat of sexually transmitted diseases or unwanted pregnancy and is recast into a collective or nationalized threat. The young boy is no longer signifying only sexual innocence but represents national innocence, with religious sacrilege and illegal aliens posing equal threats to national security and eternal salvation. The last verse of the Mum's song raises the stakes even higher by drawing on the global threat of nuclear war. After the mother permits her son to build a nuclear weapon, the bomb explodes and the video depicts real, graphic images of land, buildings, and people turning to dust and crumbling in submission. These images are accompanied by the lyrics "The world says use a condom / If we told you you'd be fine, we'd be lying to your face / It's like playing with a nuclear bomb / You could wipe out the whole human race."[20]

The hyperbolic and humorous language of this song indicates a metaphorical message that supports its position in the new paradigm. However, it is also the final investment in the moral economy that places the demarcation between pure and impure within the theater of spiritual warfare. Sexual immorality leads to the emotional and spiritual apocalypse of the individual, a fate that separates the believer from God, casting one into emotional desolation and threatening one's personal salvation. For adolescent audience members, individualized fears of relational hardship and eternal damnation shape the final moments of the live performance just prior to an invitation to "get right with God" and make a pledge of sexual abstinence.

This final refrain reveals a mapping sequence in which purity culture and rapture culture are shown to share a similar terrain. Audience members who are invested in at least one of these expressions of the evangelical subculture are given a theological formulation that allows them to map their apocalyptic beliefs onto sexual purity, or to imbue their commitment to sexual purity with apocalyptic significance. Either way, this mapping performs the kind of "truth-making" exercise that other scholars have found to be characteristic of rapture culture.[21] Direct references to end-times theology, rapture, or tribulation are absent from the live performance and the group's formal statement of faith. The purity culture of contemporary evangelicalism, like its predecessors, attends to widespread cultural anxieties. Unlike its predecessors, however, it provides answers that are most relevant to the individual's quest for personal fulfillment and security. But, because the moral economy of the contemporary movement is arranged in order to demonstrate the correlation between an individual's sexual immorality and the collective well-being, the distinctions between purity culture and rapture culture become less indiscernible.

Sexual Purity and American Apocalypse

Contemporary sexual purity groups, as impactful as they have been, are the beneficiaries, not the progenitors, of a moral economy that links the purity and rapture camps of Protestant evangelicalism. Most notably, the discourse of sexual fear that pervaded the Cold War era established a seemingly natural link between sexual deviance and national instability. Fundamentalist leaders such as Billy Graham lauded the government's decision to expunge homosexuals from federal offices because of their presumed susceptibility to blackmail.[22] Graham's endorsement was not a lark, but an early contribution to a uniquely twentieth-century millennialist theology rooted in newfound sexual fears.

Over several decades, evangelical and fundamentalist leaders such as Graham, Carl F. H. Henry, Francis Schaeffer, and James Dobson wove together theories of civilizations' rise and decline with a rhetoric of sexual fear that asserted a divinely designed connection between sexual immorality, national decline, and apocalyptic anticipation. As a foundational rhetoric that underscored much of popular evangelicalism, sexual fear provided the ideal opening for a sexual purity movement to emerge and mark adolescent sexuality as a venue rife with opportunity for personal transformation, national revitalization, and, quite possibly, the salvation of civilization.

Though seemingly far from a church sanctuary populated with ogling adolescents and images of scantily clad reality-show contestants, apocalyptic anticipation underscores the evangelical purity culture, providing believers with a cohesive strategy for procuring individual and collective salvation. In the moral economy of sexual purity, the rapture of sexual ecstasy is only offered to those who wait for divine beneficence. Waiting is the mantra of purity seekers, who believe they are participating in a divine design, one that mirrors the more significant narrow pathway toward the rapture of human-divine union. In millennialist theologies, the promise of rapture is never without the threat of destruction, an axiom that abstinence organizations have expertly mapped onto the adolescent experience. Consequently, the moral economy of sexual purity is doubly charged with individual and collective implications. The evangelical purity culture not only cultivates the spiritual formation of adolescents; it also elevates this experience to exemplify the universal quest of all Christian believers. Thus, young people who pledge themselves to sexual purity are tasked with far more than saving themselves for a future spouse. In the moral economy of sexual purity, these adolescents are the salvation of American civilization.

Notes

INTRODUCTION

1. For this argument, see Stephen J. Whitfield, *The Culture of the Cold War* (Baltimore: John Hopkins University Press, 1991); Fred Fejes, *Gay Rights and Moral Panic: The Origins of America's Debate on Homosexuality* (New York: Palgrave Macmillan, 2011); Tina Fetner, *How the Religious Right Shaped Gay and Lesbian Activism* (Minneapolis: University of Minnesota Press, 2008).

2. Heather Rachelle White, "Virgin Pride: Born Again Faith and Sexual Identity in the Faith-Based Abstinence Movement." In *Ashgate Research Companion to Contemporary Religion and Sexuality*, edited by Stephen J. Hunt and Andrew Yip (Farnham, UK: Ashgate, 2012), 243.

3. Christine Gardner, *Making Chastity Sexy: The Rhetoric of Evangelical Chastity Campaigns* (Berkeley: University of California Press, 2011); Donna Freitas, *Sex and the Soul: Juggling Sexuality, Spirituality, Romance, and Religion on America's College Campuses* (New York: Oxford University Press, 2008); Mark Regnerus, *Forbidden Fruit: Sex and Religion in the Lives of American Teenagers* (New York: Oxford University Press, 2007); Peter Bearman and Hannah S. Brückner, "Promising the Future: Virginity Pledges and First Intercourse," *American Journal of Sociology* 106, no. 4 (2001): 859–912; Peter Bearman and Hannah S. Brückner, "After the Promise: The STD Consequences of Adolescent Virginity Pledges," *Journal of Adolescent Health* 36, no. 4 (2005): 271–278.

4. David Pivar, *Purity Crusade: Sexual Morality and Social Control, 1868–1900* (Westport, CT: Greenwood, 1973).

5. Though historians of adolescence indicate that he was not the first to address a life stage in between childhood and adulthood, Hall's work introduced the terminology and the definition into common usage beyond the psychological laboratories and professional journals of his academic field.

6. Heather Hendershot, *Shaking the World for Jesus: Media and Conservative Evangelical Culture* (Chicago: University of Chicago Press, 2004). Hendershot's study of True Love Waits and the literature that accompanies the movement is especially helpful for understanding how purity culture is heavily indebted to secular therapeutic and psychological discourses.

7. Amy Kaplan, "Manifest Domesticity," *American Literature* 70, no. 3 (1998): 582, 586, 592.

8. See Pivar, *Purity Crusade*, and his *Purity and Hygiene: Women, Prostitution, and the "American Plan," 1900–1930* (Westport, CT: Greenwood, 2002); Alan Hunt, *Governing Morals: A Social History of Moral Regulation* (Cambridge, UK: Cambridge University Press: 1999); Beryl Satter, *Each Mind a Kingdom: American Women, Sexual Purity, and the New Thought Movement, 1975–1920* (Berkeley: University of California Press, 1999).

9. Billy Graham, *World Aflame* (New York: Doubleday, 1965), 20; Tina Fetner, *How the Religious Right Shaped Gay and Lesbian Activism* (Minneapolis: Univesity of Minnesotta Press, 2008), 7.

10. Stephen J. Whitfield, *The Culture of the Cold War* (Baltimore: John Hopkins University Press, 1991), 45.

11. Jason Bivins, *Religion of Fear: The Politics of Horror in Conservative Evangelicalism* (New York: Oxford University Press, 2008).

12. See Angela Lahr, *Millennial Dreams and Apocalyptic Nightmares: The Cold War Origins of Political Evangelicalism* (New York: Oxford University Press, 2007).

13. Socially conservative evangelicals and neofundamentalism are situated closely, though not exactly at the same point, on the cultural and theological spectrum of American Protestantism. This project is not necessarily concerned with the various distinctions, as evangelicals of all stripes are part of the evangelical purity culture.

14. See David Harrington Watt, "The Private Hopes of American Fundamentalists and Evangelicals, 1925–1975," *Religion and American Culture: A Journal of Interpretation* 1, no. 2 (1991): 155–175.

15. Donald E. Miller, *Reinventing American Protestantism: Christianity in the New Millennium* (Berkeley: University of California Press, 1999.)

16. Darren Dochuk, *From Bible Belt to Sun Belt: Plain-Folk Religion, Grassroots Politics, and the Rise of Evangelical Conservatism* (New York: W. W. Norton, 2011); Randall Stephens and Karl W. Giberson, *The Anointed: Evangelical Truth in a Secular Age* (Cambridge, MA: Belknap Press of Harvard University Press, 2011); Daniel K. Williams, *God's Own Party: The Making of the Christian Right* (New York: Oxford University Press, 2010); Seth Dowland, "'Family Values' and the Formation of a Christian Right Agenda," *Church History* 78, no. 3 (2009): 606–631; George M. Marsden, *Fundamentalism and American Culture*, 2nd ed. (New York: Oxford University Press, 2006); Lisa McGirr, *Suburban Warriors: The Origins of the New American Right* (Princeton, NJ: Princeton

University Press, 2001); Susan Harding, *The Book of Jerry Falwell: Fundamentalist Language and Politics* (Princeton, NJ: Princeton University Press, 2000); Margaret Lamberts Bendroth, *Fundamentalism and Gender: 1875–Present* (New Haven, CT: Yale University Press, 1996); Michael Lienesch, *Redeeming America: Politics and Piety in the New Christian Right* (Chapel Hill: University of North Carolina Press, 1993).

17. Lynn Gerber, *Seeking the Straight and Narrow: Weight Loss and Sexual Reorientation in Evangelical America* (Chicago: University of Chicago Press, 2011), 6–7.

18. The group has edited its performance content over the years, though, when I first started attending, shows were often concluded at the three-hour mark.

CHAPTER 1

1. Marie Griffin, *Born Again Bodies: Flesh and Spirit in American Christianity* (Berkeley: University of California Press, 2004), 4.

2. Sue Morgan, "'Wild Oats or Acorns?': Social Purity, Sexual Politics, and the Response of the Late-Victorian Church," *Journal of Religious History* 31, no. 2 (2007): 151–168; Sue Morgan, "'Knights of God': Ellice Hopkins and the White Cross Army, 1883–95," in *Gender and Christian Religion*, edited by R. N. Swanson. Studies in Church History 34 (Suffolk: Ecclesiastical History Society and Boydell Press, 1998); John D'Emilio and Estelle Freedman, *Intimate Matters: A History of Sexuality in America* (Chicago: University of Chicago Press, 1988), 153–156 and illustration 39; David Pivar, *Purity Crusade: Sexual Morality and Social Control, 1868–1900* (Westport, CT: Greenwood Press, 1973), 110–117; Frances E. Willard, "Social Purity Work for 1887," *Union Signal* 13 (January 1887): 12.

3. Julia Ward Howe, "Moral Equality between the Sexes," and Reverend J. B. Welty, "The Need for White Cross Work," both in *The National Purity Congress: Its Papers, Addresses, Portraits* (New York: American Purity Alliance, 1896), 66–71 and 240–249; Frances Willard, *Glimpses of Fifty Years: The Autobiography of an American Woman* (Toronto: Rose Publishing, 1898), PDF e-book.

4. Pivar, *Purity Crusade*, 157–158.

5. Louise Michele Newman, *White Women's Rights: The Racial Origins of Feminism in the United States* (New York: Oxford University Press, 1999), 7–8; Amy Kaplan, "Manifest Domesticity," *American Literature* 70, no. 3 (1998): 581; Brian Donovan, *White Slave Crusaders: Race, Gender, and Anti-Vice Activism, 1887–1917* (Chicago: University of Illinois Press, 2006), 18, 37, 46; Peggy Pascoe, *Relations of Rescue: The Search for Female Moral Authority in the American West, 1874–1939* (New York: Oxford University Press, 1990), 55–58, 68.

6. Newman, *White Women's Rights*, 34; Donovan, *White Slave Crusaders*, 46; Pascoe, *Relations of Rescue*, 32–36.

7. Jennifer Pierce Burek, "What Young Readers Ought to Know: The Successful Selling of Sexual Health Texts in the Early Twentieth Century," *Book History* 14(2011): 110–136.

8. G. Stanley Hall, *Adolescence: Its Psychology and Its Relations to Physiology, Anthropology, Sociology, Sex, Crime, Religion, and Education* (New York: D. Appleton, 1904), xii–xviii, 304, 648–749. See also "The Awkward Age," *Appleton's Magazine* 12 (August 1908): 149–156; "From Generation to Generation: With Some Plain Language about Race Suicide and the Instruction of Children during Adolescence," *American Magazine* 66 (July): 248–254. "Education in Sex Hygiene" *Eugenic Review* 1 (January 1910): 242–253.

9. Willard, *Glimpses*, 418.

10. Thekla Ellen Joiner, *Sin in the City: Chicago and Revivalism, 1880–1920* (Columbia: Missouri University Press, 2007) 71; Newman, *White Women's Rights*, 7–8; Kaplan, "Manifest Domesticity," 567. See also Beryl Satter, *Each Mind a Kingdom: American Women, Sexual Purity, and the New Thought Movement, 1875–1920* (Berkeley: University of California Press,1999) and Barbara Leslie Epstein, *The Politics of Domesticity: Women, Evangelism, and Temperance in Nineteenth-Century America* (Middleton, CT: Wesleyan University Press, 1986).

11. Elizabeth Blackwell, "Cruelty and Lust—Appeal to Women," *Philanthropist* 6, no. 12 (December 1891): 1–2.

12. Willard, *Glimpses*, 426.

13. Elizabeth Powell Bond, "The Sacredness of Motherhood," *Philanthropist* 1, no. 7 (July 1886): 1–2.

14. J. W. Richardson, "The Ideal Woman," *Philanthropist* (ca. 1893); Grace A. Dodge, "A Portion of a Confidential Letter to Girls," *Philanthropist* 3, no. 7 (July 1889): 1–3.

15. "The Responsibilities of Men," *Philanthropist* 1, no. 5 (May 1886): 4.

16. Hall, *Adolescence*, 493.

17. The shift from sexual purity to sexual hygiene parallels the shift in the locus of morality at the end of the nineteenth century. As scientific and medical advances provided more compelling explanations for physical and psychological degeneration, medicine, not religion, became the primary arbiter of morality. See Heidi Rimke and Alan Hunt, "From Sinners to Degenerates: The Medicalization of Morality in the Nineteenth Century," *History of Human Sciences* 15, no. 1 (2002): 59.

18. Tony Ladd and James A. Mathisen, *Muscular Christianity: Evangelical Protestants and the Development of American Sport* (Grand Rapids, MI: Baker Book House, 1999); Chad Alan Gregory, "Revivalism, Fundamentalism, and Masculinity in the United States, 1880–1930" (PhD diss., University of Kentucky,

1999), 49–50; Clifford Putney, *Muscular Christianity: Manhood and Sports in Protestant America, 1880–1920* (Cambridge, MA: Harvard University Press, 2001), 12.

19. Gail Bederman, *Manliness and Civilization: A Cultural History of Gender and Race in the United States, 1880–1917* (Chicago: University of Chicago Press, 1995), 79.

20. Putney, *Muscular Christianity*, 3–6.

21. Putney, *Muscular Christianity*; Ladd and Mathisen, *Muscular Christianity*, 33–41.

22. Ladd and Mathisen, *Muscular Christianity*, 33–41.

23. Ladd and Mathisen, *Muscular Christianity*, 33–41.

24. Joiner, *Sin in the City*, 82.

25. Joiner, *Sin in the City*, 89.

26. Joiner, *Sin in the City*, 55, 57; Margaret Lamberts Bendroth, *Gender and Fundamentalism: 1875–Present* (New Haven, CT: Yale University Press, 1996), 20, 26, 29; Ruth Bordin, *Frances Willard: A Biography* (Chapel Hill: University of North Carolina Press, 1987), 88.

27. Willard, *Glimpses*, 426.

28. Willard, *Glimpses*, 420.

29. Morgan, "Knights of God," 434, 436, 439.

30. Willard, *Glimpses*, 429.

31. "The Triumph of Manhood," *Philanthropist* 6, no. 6 (June 1892): 1–3.

32. Joseph F. Flint, "The Science of Domestic Happiness," *Philanthropist* 6, no. 7 (July 1892): 1–2.

33. "The Triumph of Manhood."

34. "The Triumph of Manhood."

35. Stephen Prothero, "Manly Redeemer," chap. 3 in *American Jesus: How the Son of God Became a National Icon* (New York: Farrar, Straus & Giroux, 2003).

36. Joseph F. Flint, "Social Purity Code," *Philanthropist* 5, no. 7 (July, 1891): 3.

37. "The Triumph of Manhood."

38. Flint, "Science of Domestic Happiness."

39. "The Triumph of Manhood."

40. Kaplan, "Manifest Domesticity," 567, 582, 586, 592.

41. Frances Willard, "A White Life for Two," *Philanthropist* 5, no. 7 (July 1890): 1–3.

42. Morgan, "Wild Oats or Acorns," 445.

43. Emily Blackwell, "The Responsibilities of Women in Regard to Questions Concerning Public Morality," *The National Purity Congress: Its Papers, Addresses, Portraits* (New York: American Purity Alliance, 1896), 73.

44. "The Responsibilities of Men."

45. Willard, "A White Life for Two"; Ward Howe, "Moral Equality between the Sexes"; Welty, "The Need for White Cross Work."

46. Susan B. Anthony, "Social Purity" (1875), PBS, http://www.pbs.org/stantonanthony/resources/index.html?body=social_purity.html.

47. Dodge, "A Portion of a Confidential Letter to Girls."

48. According to a footnote in the publication, this article was written anonymously by "a devoted Christian woman of Cincinnati, of large experience among the unfortunate." Her anonymity suggests that the author herself had been victimized by the dangers she described. "An Earnest Appeal to Young Women," *Philanthropist* 6, no. 1 (January 1891): 1–3.

49. Mrs. Ballington Booth, *Chicago Tribune*, June 25, 1893, quoted in Joiner, *Sin in the City*, 72.

50. Morgan, "Wild Oats or Acorns" (2007), and Rev. J. P. Gledstone, "Message to Young Men—Wild Oats," *Philanthropist* 8, no. 2 (February 1894): 1–3.

51. Gledstone, "Message to Young Men—Wild Oats."

52. Willard, *Glimpses*, 418.

53. Willard, "Social Purity Work for 1887," *Union Signal* (January 13, 1887): 12.

54. Aaron Macy Powell, "Moral Elevation of Women," *Philanthropist* 1, no. 2 (February 1886): 5–6.

55. Robert A. Woods and Albert J. Kennedy, "The Morality of Sex," chap. 7 in *Young Working Girls: A Summary of Evidence from Two Thousand Social Workers* (Boston: Houghton Mifflin, 1913), 84–100.

56. Richardson, "The Ideal Woman."

57. Reverend Anna Garlin Spencer, "The Care of the Prostitute," *Philanthropist* 6, no. 8 (August 1891): 2.

58. Willard, *Glimpses*, 418.

59. Paul S. Boyer, *Purity in Print: Book Censorship in American from the Gilded Age to the Computer Age*, 2nd ed. (Madison: University of Wisconsin Press, 2002), 17.

60. Willard, *Glimpses*, 420.

61. Leigh Eric Schmidt, "The Easter Parade: Piety, Fashion, and Display," in *Religion and American Culture*, ed. David Hackett (New York: Routledge, 2003), 245–269.

62. Colleen McDannell, *Material Christianity: Religion and Popular Culture in America* (New Haven, CT: Yale University Press, 1995), 89; Paul Gutjahr, *An American Bible: A History of the Good Book in the United States, 1777–1880* (Stanford, CA: Stanford University Press, 1999), 36. Peter J. Wosh, *Spreading the Word: The Bible Business in Nineteenth-Century America* (Ithaca, NY: Cornell University Press, 1994), 19–20.

63. Gail Bederman, "'The Women Have Had Charge of the Church Work Long Enough': The Men and Religion Forward Movement of 1911–1912 and the Masculinization of Middle-Class Protestantism," in *A Mighty Baptism: Race, Gender, and the Creation of American Protestantism*, ed. Susan Juster and Lisa MacFarlane (Ithaca, NY: Cornell University Press, 1996), 112; Joiner, *Sin in the City*, 9.

64. Benjamin F. DeCosta, "The Capitalists of Vice," *Philanthropist* 7, no. 6 (June 1892): 6.
65. Kate C. Bushnell, "The White Cross and White Shield," *Philanthropist* 2, no. 11 (November 1888): 1–2, 6.
66. Bushnell, "The White Cross and White Shield."
67. Many were inspired by William T. Stead, a British journalist who entered the London red-light district posing as a pimp in order to collect evidence for his story "The Maiden Voyage of Modern Babylon," which detailed the exploitation of young women in the London sex trade. Donovan, *White Slave Crusaders*, 39–43; Pascoe, *Relations of Rescue*, 32–72.
68. Pascoe, *Relations of Rescue*, 55.
69. Pascoe, *Relations of Rescue*, 58.
70. Pascoe, *Relations of Rescue*, 68.
71. Mary L. Sawyer, *American Missionary* 36, no. 1 (January 1881): 10. At the annual meeting a year prior, the same topic was addressed by a Mary E. Sawyer of the Talladega School. However, Mary L. Sawyer of Boxford, Massachusetts, appears on the Talladega instructors' roster in 1879, suggesting that these individuals were the same person.
72. Mary E. Sawyer, "Woman's Work for Woman," *American Missionary* 35, no. 1 (January 1882): 9–10.
73. Laura A. Parmelee, "Woman's Work for Woman," *American Missionary* 34 no. 1 (January 1880): 12.
74. "The Legacy of Slavery," *Philanthropist* 2, no. 2 (February 1888): 1; "The Immoral Legacy of Slavery," *Philanthropist* 5, no. 4 (April 1891): 1.
75. Parmelee, "Woman's Work for Woman," 14.
76. Sawyer, "Woman's Work for Woman," 52.
77. "Colored Men on the Moral Status of the Colored Race," *Philanthropist* 2, no. 10 (October 1888): 3.
78. One example of this problematic correlation occurred when purity reformer Aaron Macy Powell hailed William Stead, the journalist whose unconventional reporting uncovered the extent of prostitution in London, as the John Brown of white slavery. Like Brown, Stead was a brave force whose rash behavior offered new hope for the "emancipation of an enslaved race." See Powell's article about Stead in *Philanthropist* 1, no. 1 (January 1886): 1–3.
79. "Colored Men."
80. Fannie B. Williams, "Religious Duty to the Negro," in *The World's Congress of Religion; the Addresses and Papers Delivered before the Parliament and an Abstract of the Congresses held in the Art Institute Chicago, Illinois, USA, August 25 to October 15, 1893 under the Auspices of the World's Columbian Exposition*, ed. J. W. Hanson, quoted in Joiner, *Sin in the City*, 78.
81. Newman, *White Women's Rights*.
82. Newman, *White Women's Rights*, 9

83. See Heidi Rimke and Alan Hunt, "From Sinners to Degenerates: The Medicalization of Morality in the Nineteenth Century," *History of Human Sciences* 15, no. 1 (2002): 59–88.

84. Beryl Satter, *American Women, Sexual Purity, and the New Thought Movement, 1875–1920* (Berkeley: University of California Press, 1999), 10–13, 48.

85. Newman, *White Women's Rights*, 34.

86. John C. Burnham, "The Progressive Era Revolution in American Attitudes toward Sex," *Journal of American History* 59, no. 4 (March 1973), 900.

87. "Education in Sex Hygiene," 243.

88. "Eduation in Sex Hygiene," 253.

89. "Education in Sex Hygiene," 253.

90. Newman, *White Women's Rights*, 34

91. Sabine gave at least three versions of a talk entitled "Social Vice and National Decay," two of which were reprinted in the *Philanthropist* and another that appeared in *The National Purity Congress: Its Papers, Addresses, Portraits*, 41–56.

92. Sabine, "Social Vice and National Decay," 42.

93. Joseph Cook, quoted in Sabine, "Social Vice and National Decay."

94. Joseph Cook, quoted in Sabine, "Social Vice and National Decay."

95. Donovan, *White Slave Crusaders*, 45–46.

96. Willard, *Glimpses*, 418.

97. The foreshadowing of the eugenics movement is evident. Given the scope of this topic and its decreasing relevance to religiously based sexual purity work and rhetoric, I leave the topic to other scholars.

98. Hall, *Adolescence*, xii–xviii, 304, 648–749. See also "The Awkward Age," *Appleton's Magazine* 12 (August 1908): 149–156; "From Generation to Generation: With Some Plain Language about Race Suicide and the Instruction of Children during Adolescence," *American Magazine* 66 (July 1908): 248–254; "Education in Sex Hygiene," 242–253.

99. See Hall, "The Adolescent Psychology of Conversion," in *Adolescence*. This follows traditional interpretations of the Edenic myth, in which Eve and Adam become aware of their sinfulness only after acknowledging their nakedness.

100. George Coe, quoted in Hall, *Adolescence*, 291.

101. See George M. Marsden, *Jonathan Edwards: A Life* (New Haven, CT: Yale University Press, 2003), and Frank Lambert, *Inventing the "Great Awakening"* (Princeton, NJ: Princeton University Press, 2001).

102. Hall, *Adolescence*, xv.

103. Hall, *Adolescence*, xv; Dorothy Ross, *G. Stanley Hall: The Psychologist as Prophet* (Chicago: University of Chicago Press, 1972), 326.

104. Bederman, *Manliness and Civilization*, 103.

CHAPTER 2

1. Matthew Avery Sutton, *American Apocalypse: A History of Modern Evangelicalism* (Cambridge: Belknap Press, 2014), xii.

2. During the early twentieth century, the labels *adolescent, teenager,* and *young adult* were often used interchangeably. See Elizabeth Ellen Young Barstow, "'These Teenagers Are Not Delinquent': The Rhetoric of Maturity for Evangelical Young-Adults" (PhD diss., Harvard University, 2010).

3. Bruce Shelley, "The Rise of Evangelical Youth Movements," *Fides et Historia* 18, no. 1 (1986): 60.

4. John D'Emilio and Estelle Freedman, *Intimate Matters: A History of Sexuality in America* (Chicago: University of Chicago Press, 1997), 223.

5. "Wanted: A Miracle of Good Weather and the 'Youth for Christ' Rally Got It," *Newsweek* (June 11, 1945), Wheaton College, http://www2.wheaton.edu/bgc/archives/exhibits/YFC%201945/07%20coverage%2009.html.

6. "Wanted: A Miracle of Good Weather and the 'Youth for Christ' Rally Got It."

7. "Program for the Victory Youth Rally Held at Chicago Stadium on October 21, 1944," Wheaton College, http://www2.wheaton.edu/bgc/archives/exhibits/YFC%201945/02%20background%2004.html.

8. Charles Neville, *Saturday Home Magazine*, August 18, 1945, quoted in Bruce L. Shelley, "The Young and the Zealous," *Christianity Today* (October 1, 2006), http://www.christianitytoday.com/ch/2006/issue92/4.20.html.

9. "Copies of the Texts of Telegrams from Newspaper Publisher William Randolph Hearst to his Newspaper Editors around the Country," Wheaton College, http://www2.wheaton.edu/bgc/archives/exhibits/YFC%201945/07%20coverage%2008.htmlBGA.

10. "Pamphlet Advertising YFC Saturday Night Meetings at Orchestra Hall," Wheaton College, http://www2.wheaton.edu/bgc/archives/exhibits/YFC%201945/02%20background%2007.html.

11. According to Eliza Young Barstow, in the postwar era, evangelicals strongly encouraged teenagers to date as preparation for marriage. Barstow, "These Teenagers Are Not Delinquent," 81. Organizations like YFC became popular because of the increased opportunities for finding a suitable marriage partner.

12. Candy Gunther Brown, *The Word in the World: Evangelical Writing, Publishing and Reading in America, 1789–1990* (Chapel Hill: University of North Carolina Press, 2004); Jeanne Halgren Kilde, *When Church Became Theatre: The Transformation of Evangelical Architecture and Worship in Nineteenth-Century America* (Oxford: Oxford University Press, 2002).

13. Carpenter, *Revive Us Again*, 169.

14. Torrey Johnson, Youth for Christ International, "Minutes of the First Annual Convention, 22–29, July 1945," 30, quoted in Carpenter, *Revive Us Again*, 168.

15. "Program for the Victory Youth Rally Held at Chicago Stadium on October 21, 1944."

16. "Reverend John Evans, *Chicago Tribune*, May 31, 1945," Wheaton College, http://www2.wheaton.edu/bgc/archives/exhibits/YFC%201945/02%20background%2004.html.

17. "Press Release for the Memorial Day Rally, ca. March 1945," Wheaton College, http://www2.wheaton.edu/bgc/archives/exhibits/YFC%201945/03%20preparation%2003.html.

18. Joel Carpenter, "Geared to the Times, but Anchored to the Rock," *Christianity Today* 16, no. 8 (1985): 44–47.

19. Carpenter, *Revive Us Again*, 161–162.

20. Torrey M. Johnson, introduction, in Billy Graham, *Calling Youth to Christ* (Grand Rapids, MA: Zondervan, 1947).

21. Graham, "Youth's Hero," in *Calling Youth to Christ*, 90.

22. Graham, "Retreat! Stand! Advance!," in *Calling Youth to Christ*, 32.

23. Graham, "Youth's Hero," 91.

24. Gail Bederman, "'The Women Have Had Charge of the Church Work Long Enough': The Men and Religion Forward Movement of 1911–1912 and the Masculinization of Middle-Class Protestantism," in *A Mighty Baptism: Race, Gender, and the Creation of American Protestantism*, ed. Susan Juster and Lisa MacFarlane (Ithaca, NY: Cornell University Press, 1996), 112.

25. Bederman, "The Women Have Had Charge of the Church Work Long Enough," 112.

26. Betty DeBerg, *Ungodly Women: Gender and the First Wave of American Fundamentalism* (Minneapolis: Fortress, 1990), 17–20; Randall Balmer, "American Fundamentalism: The Ideal of Femininity," in *Fundamentalism and Gender*, ed. John Stratton Hawley (New York: Oxford University Press, 1994), 53.

27. Margaret Lamberts Bendroth, *Fundamentalism and Gender: 1875 to the Present* (New Haven, CT: Yale University Press, 1996), 3.

28. Bendroth, *Fundamentalism and Gender*, 3.

29. Graham, "Retreat! Stand! Advance!," 33.

30. Graham, "Retreat! Stand! Advance!," 40.

31. Graham, "Midnight Tragedy," in *Calling Youth to Christ*, 70.

32. Barstow, "These Teenagers Are Not Delinquents," 81.

33. Billy Graham, *Secret to Happiness* (Minneapolis: Grason, 1956), 140.

34. Billy Graham, *My Answer* (New York: Doubleday, 1960), 63, 222.

35. Graham, *My Answer*, 63.

36. In the Roman scenario, it becomes clear that Graham adapted his formula from Gibbon's *Rise and Fall of the Roman Empire*.

37. Graham, *Peace with God* (1952), quoted in Jason Stevens, *God-Fearing and Free: A Spiritual History of America's Cold War* (Cambridge, MA: Harvard University Press, 2010), 49.

38. Graham, "America's Hope," 20.

39. Graham, "America's Hope," 27.

40. Graham, quoted in William G. McLoughlin, *Revivals, Awakenings, and Reform* (Chicago: University of Chicago Press, 1980), 190.

41. Graham, "We Need a Revival," in *The Early Billy Graham: Sermon and Revival Accounts*, ed. Joel A. Carpenter (New York: Garland, 1988), 55.

42. Stephen J. Whitfield, *The Culture of the Cold War* (Baltimore: John Hopkins University Press, 1991), 77.

43. Whitfield, *The Culture of the Cold War*, 53.

44. Graham, "The Home God Honors," in Carpenter, *Revive Us Again*, 79–74.

45. Graham, "The Home God Honors," 65.

46. Graham, "The Home God Honors," 72.

47. Truman had strong aversions to traditional religion and disliked Graham upon their first meeting. Jonathan P. Herzog, *The Spiritual-Industrial Complex: America's Religious Battle against Communism in the Early Cold War* (New York: Oxford University Press, 2011), 76, 95.

48. Angela Lahr, *Millennial Dreams and Apocalyptic Nightmares* (New York: Oxford University Press, 2007), 23, 54, 200.

49. Paul Boyer, *When Time Shall Be No More: Prophecy Belief in Modern American Culture* (Cambridge, MA: Belknap Press, 1992), 117, 122.

50. Herzog, *The Spiritual-Industrial Complex*, 8, 179, 209.

51. Boyer, *When Time Shall Be No More*, 315.

52. Herzog, *The Spiritual-Industrial Complex*, 15.

53. Arnold Toynbee, *A Study of History*, vol. 2, *Abridgement of Volumes VII–X* (Oxford: Oxford University Press, 1957), 112.

54. Arnold Toynbee, "I Agree with a Pagan," http://thisibelieve.org/essay/17053/.

55. Kenneth O. Gangel, "Arnold Toynbee: An Evangelical Evaluation," *Bibliotheca Sacra* (April–June 1977): 149.

56. Gangel, "Arnold Toynbee," 145.

57. Gangel, "Arnold Toynbee," 152.

58. Carpenter, *Revive Us Again*, 201.

59. Carl F. H. Henry, *Remaking the Modern Mind* (Grand Rapids, MI: Eerdmans, 1948), 44.

60. Carl F. H. Henry, *Twilight of a Great Civilization: The Drift toward Neo-Paganism* (Westchester, IL: Crossway Books, 1988), 28.

61. Romans 1:24–28.

62. Henry, *Twilight of a Great Civilization*, 27.

63. Henry, *Twilight of a Great Civilization*, 172.

64. Henry, *Twilight of a Great Civilization*, 41.

65. Henry, *Twilight of a Great Civilization*, 71.

66. Henry, *Twilight of a Great Civilization*, 72.

67. Billy Graham, "Sermon #8: Now Is the Acceptable Time," Charlotte Evangelistic Campaign, September 28, 1958, Wheaton College, http://www.wheaton.edu/bgc/archives/docs/bg-charlotte/0928-1.htm.

68. Billy Graham, "Sermon #14: The Second Coming of Christ," Charlotte Evangelistic Campaign, October 5, 1958, Wheaton College, http://www.wheaton.edu/bgc/archives/docs/bg-charlotte/1005.html.

69. Billy Graham, "Sermon #14: The Second Coming of Christ."

70. Pitirim Sorokin, *The American Sex Revolution* (Boston: Porter Sargent, 1956). Sorokin also notes that the Soviets, while initially falling prey to the dissolution of marriage, had since overcome the trend.

71. Sorokin, *The American Sex Revolution*, 78.

72. Sorokin, *The American Sex Revolution*, 98.

73. Graham, "The Second Coming of Christ."

74. "Homosexuals in Government," 96 Cong. Rec. (1950), http://www.writing.upenn.edu/~afilreis/50s/gays-in-govt.html.

75. Whitfield, *The Culture of the Cold War*, 44.

76. Whitfield, *The Culture of the Cold War*, 45.

77. Whitfield, *The Culture of the Cold War*, 80.

78. Whitfield, *The Culture of the Cold War*, 77.

79. Billy Graham, *World Aflame* (New York: Doubleday, 1965), 22.

80. Graham, *World Aflame*, 22.

81. Graham, *World Aflame*, 28.

82. Graham, *World Aflame*, 233.

CHAPTER 3

1. Jason Stevens, *God-Fearing and Free: A Spiritual History of America's Cold War* (Cambridge, MA: Harvard University Press, 2010), 10; Jeffrey P. Moran, *Teaching Sex: The Shaping of Adolescence in the 20th Century* (New York: Oxford University Press, 2002), 179. See also David K. Johnson, *The Lavender Scare: The Cold War Persecution of Gays and Lesbians in the Federal Government* (Chicago: University of Chicago Press, 2006).

2. Jason Bivins, *Religion of Fear: The Politics of Horror in Conservative Evangelicalism* (New York: Oxford University Press, 2008), 8.

3. Angela Lahr, *Millennialist Dreams, Apocalyptic Nightmares: The Cold War Origins of Political Evangelicalism* (New York: Oxford University Press, 2007), 4, 23, 31–34, 53, 84, 144, 199.

4. See David Nord, *Faith in Reading, Religious Publication and the Birth of Mass Media* (Oxford: Oxford University Press, 2004); Candy Gunther Brown, *The Word in the World: Evangelical Writing, Publishing, and Reading in America,*

1789–1990 (Chapel Hill: University of North Carolina Press, 2004); Jeanne Halgren Kilde, *When Church Became Theatre: The Transformation of Evangelical Architecture and Worship in Nineteenth-Century America* (Oxford: Oxford University Press, 2002); Paul Gutjahr, *An American Bible: The History of the Good Book in America* (Stanford, CA: Stanford University Press, 1999), for examples of nineteenth- and twentieth-century Protestant evangelicals utilizing mass media, consumer market analysis, popular culture, and technological advancement in order to spread their message to the widest possible audience.

5. Donald E. Miller, *Reinventing American Protestantism: Christianity in the New Millennium* (Berkeley: University of California Press), 21–22.

6. Eileen Luhr, *Witnessing Suburbia: Conservatives and Christian Youth Culture* (Berkeley: University Of California Press, 2009), 80.

7. Miller, *Reinventing American Protestantism*, 17–18; Wade Clark Roof, *A Generation of Seekers: The Spiritual Journeys of the Baby Boom Generation* (San Francisco: HarperCollins, 1993), 60–70; Stewart Hoover, *Religion in the Media Age* (New York: Routledge, 2006), 85; Mara Einstein, *Brands of Faith: Marketing Religion in a Commercial Age* (New York: Routledge, 2008), 21.

8. Axel R. Schafer, *Countercultural Conservatives: American Evangelicalism from the Postwar Revival to the New Christian Right* (Madison: University of Wisconsin Press, 2011), PDF e-book; Darren Dochuk, *From Bible Belt to Sun Belt: Plain-Folk Religion, Grassroots Politics, and the Rise of Evangelical Conservatism* (New York: Norton, 2011); Randall Stephens and Karl W. Giberson, *The Anointed: Evangelical Truth in a Secular Age* (Cambridge, MA: Belknap Press of Harvard University Press, 2011); Daniel K. Williams, *God's Own Party: The Making of the Christian Right* (New York: Oxford University Press, 2010); Seth Dowland, "'Family Values' and the Formation of a Christian Right Agenda," *Church History* 78, no. 3 (2009): 606–631.

9. David Harrington Watt, *A Transforming Faith: Explorations of Twentieth-Century American Evangelicalism* (New Brunswick, NJ: Rutgers University Press, 1991), 154.

10. George M. Marsden, *Fundamentalism and American Culture* (Oxford: Oxford University Press, 2006), 236.

11. Schafer, *Countercutural Conservatives*, 70.

12. Schafer, *Countercultural Conservatives*, 96.

13. Wade Clark Roof, *Spiritual Marketplace: Baby Boomers and the Re-making of American Religion* (Princeton, NJ: Princeton University Press, 1999), 186, 189.

14. Miller, *Reinventing American Protestantism*, 32–33; Lisa McGirr, *Suburban Warriors: The Origins of the New American Right* (Princeton, NJ: Princeton University Press, 2001), 242.

15. Eileen Luhr, *Witnessing Suburbia: Conservatives and Christian Youth Culture* (Berkeley: University of California Press, 2009), 77.

16. Luhr, *Witnessing Suburbia*, 71.

17. David W. Stowe, *No Sympathy for the Devil: Christian Pop Music and the Transformation of American Evangelicalism* (Chapel Hill: University of North Carolina Press, 2011), 2–3.

18. Stowe, *No Sympathy for the Devil*, 77.

19. Dochuk, *From Bible Belt to Sun Belt*, 295.

20. Luhr, *Witnessing Suburbia*, 27, 73; Stephen Prothero, *American Jesus: How the Son of God Became a National Icon* (New York: Farrar, Straus & Giroux, 2003), 131.

21. Peter Goodwin Heltzel, *Jesus and Justice: Evangelicals, Race, and American Politics* (New Haven, CT: Yale University Press, 2009), 103; Watt, *A Transforming Faith*, 70.

22. Dowland, "Family Values," 608, 616; Watt, *Transforming Faith*, 49.

23. Dochuk, *From Bible Belt to Sun Belt*, 316; Shafer, *Countercultural Conservatives*, 70.

24. Dochuk, *From Bible Belt to Sun Belt*, 295, 316; Shafer, *Countercultural Conservatives*, 98; Dowland, "Family Values," 616.

25. McGirr, *Suburban Warriors*, 221.

26. Quoted in McGirr, *Suburban Warriors*, 229.

27. McGirr, *Suburban Warriors*, 228; D. G. Hart, *That Old-Time Religion in Modern America: Evangelical Protestantism in the Twentieth Century* (Chicago: Ivan R. Dee, 2002), 156; Dochuk, *From Bible Belt to Sun Belt*, 300.

28. Dochuk, *From Bible Belt to Sun Belt*, 306.

29. Antigay campaigns like Anita Bryant's argued that homosexuals recruited young people and should therefore be kept from occupations that allowed them access to children and adolescents.

30. Francis Schaeffer, *How Should We Then Live: The Rise and Decline of Western Thought and Culture* (Old Tappan, NJ: Fleming H. Revell, 1976), 210.

31. Hart, *That Old-Time Religion*, 137.

32. Hart, *That Old-Time Religion*, 161.

33. Hart, *That Old-Time Religion*, 137.

34. Schaeffer, *How Should We Then Live*, 218.

35. Hart, *That Old-Time Religion*, 140.

36. Hart, *That Old-Time Religion*, 161; Dowland, "Family Values," 613.

37. Barry Hankins, *Francis Schaeffer and the Shaping of Evangelical America* (Grand Rapids, MI: Eerdmans, 2008), 114.

38. Schaeffer, *How Should We Then Live*, 224.

39. Schaeffer, *How Should We Then Live*, 168.

40. Schaeffer, *How Should We Then Live*, 227.

41. Schaeffer, *How Should We Then Live*, 49.

42. Schaeffer, *How Should We Then Live*, 224.

43. David Harrington Watt, "The Private Hopes of American Fundamentalists and Evangelicals, 1925–1975," *Religion and American Culture: A Journal of Interpretation* 1, no. 2 (1991): 32.

44. Stowe, *No Sympathy for the Devil*, 68–69.

45. Randall J. Stephens and Karl W. Giberson, *The Anointed: Evangelical Truth in a Secular Age* (Cambridge, MA: Belknap Press of Harvard University Press, 2011), 156.

46. George M. Marsden, *Fundamentalism and American Culture* (new ed.; New York: Oxford University Press, 2006), 49.

47. Joel Carpenter, *Revive Us Again: The Reawakening of American Fundamentalism* (New York: Oxford University Press), 1997.

48. Marsden, *Fundamentalism and American Culture*, 52.

49. Stephens and Giberson, *The Anointed*, 154.

50. Stowe, *No Sympathy for the Devil*, 68–72.

51. Watt, "The Private Hopes," 164.

52. Amy Kaplan, "Manifest Domesticity," *American Literature* 70, no. 3 (1998): 582, 586, 592.

53. Dochuk, *From Bible Belt to Sun Belt*; Stephens and Giberson, *The Anointed*; Williams, *God's Own Party*; Dowland, "Family Values," 606–631; Marsden, *Fundamentalism and American Culture*; McGirr, *Suburban Warriors*; Susan Harding, *The Book of Jerry Falwell: Fundamentalist Language and Politics* (Princeton, NJ: Princeton University Press, 2000); Margaret Lamberts Bendroth, *Fundamentalism and Gender: 1875–Present* (New Haven, CT: Yale University Press, 1996); Michael Lienesch, *Redeeming America: Piety and Politics in the New Christian Right* (Chapel Hill: University of North Carolina Press, 1993).

54. James Davidson Hunter, *Evangelicals: The Coming Generation* (Chicago: University of Chicago Press, 1987), 64; Watt, "The Private Hopes," 138; Stephens and Giberson, *The Anointed*, 100.

55. Watt, "The Private Hopes," 145.

56. Stephens and Giberson, *The Anointed*, 101–102.

57. Susan E. Shirk-Myers, *Helping the Good Shepherd: Pastoral Counselors in a Psychotherapeutic Culture, 1925–1975* (Baltimore: Johns Hopkins University Press, 2009), 213; Stephens and Giberson, *The Anointed*, 102.

58. Heather Hendershot, *Shaking the World for Jesus: Media and Conservative Evangelical Culture* (Chicago: University of Chicago Press, 2004), 68; Shirk-Myers, *Helping the Good Shepherd*, 213.

59. Shirk-Myers, *Helping the Good Shepherd*, 208, 216, 220

60. Roof, *Spiritual Marketplace*, 69, 134; Watt, "The Private Hopes," 139.

61. Carl F. H. Henry, *Twilight of a Great Civilization: The Drift toward Neo-Paganism* (Westchester, IL: Crossway Books, 1988), 40. Though published in the 1980s, this text was based on a convocation speech Henry gave in 1969 entitled "The Barbarians Are Coming." James Patterson, "Cultural Pessimism in Modern Evangelical Thought: Francis Schaeffer, Carl Henry, and Charles Colson," *Journal of Evangelical Theology* 49, no. 4 (2006): 813.

62. Hunter, *Evangelicals*, 68.

63. Hunter, *Evangelicals*, 65.

64. Hunter, *Evangelicals*, 67. Also, Wade Clark Roof notes that 63 percent of conservative and 68 percent of moderate churchgoers in his study of the baby-boom generation provide psychological explanations for their own church attendance. See Roof, *A Generation of Seekers*, 110.

65. Hendershot, *Shaking the World for Jesus*, 89.

66. In *Children At Risk: Winning the Battle for the Hearts and Minds of Your Children* (Dallas: Word, 2000), he and coauthor Gary Bauer refer to it as a "Civil War of Values."

67. Stephens and Giberson, *The Anointed*, 113; John P. Bartkowski and Christopher G. Ellison, "Divergent Models of Child-Rearing in Popular Manuals: Conservative Protestants vs. the Mainstream Experts," *Sociology of Religion* 56, no. 1 (1995): 25.

68. Charles W. Phillips, "Focus on the Family," *Saturday Evening Post*, April 1982, 34, reprinted as the introduction to *Dr. Dobson Answers Your Questions* (Wheaton, IL: Tyndale House Publishers, 1982).

69. Colleen McDannell. "Beyond Dr. Dobson: Women, Girls, and Focus on the Family," in *Women and Twentieth-Century Protestantism*, ed. Margaret Lamberts Bendroth and Virginia Lieson Brereton (Chicago: University of Illinois Press, 2002), 116; Stephens and Giberson, *The Anointed*, 98, 117. In 1992, Dobson claimed that since 1970 he had sold over two million copies of *Dare to Discipline*, first published in 1970. James Dobson, *The New Dare to Discipline* (Wheaton, IL, Tyndale House Publishers, 1992), 3.

70. James Dobson, *Love for a Lifetime* (Portland, OR: Multnomah, 1987), 43.

71. Heltzel, *Jesus and Justice*, 113–114.

72. Heltzel, *Jesus and Justice*, 116; Dobson, *Love for a Lifetime*, 34.

73. James Dobson, *Straight-Talk to Men and Their Wives / What Wives Wish Their Husbands Knew about Women: A Guideposts Two-Volume Book for Christian Families* (Danbury, CT: Guideposts, 1979), 155.

74. James Dobson, *Dr. Dobson Answers Your Questions* (Wheaton, IL: Tyndale House Publishers, 1982), 54, 92.

75. Dobson, *Dr. Dobson Answers Your Questions*, 92, 451–452.

76. Purity balls are elaborate father-daughter dances developed by Randy Wilson, an employee at the Family Research Council, the political arm of Focus on the Family. They exemplify the process of heterosexual socialization that reinforces male headship and female subservience. See Hilde Løvdal, "Family Matters: James Dobson and Focus on the Family's Message to Evangelicals," *1970–2010* (PhD diss., University of Oslo, 2012), 142–143.

77. James Dobson, *Marriage under Fire* (Portland, OR: Multnomah, 2004), 12.

78. James Dobson, *Straight-Talk to Men and Their Wives* (Guideposts, 1979), 157.

79. George Gilder, *Men and Marriage* (New York: Quadrangle / New York Times Book Company, 1986), 38–39.

80. Gilder, *Men and Marriage*, 5.

81. See McDannell, "Beyond Dr. Dobson," and Dan Gilgoff, *The Jesus Machine: How James Dobson, Focus on the Family, and Evangelical America Are Winning the Culture War* (New York: St. Martin's Press, 2007), xv.

82. "History of Family Research Council: Thirty Years of Advancing Faith, Family, and Freedom," Family Research Council, http://www.frc.org/historymission.

83. Dobson, *Dr. Dobson Answers Your Questions*, 167; Dobson, *The New Dare to Discipline*, 154–155.

84. James Dobson, *Dare to Discipline* (Wheaton, IL: Tyndale House Publishers, 1970), 28; *Dr. Dobson Answers Your Questions*, 92; *The New Dare to Discipline*, 150.

85. Dobson, *The New Dare to Discipline*, 210.

86. James Dobson and Gary Bauer, *Children at Risk: Winning the Battle for the Hearts and Minds of Your Children* (Dallas: Word, 2000), 38.

87. Dobson and Bauer, *Children at Risk*, 47–48.

88. Dobson, *Love for a Lifetime*, 87.

89. Dobson, *Love for a Lifetime*, 36.

90. Dobson, *The New Dare to Discipline*, 156; James Dobson, *Complete Marriage and Home Reference Guide* (Wheaton, IL: Tyndale House Publishers, 2000), 154.

91. Dobson, *Complete Marriage*, 156.

92. Gilder, *Men and Marriage*, 198.

93. Gilder, *Men and Marriage*, 177.

94. Dobson, *Marriage Under Fire*, 12.

95. Gilder, *Men and Marriage*, 47.

96. Unwin, *Sexual Regulations*, 15, 21. As cited in Hilda Løvdal, "Sex and the Civilization: From the Cold War to the Culture Wars." Paper presented at the American Academy of Religion, Rock Island, IL, March 2011.

97. Unwin, *Sexual Regulations*, 5, 15.

98. For Sorokin's use of Unwin, see Pitirim Sorokin, *The American Sex Revolution* (Boston: Porter Sargent, 1956), 108–113.

99. Dobson, *The New Dare to Discipline*, 236.

100. Ibid.

101. Dobson and Bauer, *Children at Risk*, 59.

102. Dobson, *Marriage under Fire*, 8.

103. Dobson, *What Wives Wish Their Husbands Knew about Women*, 97. This metaphor is repeated in his later publication, *Head over Heels* (Ventura, CA: Regal, 2011); Løvdal, "Family Matters," 72–75.

104. Dobson, *What Wives Wish Their Husbands Knew about Women*, 96.

105. Dobson, *Dr. Dobson Answers Your Questions*, 1982 (introduction reprinted from *Saturday Evening Post*, April 1982); Dobson, *The New Dare to Discipline*, introduction.

CHAPTER 4

1. This chapter makes use of ethnographic research conducted from 2006 to 2008. Combined with historical documentation and media reports, my participant-observation of several Silver Ring Thing events, survey data from thirty evangelical college students, and interviews with Richard Ross of True Love Waits and Denny Pattyn and two other staff members of Silver Ring Thing aided me significantly in the development of my portrayal of the movement.

2. Richard Vara, "Texas Youths Sign Cards, Vow to Abstain from Sex," *Houston Chronicle*, November 13, 1993; Esme M. Infante, "Teens: Sex Can Wait for Wedding Bells," *USA Today*, July 29, 1994; Rebekah Scott Schreffler, "True Love Waits," *Pittsburgh Post-Gazette*, July 27, 1994; Laurie Goodstein, "Saying No to Teen Sex in No Uncertain Terms," *Washington Post*, July 30, 1994; Colman McCarthy, "No 'Safe' Teenage Sex," *Washington Post*, August 20, 1994.

3. "True Love Waits: Baptist Teens Asked to Pledge to Delay Sex until Marriage," *Houston Chronicle*, April 22, 1993; "Teens Pledge Abstinence," *St. Petersburg Times*, May 1, 1993; "A History of True Love Waits," True Love Waits, http://www.lifeway.com/Article/true-love-waits-history.

4. Though Ross still serves as one of TLW's spokespeople, he now holds a faculty position in student ministry at Southwestern Baptist Theological Seminary.

5. Denny Pattyn, phone interview by author, October 31, 2006.

6. In 2005, this program was renamed Community Based Abstinence Education (CBAE) after the Administration for Children and Families took on its administrative responsibilities.

7. Though the idea is not new, the phrase "evangelical purity culture" was introduced by Donna Freitas in *Sex and the Soul: Juggling Sexuality, Spirituality, Religion and Romance on America's College Campus* (New York: Oxford University Press, 2008) to describe the constellation of beliefs, practices, and organizations that constitute the sexual values of most evangelical subcultures in the United States.

8. Janet Benshoff, "The Chastity Act: Government Manipulation of Abortion Information and the First Amendment," *Harvard Law Review* 101, no. 8 (1988): 1916–1937.

9. "Encouraging Teen Abstinence," *CQ Researcher* 8, no. 25 (1998): 586.

10. This ratio was later reversed in 1997 with the abstinence-only provision included in the Welfare Reform Act.

11. "Encouraging Teen Abstinence," 585.

12. Julie Jones, "Money, Sex, and the Religious Right: A Constitutional Analysis of Federally Funded Abstinence-Only-until-Marriage Sexuality Education," *Creighton Law Review* 35 (June 2002): 1075–1106; Hazel Glenn Beh and Milton Diamond, "Children and Education: The Failure of Abstinence-Only Education." *Columbia Journal of Gender and Law* 15 (2006): 15–62.

13. Subcommittee on Departments of Labor, Health and Human Services, and Related Agencies, *Abstinence Education: Hearings before a Subcommittee of the Committee on Appropriations*. 104th Cong., 2nd sess. (1996), 87–91.

14. Charles Murray, "The Coming White Underclass," *Wall Street Journal*, October 29, 1993.

15. Murray, "The Coming White Underclass," 10.

16. House Committee on Government Reform-Minority Staff, Special Investigations Division, *The Content of Federally Funded Abstinence-Only Education Programs* (December 2004), 6.

17. *American Civil Liberties Union of Massachusetts v. Leavitt, Horn, and Wilson*, accessed December 8, 2007, http://www.aclu.org/FilesPDFs/teeneducomplaint.pdf.

18. *ACLU v. Leavitt*, 4.

19. Brian C. Rittmeyer, "Silver Ring Thing Says It Will Survive," *Pittsburgh Tribune Review*, August 24, 2005.

20. "Evidence-Based Programs," Office of Adolescent Health, http://www.hhs.gov/ash/oah/oah-initiatives/teen_pregnancy/db/tpp-searchable.html.

21. Elizabeth Schroeder, Debra Hauser, and Monica Rodriguez, "He-Men, Virginity Pledges, and Bridal Dreams: Obama Administration Quietly Endorses Dangerous Ab-Only Curriculum," RH Reality Check, http://rhrealitycheck.org/article/2012/05/01/he-men-virginity-pledges-and-bridal-dreams-an-hhs-endorsed-curriculum/.

22. Eileen Luhr, *Witnessing Suburbia: Conservatives and Christian Youth Culture* (Berkeley: University of California Press, 2009), 27, 73; Stephen Prothero, *American Jesus: How the Son of God Became a National Icon* (New York: Farrar, Straus & Giroux, 2003), 131; David W. Stowe, *No Sympathy for the Devil: Christian Pop Music and the Transformation of American Evangelicalism* (Chapel Hill: University of North Carolina Press, 2011).

23. Thomas Billitteri, "Sex Is a 4-Letter Word: Wait," *St. Petersburg Times*, June 15, 1994.

24. Erin Curry and Polly House, "Magazine Sees 'A New Counterculture' of Teenagers Who Choose Virginity," *Baptist Press News*, December 12, 2002.

25. "True Love Waits for Some Teen-Agers," *New York Times*, June 21, 1993.

26. Heather Rachelle White, "Virgin Pride: Born Again Faith and Sexual Identity in the Faith-Based Abstinence Movement," in *The Ashgate Research Companion to Contemporary Religion and Sexuality*, ed. Stephen J. Hunt and Andrew K. T. Yip (Surrey: Ashgate, 2012), 242.

27. Movement literature often refers to purity as a revolution through which sexually pure adolescents will lead the nation to religious and social renewal. Foreword to *The NIV True Love Waits Youth Bible* (Nashville: Broadman and Holman, 1996).

28. McCarthy, "No 'Safe' Teenage Sex."

29. Roof asserts that much of contemporary evangelicalism is characterized by a "quest culture" in which believers are seeking to find answers to both spiritual and moral questions. They achieve this through special-purpose groups and, most prominently, through the seeker churches that often provide numerous self-help programs along with traditional church offerings such as Sunday worship and school. See Roof, *Spiritual Marketplace: Baby Boomers and the Re-Making of American Religion* (Princeton, NJ: Princeton University Press, 1999), 95.

30. Heather Hendershot, *Shaking the World for Jesus: Media and Conservative Evangelical Culture* (Chicago: University of Chicago Press, 2004), 88.

31. Hendershot, *Shaking the World for Jesus*, 89.

32. Hendershot, *Shaking the World for Jesus*, 90.

33. Matt and Tracy Webster are pseudonyms for a married couple who worked for SRT during the years of my ethnographic research (2005–2007).

34. Julie Breyer (pseudonym), questionnaire by author, November 2006.

35. Jonathan Pierce (pseudonym), questionnaire by author, November 2006.

36. Walter Newsome (pseudonym), questionnaire by author, December 2006.

37. Heather Hendershot's argument is that, given the belief that sin can never be fully "cured," sin "goes into remission." Hendershot, *Shaking the World for Jesus*, 88.

38. Silver Ring Thing, *It's Time / Silver Ring Thing Newsletter*, June/July 2006.

39. Silver Ring Thing, *It's Time / Silver Ring Thing Newsletter*, June/July 2006.

40. Doug Herman, *Time for a Pure Revolution* (Wheaton, IL: Tyndale, 2004), 19.

41. Herman, *Time for a Pure Revolution*, 19.

42. Silver Ring Thing, *Sexual Abstinence Study Bible: New Living Translation* (Sewickley, PA: Silver Ring Thing, 2002), 18.

43. Tracy Webster, phone interview by author, October 18, 2006.

44. Webster interview.

45. Pattyn interview.

46. Francis Schaeffer used the term *co-belligerents* when calling evangelicals to ally themselves with nonevangelicals in the pursuit of pro-life goals. I used this term to deploy the idea of two conflicting groups or impulses (in this case, sexuality and spirituality) used by evangelicals to promote their political and social initiatives. See Francis Schaeffer, *Plan for Action: An Action Alternative Handbook for Whatever Happened to the Human Race?* (Old Tappan, NJ: Fleming H. Revell, 1980), 68.

CHAPTER 5

1. "What Is Silver Ring Thing?," Silver Ring Thing, accessed July 20, 2011, http://www.silverringthing.com/whatissrt.asp.

2. Stewart Hoover, "The Cross at Willow Creek: Seeker Religion and the Contemporary Marketplace," in *Religion and Popular Culture in America*, ed. Bruce

David Forbes and Jeffrey Mahan (Berkeley: University of California Press, 2000,) 141.

3. Wade Clark Roof, *A Generation of Seekers: The Spiritual Journeys of the Baby Boom Generation* (San Francisco: HarperCollins, 1993), 60–70.

4. Stewart M. Hoover, *Religion in the Media Age* (New York: Routledge, 2006), 85; David Lyon, *Jesus in Disneyland: Religion in Postmodern Times* (Cambridge: Polity Press, 2004), 94; Wade Clark Roof, *Spiritual Marketplace: Baby Boomers and the Remaking of American Religion* (Princeton, NJ: Princeton University Press: 1999), 69–70.

5. For examples of nineteenth- and twentieth-century Protestant evangelicals utilizing mass media, consumer market analysis, popular culture, and technological advancement in order optimize their evangelical initiatives, see David Nord, *Faith in Reading: Religious Publication and the Birth of Mass Media* (Oxford: Oxford University Press, 2004); Candy Gunther Brown, *The Word in the World: Evangelical Writing, Publishing and Reading in America, 1789–1990* (Chapel Hill: University of North Carolina Press, 2004); Jeanne Halgren Kilde, *When Church Became Theatre: The Transformation of Evangelical Architecture and Worship in Nineteenth-Century America* (Oxford: Oxford University Press, 2002); and Paul Gutjahr, *An American Bible: The History of the Good Book in America* (Stanford, CA: Stanford University Press, 1999).

6. The purity pledge is structured as a system of exchange between God and the individual. The pledger promises to remain sexually pure in exchange for God's blessing in the forms of a spouse, marital harmony, and sexual satisfaction.

7. Christine Gardner also provides an extensive description of SRT events that highlights the role of performance and media entertainment. See *Making Chastity Sexy: The Rhetoric of Evangelical Abstinence Campaigns* (Berkeley: University of California Press, 2011), 41–47.

8. Tracy Webster, interview by author, October 18, 2006.

9. Though the organization has made efforts to reach racially diverse audiences, it has been most successful at reaching white, suburban youth, most likely because its own staff is representative of this demographic. When the group does perform shows for predominantly black audiences, Denny Pattyn is replaced with a guest speaker from the community in hopes that this will dispel any distrust the audience may feel toward the group.

10. Jonathan Gray, *Show Sold Separately: Promos, Spoilers, and Other Media Paratexts* (New York: New York University Press, 2010), 93.

11. Christian Smith, *American Evangelicals: Embattled and Thriving* (Chicago: University of Chicago Press, 1998), 118.

12. Gray, *Show Sold Separately.*

13. Jonathan Gray, "Television Teaching: Parody, *The Simpsons*, and Media Literacy Education," *Critical Studies in Media Communication* 22, no. 3 (2004): 227.

14. Silver Ring Thing homepage, accessed July 25, 2013, http://www.silverringthing.com/home.asp.

15. Studies conducted by Peter Bearman, Hannah Bruckner, and Janet Rosenbaum discussed in the previous chapter have addressed this question and concluded that abstinence pledgers show little distinction from nonpledgers. However, Denny Pattyn, founder and CEO of Silver Ring Thing, is quick to point out that these studies were not conducted on his organization.

16. Linda Hutcheon, *A Theory of Parody: The Teaching of Twentieth-Century Art Forms* (Champaign: University of Illinois Press, 1985), 75.

17. In an interview with Ed Bradley of *60 Minutes*, Pattyn claimed that he would never, under any circumstances, encourage his sixteen-year-old daughter to use a condom, because, in the long term, it would not protect her.

18. SRT DVD.

19. George Whelan, "Frown Jewels: Christian Rings Banned, Sikh Bracelets Allowed," *Daily Star*, June 19, 2006.

20. Elizabeth Day, "Sikh Bracelets, but Not Christian Rings as School Bans Pupils from Wearing 'Purity Rings,'" *Daily Telegraph*, June 18, 2006.

21. Day, "Sikh Bracelets."

22. Alan Cowell, "British High Court Wrestles with Symbol of Premarital Purity," *New York Times*, June 23, 2007.

23. Frances Gibb, "Teenage Girl Loses 'Purity Ring' Case," *Times* (London), July 17, 2007.

24. Raphael G. Satter, "British Court Hears Chastity Ring Case," CBN News, June 25, 2007, accessed December 17, 2008, http://www.cbn.com/CBNnews/183730.aspx.

25. "Purity Ring Is Not Intimately Linked to Religious Belief," *Times* (London), July 23, 2007.

26. Sam Greenhill, "Teenager Loses High Court Battle against School Ban on Chastity Ring," *Daily Mail* (London), July 17, 2007.

27. Greenhill, "Teenager Loses High Court Battle."

28. Gibb, "Teenage Girl Loses 'Purity Ring' Case."

29. Greenhill, "Teenager Loses High Court Battle"; Gibb, "Teenage Girl Loses 'Purity Ring' Case."

30. Recall R. Marie Griffith's argument that controlled bodies signify a superior faith system, as detailed in chapter three. See R. Marie Griffith, *Born Again Bodies: Flesh and Spirit in American Christianity* (Berkeley: University of California Press: 2004), 4.

31. *Silver Ring Thing Abstinence Study Bible*, New Living Translation (Wheaton, IL: Tyndale House, 2000), front matter.

32. *Silver Ring Thing Abstinence Study Bible*, 3.

33. Richard Ross, email correspondence with author, November 18, 2006.

34. "Teens Pledge Abstinence," *St. Petersburg Times*, May 1, 1993.

35. For purity ring ceremony instructions, see http://www.lifeway.com/tlw/leaders/ring_ceremony.asp.

36. Elizabeth Moore, "Teens Believe True Love Waits," *Times-Picayune,* October 9, 2004.

37. Patsy Keith, "Teens Walk the Aisle for True Love Waits," *Commercial Appeal,* February 13, 2005.

38. "God Blesses Pledges with Happiness," February 2001, http://www.lifeway.com/tlw/media/news_happiness.asp.

39. Stephanie Rosenbloom, "A Ring That Says No, Not Yet," *New York Times,* December 8, 2005.

40. For a more extended description of how religion has adapted to commercial market practices by utilizing branding and marketing strategies to promote particular belief systems and religious affiliations, see Mara Einstein's *Brands of Faith: Marketing Religion in a Commercial Age* (New York: Routledge, 2008). See also Nord, *Faith in Reading*; Brown, *The Word in the World*; Kilde, *When Church Became Theatre*; and Gutjahr, *An American Bible.*

41. Denny Pattyn, *Next: Living Out Your Commitment to Wait* (Moon Township, PA: Silver Ring Thing, 2009), 38.

42. See Nord, *Faith in Reading*; Brown, *The Word in the World*; Kilde, *When Church Became Theatre*; and Gutjahr, *An American Bible.*

43. Paul Gutjahr, "The Bible-Zine *Revolve* and the Evolution of the Culturally Relevant Bible in America," in *Religion and the Culture of Print in Modern America,* ed. Charles L. Cohen and Paul S. Boyer (Madison: University of Wisconsin Press, 2008), 326–348.

44. Webster, interview by author, October 18, 2006.

45. Stewart M. Hoover, *Religion in the Media Age* (New York: Routledge), 85.

46. Thanks to Amy DeRogatis for these insights.

47. Thomas Csordas, *The Sacred Self: A Cultural Phenomenology of Charismatic Healing* (Berkeley: University of California Press, 1994), 110.

48. Csordas, *The Sacred Self,* 149.

49. Here I distinguish between holiness evangelicals (Pentecostals, charismatics, etc.), who have traditionally integrated the healing of bodies and souls, from mainstream evangelicals, who, due to Calvinist influences, have traditionally maintained clear distinctions between bodies and souls. My argument refers to the latter. In any case, the integration of therapeutic rhetoric into discourses on healing is a relatively new development to both.

50. Roof, *Spiritual Marketplace,* 187.

51. David Lyon, *Jesus in Disneyland: Religion in Postmodern Times* (Cambridge: Polity Press, 2004), 94.

52. Roof, *Spiritual Marketplace,* 189.

53. Catherine Bell, *Ritual Theory, Ritual Practice* (New York: Oxford University Press, 1992), 98.

CONCLUSION

1. Donald E. Miller, *Reinventing American Protestantism: Christianity in the New Millennium* (Berkeley: University of California Press), 21–22.

2. See Christine Gardner, *Making Chastity Sexy: The Rhetoric of Evangelical Purity Campaigns* (Berkeley: University of California Press, 2011).

3. Donna Freitas, *Sex and the Soul: Juggling Sexuality, Spirituality, Romance, and Religion on America's College Campuses* (New York: Oxford University Press, 2008); Mark Regnerus, *Forbidden Fruit: Sex and Religion in the Lives of American Teenagers* (New York: Oxford University Press, 2007); Peter Bearman and Hannah S. Brückner, "Promising the Future: Virginity Pledges and First Intercourse," *American Journal of Sociology* 106, no. 4 (2001): 859–912; and Peter Bearman and Hannah S. Brückner, "After the Promise: The STD Consequences of Adolescent Virginity Pledges," *Journal of Adolescent Health* 36, no. 4 (2005): 271–278.

4. Miller, *Reinventing American Protestantism*, 21–22.

5. Jason Stevens, *God-Fearing and Free: A Spiritual History of America's Cold War* (Cambridge, MA: Harvard University Press, 2010), 10; Jeffrey Moran, *Teaching Sex: The Shaping of Adolescence in the 20th Century* (New York: Oxford University Press, 2002), 179; David K. Johnson, *The Lavender Scare: The Cold War Persecution of Gays and Lesbians in the Federal Government* (Chicago: University of Chicago Press, 2006).

6. Jason Bivins, *Religion of Fear: The Politics of Horror in Conservative Evangelicalism* (New York: Oxford University Press, 2008), 5–6.

7. Hell Houses are Christian haunted houses produced in various locations during Halloween season and used for evangelistic purposes. Visitors view numerous scenarios that portray sinful activities such as drug use, rape, abortion, and homosexual behavior. In each case, the main character makes a sinful choice and is cast into hell. After moving through the house and viewing each scene, visitors are then given the opportunity to pray with someone and repent of their own sins.

8. Bivins, *Religion of Fear*, 5–6, 26, 37.

9. G. Stanley Hall, *Adolescence, Its Psychology and Its Relations to Physiology, Anthropology, Sociology, Sex, Crime, Religion, and Education* (New York: D. Appleton, 1904), xii–xviii, 304, 648–749.

10. See Stephen J. Whitfield, *The Culture of the Cold War* (Baltimore: John Hopkins University Press, 1991); Susan Friend Harding, *The Book of Jerry Falwell: Fundamentalist Language and Politics* (Princeton, NJ: Princeton University Press, 2001); Fred Fejes, *Gay Rights and Moral Panic: The Origins of America's Debate over Homosexuality* (New York: Palgrave Macmillan, 2008); Mark D. Jordan, *Recruiting Young Love: How Christians Talk about Homosexuality* (Chicago: University of Chicago Press, 2011).

11. Mara Einstein, *Brands of Faith: Marketing Religion in a Commercial Age* (New York: Routledge, 2008), 21; Stewart Hoover, *Religion in the Media Age* (New York: Routledge, 2006), 85; Roof, *A Generation of Seekers*: The Spiritual Journeys of the Baby Boom Generation (San Francisco: HarperCollins, 1993), 60–70; Miller, *Reinventing American Protestantism*, 17–18.

12. See Joel Carpenter, *Revive Us Again: The Reawakening of American Fundamentalism* (New York: Oxford University Press, 1997); Margaret Lamberts Bendroth, *Gender and Fundamentalism: 1875–Present* (New Haven, CT: Yale University Press, 1996); Betty DeBerg, *Ungodly Women: Gender and the First Wave of American Fundamentalism* (Minneapolis: Fortress, 1990); George M. Marsden, *Fundamentalism and American Culture: The Shaping of Twentieth-Century Evangelicalism: 1870–1925* (New York: Oxford University Press, 1980, 2006.)

13. Grant Wacker, "Searching for Eden with a Satellite Dish," in *Religion and American Culture: A Reader*, ed. David Hackett (New York: Routledge, 2003), 427.

14. R. Marie, *Born Again Bodies: Flesh and Spirit in American Christianity* (Berkeley: University of California Press, 2004), 77.

15. Silver Ring Thing, "Laws of the Father," *Best of Silver Ring Thing Commercials*, vol. 1 (Moon Township, PA: Silver Ring Thing, 2009), DVD.

16. The most well-known example of this critique is that raised by Elizabeth Smart, the young woman who at thirteen was abducted at knifepoint from her home in Salt Lake City, raped, and held captive for nine months. Smart now runs an organization assisting victims of similar circumstances. In her public addresses, she attributes her inability to escape her captors to the purity teachings she learned as a young girl. For more on Smart, see Alex Dominguez, "Elizabeth Smart Speaks on Human Trafficking," http://www.csmonitor.com/USA/Latest-News-Wires/2013/0504/Elizabeth-Smart-speaks-on-human-trafficking; Abigail Rine, "Why Some Evangelicals Are Trying to Stop Obsessing Over Pre-Marital Sex," *The Atlantic*, May 28, 2013. Numerous evangelical writers have written to raise similar critiques. Richard Clark, "I'm an Abstinence Christian, and Yeah, It's a Struggle," http://www.xojane.com/issues/in-the-abstinence-only-crowd; Jessica Ciencin Henriques, "My Virginity Mistake," http://www.salon.com/2013/05/06/my_virginity_mistake/; Sarah Bessy, "I Am Damaged Goods," http://deeperstory.com/i-am-damaged-goods/; Rachel Evans Held, "Do Christians Idolize Virginity?" http://rachelheldevans.com/blog/christians-idolize-virginity; Carolyn Curtis James, "Why Virginity Is Not the Gospel," http://www.huffingtonpost.com/carolyn-custis-james/why-virginity-is-not-the-gospel_b_1735085.html?utm_hp_ref=tw; Elizabeth Esther, "Virginity: New & Improved," http://www.elizabethesther.com/2013/01/virginity-new-improved.html; Ally Spotts, "What's the Big Deal about Waiting until Marriage?" http://www.

relevantmagazine.com/life/relationship/features/27286-whats-the-big-deal-about-waiting-for-marriage; Emily Maynard, "The Day I Turned In My V-Card," http://www.prodigalmagazine.com/the-day-i-turned-in-my-v-card/; Christian Piatt, "The Dangers of 'Marriage Worship,'" http://www.patheos.com/blogs/christianpiatt/2013/05/the-dangers-of-christian-marriage-worship/; Jonathan Acuff, "4 Ways Christians Damage Sex," http://www.relevantmagazine.com/life/relationship/features/22742-4-ways-christians-damage-sex; Kristen Howerton, "Shame-Based Sex Education: We Can Do Better," http://www.rageagainsttheminivan.com/2013/05/shame-based-sex-education-we-can-do.html.

17. See Jessica Valenti, *The Purity Myth: How America's Obsession with Virginity Is Hurting Young Women* (Berkeley, CA: Seal Press, 2009).

18. Christine Gardner, *Making Chastity Sexy: The Rhetoric of Evangelical Abstinence Campaigns* (Berkeley: University of California Press, 2011), 86.

19. Though Pattyn did not disclose the origin of these opinions, the specific number of civilizations he used suggests that they were drawn from Arnold Toynbee.

20. Silver Ring Thing, "Mixed-Message Mum," *Best of Silver Ring Thing Commercials,* vol. 1 (Moon Township, PA: Silver Ring Thing, 2009), DVD.

21. Amy Frykholm Johnson, *Rapture Culture: Left Behind in Evangelical America* (New York: Oxford University Press, 2004), 132.

22. Stephen J. Whitfield, *The Culture of the Cold War* (Baltimore: John Hopkins University Press, 1991), 44.

Bibliography

NEWSPAPERS AND PERIODICALS

American Magazine
American Missionary
Associated Press
Boston Globe
CBN News
Chicago Herald-American
Christian Science Monitor
Christianity Today
Columbus Dispatch
Daily Star (United Kingdom)
Daily Telegraph (Australia)
Eugenics Review
Houston Chronicle
London Times
Modesto Bee
New York Times
Newsweek
The Philanthropist (1886–1914)
Pittsburgh Post-Gazette
Pittsburgh Tribune-Review
St. Petersburg Times
Union Signal
USA Today
Wall Street Journal
Washington Post
Youth For Christ magazine (1945–1960)

PRIMARY SOURCES

Acuff, Jonathan. "4 Ways Christians Damage Sex." *Relevant Magazine*, September 2, 2010. http://www.relevantmagazine.com/life/relationship/features/22742-4-ways-christians-damage-sex.

American Civil Liberties Union. "In Light of ACLU Lawsuit Charging the Federal Government with Funding Religious Activities, the Silver Ring Thing Removes Religious Content from Website." ACLU. Last modified May 19, 2005. https://www.aclu.org/religion-belief_reproductive-freedom/light-aclu-lawsuit-charging-federal-government-funding-religiou.

———. "ACLU Announces Settlement in Challenge to Government-Funded Religion in the Abstinence-Only-until-Marriage Program the 'Silver Ring Thing.'" ACLU. Last modified February 23, 2006. http://www.aclu.org/reproductiverights/sexed/24246prs20060223.html.

Anthony, Susan B. "Social Purity" (1875). PBS. http://www.pbs.org/stantonanthony/resources/index.html?body=social_purity.html.

Bailey, Julie R. "With Rings, Teens Pledge to Remain Pure until Marriage." *Columbus Dispatch*, April 15, 2005.

Beck, Richard. *Unclean: Meditations on Purity, Hospitality, and Mortality*. Eugene, OR: Cascade Books, 2011.

Bessy, Sarah. "I Am Damaged Goods." Last modified January 29, 2013. http://deeperstory.com/i-am-damaged-goods.

Billitteri, Thomas. "Sex Is a 4-Letter Word: Wait." *St. Petersburg Times*, June 15, 1994.

Blackwell, Elizabeth. "Cruelty and Lust—Appeal to Women." *Philanthropist* 6, no. 12 (December 1891), 1–3.

Bond, Elizabeth Powell. "The Sacredness of Motherhood." *Philanthropist* 1, no. 7 (July 1886), 1–2.

Bushnell, Kate C. "The White Cross and White Shield," *Philanthropist* 2, no. 11 (November 1888), 1–2, 6.

Carpenter, Joel, "Geared to the Times, but Anchored to the Rock." *Christianity Today* 16, no. 8 (1985): 44–47.

Carpenter, Joel. "We Need a Revival." In *Early Billy Graham: Sermons and Revival Accounts*. New York: Garland, 1988.

Chapman, Gary, and Tony Rankin. *True Love Waits: A Student's Guide to the Five Love Languages*. Nashville: Lifeway Press, 2003.

Clark, Richard. "I'm an Abstinence Christian, and Yeah, It's a Struggle." xoJane.com. Last modified May 3, 2013. http://www.xojane.com/issues/in-the-abstinence-only-crowd.

"Colored Men on the Moral Status of the Colored Race." *Philanthropist* 2, no. 10 (October 1888): 3.

Cowell, Alan. "British High Court Wrestles with Symbol of Premarital Purity." *New York Times*, June 23, 2007.

Crary, David. "ACLU Lawsuit Alleges That Abstinence-Only Program Uses Federal Funds to Promote Christianity." *Associated Press*, May 16, 2005.

Curry, Erin, and Polly House. "Magazine Sees 'a New Counterculture' of Teenagers Who Choose Virginity." *Baptist Press News*, December 12, 2002.

Day, Elizabeth. "Sikh Bracelets, but Not Christian Rings as School Bans Pupils from Wearing 'Purity Rings.'" *London Daily Telegraph*, June 18, 2006.

DeCosta, Benjamin F. "The Capitalists of Vice." *Philanthropist* 7, no. 6 (June 1892): 6.

Dobson, James. *The Complete Marriage and Home Reference Guide*. Wheaton, IL: Tyndale House Publishers, 2000.

———. *Dare to Discipline*, Wheaton, IL: Tyndale, 1970.

———. *Family under Fire*. Kansas City, MO: Beacon Hill, 1971.

———. *Straight-Talk to Men and Their Wives/What Wives Wish Their Husbands Knew about Women*. Danbury, CT: Guideposts, 1979.

———. *Dr. Dobson Answers Your Questions*, Wheaton, IL: Tyndale House, 1982.

———. *Love for a Lifetime*. Portland, OR: Multnomah Press, 1987.

———. *The New Dare to Discipline*. Wheaton, IL: Tyndale House, 1992.

———. *Marriage under Fire*. Portland, OR: Multnomah Press, 2004.

Dobson, James, and Gary Bauer. *Children at Risk: Winning the Battle for the Hearts and Minds of Your Children*. Dallas, TX: Word, 2000.

Dodge, Grace A. "A Portion of a Confidential Letter to Girls." *Philanthropist* 3, no. 7 (July 1889): 1–3.

Dominguez, Alex. "Elizabeth Smart Speaks on Human Trafficking." *Christian Science Monitor*, May 4, 2013. http://www.csmonitor.com/USA/Latest-News-Wires/2013/0504/Elizabeth-Smart-speaks-on-human-trafficking.

"An Earnest Appeal to Young Women," *Philanthropist* 6, no. 1 (January 1891).

Esther, Elizabeth. "Virginity: New and Improved." Last modified January 28, 2013. http://www.elizabethesther.com/2013/01/virginity-new-improved.html.

Evans Held, Rachel. "Do Christians Idolize Virginity?" Last modified January 29, 2013. http://rachelheldevans.com/blog/christians-idolize-virginity.

———. "Elizabeth Smart, Human Trafficking, and Purity Culture." Last modified May 26, 2013. http://rachelheldevans.com/blog/elizabeth-smart-purity-culture.

Flint, Joseph F. "Social Purity Code." *Philanthropist* 5, no. 7 (July 1891): 3.

———. "The Science of Domestic Happiness." *Philanthropist* 6, no. 7 (July 1892): 1–2.

Gangel, Kenneth O. "Arnold Toynbee: An Evangelical Evaluation." *Bibliotheca Sacra*, Volume 133 (April–June 1977): 144–155.

Gibb, Frances. "Teenage Girl Loses 'Purity Ring' Case." *Times* (London), July 17, 2007.

Gilder, George. *Sexual Suicide*. New York: Quadrangle / New York Times Book Company, 1973.

Gledstone Rev. J. P., "Message to Young Men—Wild Oats," *Philanthropist* 8, no. 2 (February 1894): 1–3.

"God Blesses Pledges with Happiness." Accessed September 14, 2008.. http://www.lifeway.com/tlw/media/news_happiness.asp.

Goodstein, Laurie. "Saying No to Teen Sex in No Uncertain Terms." *Washington Post*, July 30, 1994.

Graham, Billy. *Calling Youth to Christ*. Grand Rapids, MI: Zondervan, 1947.

———. Sermon #8: "Now is the Acceptable Time." *Charlotte Observer*, September 28, 1958. http://www.wheaton.edu/bgc/archives/docs/bg-charlotte/09289-1.htm.

———. Sermon #14: "The Second Coming of Christ." *Charlotte Observer*, October 5, 1958. http://www.wheaton.edu/bgc/archives/docs/bg-charlotte/1005.html.

———. *World Aflame*. New York: Doubleday, 1965.

———. *Men and Marriage*. New York: Quadrangle / New York Times Book Company, 1986.

"The Greatest Youth Gathering in History: The 1945 Youth for Christ Memorial Day Rally at Soldier Field." Wheaton College. Last modified December 31, 2011. http://www2.wheaton.edu/bgc/archives/exhibits/YFC%201945/entrance.html.

Greenhill, Sam. "Teenager Loses High Court Battle against School Ban on Chastity Ring." *Daily Mail* (London), July 17, 2007.

Hall, G. Stanley. *Adolescence, Its Psychology and Its Relations to Physiology, Anthropology, Sociology, Sex, Crime, Religion, and Education*. New York: D. Appleton, 1904.

———. "From Generation to Generation: With Some Plain Language about Race Suicide and the Instruction of Children during Adolescence." *American Magazine* 66 (July 1908): 248–254.

———. "The Awkward Age." *Appleton's Magazine* 12 (August 1908): 149–156.

———. "Education in Sex Hygiene." *Eugenics Review* 1 (January 1910): 242–253.

Henriques, Jessica Ciencin. "My Virginity Mistake." *Salon*. Last modified May 6, 2013. http://www.salon.com/2013/05/06/my_virginity_mistake/.

Henry, Carl F. H. *Remaking the Modern Mind*. Grand Rapids, MI: Eerdmans, 1948.

———. *Twilight of a Great Civilization: The Drift toward Neo-Paganism*. Westchester, IL: Crossway Books, 1988.

Herman, Doug. *Time for a Pure Revolution*. Wheaton, IL: Tyndale, 2004.

"A History of True Love Waits." Last modified 2010. http://www.lifeway.com/Article/true-love-waits-history.

Howe, Julia Ward. "Moral Equality between the Sexes." In *The National Purity Congress: Its Papers, Addresses, Portraits*, 66–71. New York: American Purity Alliance, 1896.

Howerton, Kristen. "Shame-Based Sex Education: We Can Do Better." Last modified May 6, 2013. http://www.rageagainsttheminivan.com/2013/05/shame-based-sex-education-we-can-do.html.

"The Immoral Legacy of Slavery," *Philanthropist* 5, no. 4. (April 1891): 1.

Infante, Esme M., "Teens: Sex Can Wait for Wedding Bells." *USA Today*, July 29, 1994.

James, Carolyn Curtis. "Why Virginity Is Not the Gospel." *Huffington Post*. Last modified August 7, 2012. http://www.huffingtonpost.com/carolyn-custis-james/why-virginity-is-not-the-gospel_b_1735085.html.

Johnson, Torrey. "Blame Parents for Teen Crime, Churchman Cites Orgies, Robberies." *Chicago Herald American* (Sunday, December 1, 1946). Folder 1, Box 17, Collection 48, Records of Youth for Christ/USA, Archives of the Billy Graham Center, Wheaton, Illinois.

Keith, Patsy. "Teens Walk the Aisle for True Love Waits." *Commercial Appeal*, February 13, 2005.

Kelly, Paul. [*True Love Waits*] *Sexual Resolutions*. Nashville: Lifeway, 1999.

"The Legacy of Slavery." 2, no. 2 (February 1888): 1.

Lindsey, Hal. *The Late, Great Planet Earth*. Grand Rapids, MI: Zondervan, 1970.

Maynard, Emily. "The Day I Turned In My V-Card." *Prodigal Magazine*. Last modified January 31, 2013. http://www.prodigalmagazine.com/the-day-i-turned-in-my-v-card/.

McCarthy, Colman. "No 'Safe' Teenage Sex." *Washington Post*, August 20, 1994.

Meeker, Meg. *Epidemic: How Teen Sex Is Killing Our Kids*. Washington, DC: LifeLine, 2002.

Moore, Elizabeth. "Teens Believe True Love Waits." *Times-Picayune*, October 9, 2004.

Murray, Charles. "The Coming White Underclass." *Wall Street Journal*, October 29, 1993.

Neville, Charles. *Saturday Home Magazine*, August 18, 1945.

Parmelee, Laura A. "Women's Work for Woman." *American Missionary* 34, no. 1 (January 1880).

Pattyn, Denny. *Next: Living Out Your Commitment to Wait*. Moon Township, PA: Silver Ring Thing, 2009.

Piatt, Christian. "The Dangers of 'Marriage Worship.'" *Patheos* (blog). Last modified May 22, 2013. http://www.patheos.com/blogs/christianpiatt/2013/05/the-dangers-of-christian-marriage-worship/.

Powell, Aaron Macy. "Moral Elevation of Women." *Philanthropist* 1, no. 2 (February 1886): 5–6.

The Times Law Reports. "Purity Ring Is Not Intimately Linked to Religious Belief." *Times* (London), July 23, 2007.

Rankin, Tony, and Richard Ross. *When True Love Doesn't Wait*. Nashville: Lifeway, 1998.

"The Responsibilities of Men." *Philanthropist* 1, no. 5 (May 1886): 4.

Blackwell, Emily. "The Responsibilities of Women in Regard to Questions Concerning Public Morality." In *The National Purity Congress: Its Papers, Addresses, Portraits*, 72–80. New York: American Purity Alliance, 1896.

Richardson, J. W. "The Ideal Woman." *Philanthropist* (ca. 1893).

Riddle, Sasha. "Chastity Jewelry Has Become Popular with Many Teens." *Modesto Bee*, April 26, 2007.

Rine, Abigail. "Why Some Evangelicals Are Trying to Stop Obsessing over Premarital Sex." *Atlantic*, May 28, 2013.

Rittmeyer, Brian C. "Silver Ring Thing Says It Will Survive." *Pittsburgh Tribune Review*, August 24, 2005.

Rosenbloom, Stephanie. "A Ring That Says No, Not Yet." *New York Times*, December 8, 2005.

Sabine, William T. "Social Vice and National Decay." In *The National Purity Congress: Its Papers, Addresses, Portraits*, 41–56. New York: American Purity Alliance, 1896.

Saltzman, Jonathan. "ACLU Suit Sees Religious Content in Abstinence Plan." *Boston Globe*, May 17, 2005.

Satter, Raphael G. "Teens Chastity-Ring Fight Goes to Court." The Seattle Times. Last modified June 23, 2007. http://www.seattletimes.com/nation-world/teens-chastity-ring-fight-goes-to-court/.

Sawyer, Mary E. "Woman's Work for Woman," *American Missionary* 35, no. 1 (January 1882).

Sawyer, Mary L. "Woman's Work for Woman," *American Missionary* 36, no. 1 (January 1881).

Schaeffer, Francis. *How Should We Then Live?: The Rise and Decline of Western Thought and Culture*. Old Tappan, NJ: Fleming H. Revell. 1976.

Scott Schreffler, Rebekah. "True Love Waits." *Pittsburgh Post-Gazette*, July 27, 1994.

Shelley, Bruce L. "The Young and the Zealous." *Christianity Today*, October 1, 2006. http://www.christianitytoday.com/ch/2006/issue92/4.20.html.

Silver Ring Thing. *Sexual Abstinence Study Bible: New Living Translation*. Wheaton, IL: Tyndale House, 2000.

———. *Best of Silver Ring Thing Commercials, Volume 1*. Moon Township, PA: Silver Ring Thing, 2009. DVD.

———. "What Is Silver Ring Thing?" Accessed July 20, 2011. http://www.silverringthing.com/whatissrt.asp.

———. "SRT's National Roll-Out Plan." http://www.silverringthing.com/images/SRTRolloutPlan.pdf. Accessed June 20, 2014.

Sorokin, Pitirim. *The American Sex Revolution*. Boston: Porter Sargent, 1956.

Spencer, Anna Garlin. "The Care of the Prostitute." *Philanthropist* 6, no. 8 (August 1891): 2.

Spotts, Ally. "What's the Big Deal about Waiting until Marriage?" *Relevant*, November 10, 2011. http://www.relevantmagazine.com/life/relationship/features/27286-whats-the-big-deal-about-waiting-for-marriage.

"Teens Pledge Abstinence." *St. Petersburg Times*, May 1, 1993.

Toynbee, Arnold. *A Study of History*. Vols. 1–2, abridgement of Volumes I–IV. Oxford: Oxford University Press, 1986.

"The Triumph of Manhood," *Philanthropist* 6, no. 6 (June 1892): 1–3.

"True Love Waits: Baptist Teens Asked to Pledge to Delay Sex until Marriage." *Houston Chronicle*, April 22, 1993.

"True Love Waits for Some Teen-Agers." *New York Times*, June 21, 1993.

Tullos, Matt, Paul Turner, and Kristi Cherry. *Pure Joy: God's Formula for Passionate Living*. Nashville: Lifeway, 2001.

Unwin, Joseph Daniel. *Sexual Regulations and Cultural Behaviour*. London: Oxford University Press, 1935. Reprint, Trona, CA: Darrow, 1969.

Vara, Richard. "Texas Youths Sign Cards, Vow to Abstain from Sex." *Houston Chronicle*, November 13, 1993.

Welty, J. B. "The Need for White Cross Work." In *The National Purity Congress: Its Papers, Addresses, Portraits*, 240–249. New York: American Purity Alliance, 1896.

Wetzstein, Cheryl. "Nation Headline: Federal Funds Suspended for Abstinence Program." *Washington Times*. August 24, 2005.

Whelan, George. "Frown Jewels: Christian Rings Banned, Sikh Bracelets Allowed." *Daily Star*, June 19, 2006.

Willard, Frances E. *Glimpses of Fifty Years: The Autobiography of an American Woman*. Toronto: Rose, 1898. PDF e-book.

———. "Social Purity Work for 1887." *Union Signal* 13 (January 1887): 12.

———. "A White Life for Two." *Philanthropist* 5, no. 7 (July 1890): 1–3.

Winner, Lauren. *Real Sex: The Naked Truth about Chastity*. Grand Rapids, MI: Brazos, 2006.

Woods, Robert A., and Albert J. Kennedy. *Young Working Girls: A Summary of Evidence from Two Thousand Social Workers*. Boston: Houghton Mifflin, 1913.

GOVERNMENT DOCUMENTS

81 Cong. Rec. 96, 4527–4528 [on homosexuals in government]. March 29–April 24, 1950. Last modified May 31, 2007. http://www.writing.upenn.edu/~afilreis/50s/gays-in-govt.html.

Abstinence Education: Hearings before a Subcommittee of the Committee on Appropriations. 104th Cong., 2nd sess., 1996, 87–91.

American Civil Liberties Union of Massachusetts v. Leavitt, Horn, and Wilson. Last modified May 16, 2005. http://www.aclu.org/FilesPDFs/teeneducomplaint.pdf.

House Committee on Government Reform, Minority Staff, Special Investigations Division. "The Content of Federally Funded Abstinence-Only Education Programs." December 2004.

Personal Responsibility and Work Opportunity Reconciliation Act of 1996. Public Law 104–193, § 501b.

United States Government Accountability Office Report to Congressional Requesters. "Abstinence Education: Efforts to Assess the Effectiveness and Accuracy of Federally Funded Programs." October 2006.

SECONDARY SOURCES

Balmer, Randall. "American Fundamentalism: The Ideal of Femininity." In *Fundamentalism and Gender*, edited by John Stratton Hawley, 47–62. New York: Oxford University Press, 1994.

Bartkowski, John P., and Christopher G. Ellison. "Divergent Models of Child-Rearing in Popular Manuals: Conservative Protestants vs. the Mainstream Experts." *Sociology of Religion* 56, no. 1 (1995): 21–34.

Bearman, Peter, and Hannah S. Bruckner. "Promising the Future: Virginity Pledges and First Intercourse." *American Journal of Sociology* 106, no. 4 (2001): 859–912.

———. "After the Promise: The STD Consequences of Adolescent Virginity Pledges." *Journal of Adolescent Health* 36, no. 4 (2005): 271–278.

Bederman, Gail. *Manliness and Civilization: A Cultural History of Gender and Race in the United States, 1880–1917*. Chicago: University of Chicago Press, 1995.

———. "'The Women Have Had Charge of the Church Work Long Enough': The Men and Religion Forward Movement of 1911–1912 and the Masculinization of Middle-Class Protestantism." In *A Mighty Baptism: Race, Gender, and the Creation of American Protestantism*, edited by Susan Juster and Lisa MacFarlane, 107–141. Ithaca, NY: Cornell University Press, 1996.

Beh, Hazel Glenn, and Milton Diamond. "Children and Education: The Failure of Abstinence-Only Education." *Columbia Journal of Gender and Law* 15, no. 1 (2006): 12–62.

Bell, Catherine. *Ritual Theory, Ritual Practice*. New York: Oxford University Press, 1992.

Bendroth, Margaret Lamberts. *Fundamentalism and Gender: 1875–Present*. New Haven, CT: Yale University Press, 1996.

Benshoff, Janet. "The Chastity Act: Government Manipulation of Abortion Information and the First Amendment." *Harvard Law Review* 101, no. 8 (1988): 1916–1937.

Bivins, Jason. *Religion of Fear: The Politics of Horror in Conservative Evangelicalism*. New York: Oxford University Press, 2008.

Bordin, Ruth. *Frances Willard: A Biography*. Chapel Hill: University of North Carolina Press, 1987.

Boyer, Paul S. *When Time Shall Be No More: Prophecy Belief in Modern American Culture*. Cambridge, MA: Belknap Press of Harvard University Press, 1992.

———. *Purity in Print: Book Censorship in America from the Gilded Age to the Computer Age*. 2nd ed. Madison: University of Wisconsin Press, 2002.

Brown, Candy Gunther. *The Word in the World: Evangelical Writing, Publishing, and Reading in America, 1789–1990*. Chapel Hill: University of North Carolina Press, 2004.

Burek Pierce, Jennifer. "What Young Readers Ought to Know: The Successful Selling of Sexual Health Texts in the Early Twentieth Century." *Book History* 14 (2011): 110–136.

Burnham, John C. "The Progressive Era Revolution in American Attitudes toward Sex." *Journal of American History* 59, no. 4 (1973): 885–908.

Carpenter, Joel. *Revive Us Again: The Reawakening of American Fundamentalism.* New York: Oxford University Press, 1997.

Coble, Christopher. "The Role of Young People's Societies in the Training of Christian Womanhood (and Manhood), 1880–1910." In *Women and Twentieth-Century Protestantism*, edited by Margaret Lamberts Bendroth and Virginia Lieson Brereton, 74–92. Urbana: University of Illinois Press, 2002.

Csordas, Thomas. *The Sacred Self: A Cultural Phenomenology of Charismatic Healing.* Berkeley: University of California Press, 1994.

DeBerg, Betty. *Ungodly Women: Gender and the First Wave of American Fundamentalism.* Minneapolis: Fortress, 1990.

D'Emilio, John, and Estelle Freedman. *Intimate Matters: A History of Sexuality in America.* Chicago: University of Chicago Press, 1988.

Diamond, Sara. *Not by Politics Alone: The Enduring Influence of the Christian Right.* New York: Guilford Press, 1998.

Dochuk, Darren. *From Bible Belt to Sun Belt: Plain-Folk Religion, Grassroots Politics, and the Rise of Evangelical Conservatism.* New York: W. W. Norton, 2011.

Donovan, Brian. *White Slave Crusaders: Race, Gender, and Anti-Vice Activism, 1887–1917.* Urbana: University of Illinois Press, 2006.

Douglas, Ann. *The Feminization of American Culture.* New York: Anchor Books, 1977.

Dowland, Seth. "'Family Values' and the Formation of a Christian Right Agenda." *Church History* 78, no. 3 (2009): 606–631.

Einstein, Mara. *Brands of Faith: Marketing Religion in a Commercial Age.* New York: Routledge, 2008.

Epstein, Barbara Leslie. *Women and the Politics of Domesticity: Women, Evangelism, and Temperance in Nineteenth-Century America.* Middleton, CT: Wesleyan University Press, 1986.

Fejes, Fred. *Gay Rights and Moral Panic: The Origins of America's Debate on Homosexuality.* New York: Palgrave Macmillan, 2008.

Freitas, Donna. *Sex and the Soul: Juggling Sexuality, Spirituality, Romance, and Religion on America's College Campuses.* New York: Oxford University Press, 2008.

Frykholm, Amy Johnson. *Rapture Culture: Left Behind in Evangelical America.* New York: Oxford University Press, 2004.

Gardner, Christine. *Making Chastity Sexy: The Rhetoric of Evangelical Abstinence Campaigns.* Berkeley: University of California Press, 2011.

Gilgoff, Dan. *The Jesus Machine: How James Dobson, Focus on the Family, and Evangelical America Are Winning the Culture War.* New York: St. Martin's Griffin, 2007.

Gray, Jonathan. "Television Teaching: Parody, *The Simpsons*, and Media Literacy Education." *Critical Studies in Media Communication* 22, no. 3 (2004): 223–238.

Gray, Jonathan. *Show Sold Separately: Promos, Spoilers, and Other Media Paratexts.* New York University Press, 2010.

Green, Steven K. "'A Legacy of Discrimination'? The Rhetoric and Reality of the Faith-Based Initiative: Oregon as a Case Study." *Oregon Law Review* 84, no. 3 (2005): 725–730.

Gregory, Chad Alan. "Revivalism, Fundamentalism, and Masculinity in the United States, 1880–1930." PhD diss., University of Kentucky, 1999.

Griffith, R. Marie. *Born Again Bodies: Flesh and Spirit in American Christianity.* Berkeley: University of California Press, 2004.

Gutjahr, Paul. *An American Bible: A History of the Good Book in the United States, 1777–1880.* Stanford, CA: Stanford University Press, 1999.

———. "The Bible-zine *Revolve* and the Evolution of the Culturally Relevant Bible in America." In *Religion and the Culture of Print in Modern America*, edited by Charles L. Cohen and Paul S. Boyer, 326–348. Madison: University of Wisconsin Press, 2008.

Hankins, Barry. *Uneasy in Babylon: Southern Baptist Conservatives and American Culture.* Tuscaloosa: University of Alabama Press, 2002.

———. *Francis Schaeffer and the Shaping of Evangelical America.* Grand Rapids, MI: Eerdmans, 2008.

Harding, Susan Friend. *The Book of Jerry Falwell: Fundamentalist Language and Politics.* Princeton, NJ: Princeton University Press, 2001.

Hart, D. G. *That Old-Time Religion in Modern America: Evangelical Protestantism in the Twentieth Century.* Chicago: Ivan R. Dee, 2002.

Hendershot, Heather. *Shaking the World for Jesus: Media and Conservative Evangelical Culture.* Chicago: University of Chicago Press, 2004.

Herzog, Jonathan P. *The Spiritual-Industrial Complex: America's Religious Battle against Communism in the Early Cold War.* New York: Oxford University Press, 2011.

Hoover, Stewart. "The Cross at Willow Creek: Seeker Religion and the Contemporary Marketplace." In *Religion and Popular Culture in America*, edited by Bruce David Forbes and Jeffrey Mahan. Berkeley: University of California Press, 2000.

———. *Religion in the Media Age.* New York: Routledge, 2006.

Hunt, Alan, *Governing Morals: A Social History of Moral Regulation.* Cambridge: Cambridge University Press, 1999.

Hunter, James Davidson. *The Culture Wars: The Struggle to Define America.* New York: Basic Books, 1991.

Hutcheon, Linda. *A Theory of Parody: The Teachings of Twentieth-Century Art Forms.* Urbana: University of Illinois Press, 1985.

Johnson, David K. *The Lavender Scare: The Cold War Persecution of Gays and Lesbians in the Federal Government.* Chicago: University of Chicago Press, 2006.

Johnson, Eithne. "Dr. Dobson's Advice to Christian Women: The Story of Strategic Motherhood." *Social Text* 16, no. 4 (1998): 55–82.

Joiner, Thekla Ellen. *Sin in the City: Chicago and Revivalism, 1880–1920.* Columbia: University of Missouri Press, 2007.

Jones, Julie. "Money, Sex, and the Religious Right: A Constitutional Analysis of Federally Funded Abstinence-Only-until-Marriage Sexuality Education." *Creighton Law Review* 35 (June 2002): 1075–1106.

Jordan, Mark D. *Recruiting Young Love: How Christians Talk about Homosexuality.* Chicago: University of Chicago Press, 2011.

Kaplan, Amy. "Manifest Domesticity." *American Literature* 70, no. 3 (1998): 581–606.

Kilde, Jeanne Halgren. *When Church Became Theatre: The Transformation of Evangelical Architecture and Worship in Nineteenth-Century America.* Oxford: Oxford University Press, 2002.

Koch, Kathy. "Encouraging Teen Abstinence." *CQ Researcher* 8, no. 25 (1998): 577–600.

Ladd, Tony, and James A. Mathisen. *Muscular Christianity: Evangelical Protestants and the Development of American Sport.* Grand Rapids, MI: Baker, 1999.

Lahr, Angela. *Millennial Dreams and Apocalyptic Nightmares: The Cold War Origins of Political Evangelicalism.* New York: Oxford University Press, 2007.

Lambert, Frank. *Inventing the "Great Awakening."* Princeton, NJ: Princeton University Press, 2001.

Lienesch, Michael. *Redeeming America: Piety and Politics in the New Christian Right.* Chapel Hill: University of North Carolina Press, 1993.

Løvdal, Hilda. "Family Matters: James Dobson and Focus on the Family's Message to Evangelicals, 1970–2010." PhD diss., University of Oslo, 2012.

Luhr, Eileen. *Witnessing Suburbia: Conservatives and Christian Youth Culture.* Berkeley: University of California Press, 2009.

Lupu, Ira C., and Tuttle, Robert W., "The Faith-Based Initiative and the Constitution." *DePaul Law Review* 55, no. 1 (2005). http://ssrn.com/abstract=727744.

Lyon, David. *Jesus in Disneyland: Religion in Postmodern Times.* Cambridge: Polity Press, 2004.

Marsden, George M. *Fundamentalism and American Culture: The Shaping of Twentieth-Century Evangelicalism: 1870–1925.* 1980; New York: Oxford University Press, 2006.

———. *Jonathan Edwards: A Life.* New Haven, CT: Yale University Press, 2003.

McDannell, Colleen. *The Christian Home in Victorian America, 1840–1900.* Bloomington: Indiana University Press, 1986.

———. *Material Christianity: Religion and Popular Culture in America.* New Haven, CT: Yale University Press, 1995.

———. "Beyond Dr. Dobson: Women, Girls, and Focus on the Family." In *Women and Twentieth-Century Protestantism*, edited by Margaret Lamberts Bendroth and Virginia Lieson Brereton, 113–131. Chicago: University of Illinois Press, 2002.

McGirr, Lisa. *Suburban Warriors: The Origins of the New American Right*. Princeton, NJ: Princeton University Press, 2001.

McLoughlin, William G. *Revivals, Awakenings, and Reform*. Chicago: University of Chicago Press, 1980.

Miller, Donald E. *Reinventing American Protestantism: Christianity in the New Millennium*. Berkeley: University of California Press, 1997.

Moran, Jeffery. *Teaching Sex: The Shaping of Adolescence in the 20th Century*. New York: Oxford University Press, 2002.

Morgan, Sue. "'Knights of God': Ellice Hopkins and the White Cross Army, 1883–95." In *Gender and Christian Religion*, edited by R. N. Swanson. Studies in Church History 34. Suffolk: Ecclesiastical History Society and Boydell Press, 1998.

———. "'Wild Oats or Acorns?' Social Purity, Sexual Politics, and the Response of the Late-Victorian Church." *Journal of Religious History* 31, no. 2 (2007): 151–168.

Newman, Louise Michele. *White Women's Rights: The Racial Origins of Feminism in the United States*. New York: Oxford University Press, 1999.

Nord, David. *Faith in Reading: Religious Publication and the Birth of Mass Media*. Oxford: Oxford University Press, 2004.

Pascoe, Peggy. *Relations of Rescue: The Search for Female Moral Authority in the American West, 1874–1939*. New York: Oxford University Press, 1990.

Patterson, James A. "Cultural Pessimism in Modern Evangelical Thought." *Journal of the Evangelical Theology Society* 49, no. 4 (2006): 807–820.

Pivar, David. *Purity Crusade: Sexual Morality and Social Control, 1868–1900*. Westport, CT: Greenwood Press, 1973.

———. *Purity and Hygiene: Women, Prostitution, and the "American Plan," 1900–1930*. Westport, CT: Greenwood Press, 2002.

Prothero, Stephen. *American Jesus: How the Son of God Became a National Icon*. New York: Farrar, Straus & Giroux, 2003.

Putney, Clifford. *Muscular Christianity: Manhood and Sports in Protestant America, 1880–1920*. Cambridge, MA: Harvard University Press, 2001.

Regnerus, Mark. *Forbidden Fruit: Sex and Religion in the Lives of American Teenagers*. New York: Oxford University Press, 2007.

Rimke, Heidi, and Alan Hunt. "From Sinners to Degenerates: The Medicalization of Morality in the Nineteenth Century." *History of Human Sciences* 15, no. 1 (2002): 59–88.

Roof, Wade Clark. *A Generation of Seekers: The Spiritual Journeys of the Baby Boom Generation*. San Francisco: HarperCollins, 1993.

———. *Spiritual Marketplace: Baby Boomers and the Remaking of American Religion*. Princeton, NJ: Princeton University Press, 1999.

Ross, Dorothy. *G. Stanley Hall, the Psychologist as Prophet*. Chicago: University of Chicago Press, 1972.

Satter, Beryl. *Each Mind a Kingdom: American Women, Sexual Purity, and the New Thought Movement, 1875–1920*. Berkeley: University of California Press, 1999.

Schafer, Axel R. *Countercultural Conservatives: American Evangelicalism from the Postwar Revival to the New Christian Right.* Madison: University of Wisconsin Press, 2011. PDF e-book.

Schmidt, Leigh Eric. "The Easter Parade: Piety, Fashion, and Display." In *Religion and American Culture,* edited by David Hackett, 245–269. New York: Routledge, 2003.

Shelley, Bruce. "The Rise of Evangelical Youth Movements." *Fides et Historia* 18, no. 1 (1986): 47–63.

Shibley, Mark A. *Resurgent Evangelicalism in the United States: Mapping Cultural Change since 1970.* Columbia: University of South Carolina Press, 1996.

Shirk-Myers, Susan E., *Helping the Good Shepherd: Pastoral Counselors in a Psychotherapeutic Culture, 1925–1975.* Baltimore: Johns Hopkins University Press, 2009. PDF e-book.

Smith, Christian, *American Evangelicals: Embattled and Thriving.* Chicago: University of Chicago Press, 1998.

Stephens, Randall J., and Karl W. Giberson. *The Anointed: Evangelical Truth in a Secular Age.* Cambridge, MA: Belknap Press of Harvard University Press, 2011.

Stevens, Jason. *God-Fearing and Free: A Spiritual History of America's Cold War.* Cambridge, MA: Harvard University Press, 2010.

Stowe, David W. *No Sympathy for the Devil: Christian Pop Music and the Transformation of American Evangelicalism.* Chapel Hill: University of North Carolina Press, 2011.

Wacker, Grant. "Searching for Eden with a Satellite Dish." In *Religion and American Culture: A Reader,* edited by David Hackett, 437–458. New York: Routledge, 2003.

Watt, David Harrington. "The Private Hopes of American Fundamentalists and Evangelicals, 1925–1975." *Religion and American Culture: A Journal of Interpretation* 1, no. 2 (1991): 155–175.

———. *A Transforming Faith: Explorations of Twentieth-Century American Evangelicalism.* New Brunswick, NJ: Rutgers University Press, 1991.

Welter, Barbara. "Cult of True Womanhood: 1820–1860." *American Quarterly* 18, no. 2 (1966): 151–174.

White, Heather Rachelle. "Virgin Pride: Born Again Faith and Sexual Identity in the Faith-Based Abstinence Movement." In *Ashgate Research Companion to Contemporary Religion and Sexuality,* edited by Stephen J. Hunt and Andrew Yip. Farnham, UK: Ashgate, 2012.

Whitfield, Stephen J. *The Culture of the Cold War.* Baltimore: Johns Hopkins University Press, 1991.

Williams, Daniel K. *God's Own Party: The Making of the Christian Right.* New York: Oxford University Press, 2010.

Wosh, Peter J. *Spreading the Word: The Bible Business in Nineteenth-Century America.* Ithaca, NY: Cornell University Press, 1994.

Young Barstow, Elizabeth Ellen. "'These Teenagers Are Not Delinquent': The Rhetoric of Maturity for Evangelical Young Adults." PhD diss., Harvard University, 2010.

Index

The "n" refers to the note numbers on those pages.

Willard, Frances
  on gender equality, 24–25,
    28, 41
  Moody and, 23–24
  on promiscuity, 19, 31
  racial beliefs of, 45
  on White Cross, 25–26
  Woman's Christian Temperance
    Union presidency of, 19, 23
Williams, Fannie Barrier, 40

Woman's Christian Temperance Union,
  7, 17, 19–20, 23–24, 36
World's Fair, Chicago, 23, 40

Young Men's Christian Association, 7,
  17, 23, 58
Youth for Christ, 8, 49–54
  Graham and, 54, 62, 157
  as model, 160
  True Love Waits and, 109–110